The American Society
for Public Administration (ASPA)

The American Society for Public Administration (ASPA) is a nationwide nonprofit educational and professional membership organization dedicated to excellence in public management and the promotion of public service. The Society seeks to achieve these objectives through

- The advancement of the science, art, and processes of public administration
- The development and exchange of public administration literature and information
- Advocacy on behalf of public service and high ethical standards in government

With more than eighteen thousand members and subscribers, ASPA represents a broad array of professional interests and disciplines from all levels of government, the nonprofit and private sectors, and the academic community, both in the United States and abroad.

ASPA has provided national leadership in the areas of public administration and management since its inception in 1939. The Society and its members have been involved and influential in virtually every significant development in the theories and practice of public administration for half a century.

Through its network of 124 local chapters, 17 national special-focus sections, individual and agency members, and organizational supporters, ASPA promotes recognition of public service achievements, develops a substantive dialogue on relevant issues, and enhances the professional development of its membership. To further its mission, ASPA

- Communicates the importance and value of public service
- Promotes high ethical standards in public administration
- Speaks out in support of public service and seeks to improve the public's perception of government and to restore confidence in public servants
- Develops positions on significant public management and public interest issues
- Publishes a prestigious journal—*Public Administration Review*—an issues-oriented newspaper—*PA Times*—and other special books and publications
- Recognizes excellence in public service through annual awards for special accomplishments in the literature or practice of public administration

For additional information or membership materials, contact

*Advancing excellence
in public service. . .*

AMERICAN SOCIETY FOR PUBLIC ADMINISTRATION
1120 G STREET, N.W., SUITE 500
WASHINGTON, D.C. 20005
(202) 393-7878
FAX (202) 638-4952

The ETHICS CHALLENGE *in* PUBLIC SERVICE

Carol W. Lewis

The ETHICS CHALLENGE *in* PUBLIC SERVICE

A Problem-Solving Guide

 Jossey-Bass Publishers

THE ETHICS CHALLENGE IN PUBLIC SERVICE
A Problem-Solving Guide
by Carol W. Lewis

Copyright © 1991 by: Jossey-Bass Inc., Publishers
350 Sansome Street
San Francisco, California 94104

Library of Congress Cataloging-in-Publication Data

Lewis, Carol W. (Carol Weiss), date.
    The ethics challenge in public service : a problem-solving guide /
Carol W. Lewis. — 1st ed.
      p.   cm.—(The Jossey-Bass public administration series)
    Includes bibliographical references and index.
    ISBN 1-55542-383-3
    1. Civil service ethics—United States.   I. Title. II. Series.
JK468.E7L49   1991
172'.2'0973—dc20

                                     CIP   91-3401

Manufactured in the United States of America

The paper in this book meets the guidelines for
permanence and durability of the Committee on
Production Guidelines for Book Longevity of the
Council on Library Resources.

JACKET DESIGN BY WILLI BAUM

FIRST EDITION
HB Printing   10 9 8 7 6 5 4 3 2
Code 9185

The Jossey-Bass
Public Administration Series

Contents

Figures and Exhibits

To Norman Kugelmass, my husband,
and to the next generation:
Ari, Dov, Ruth, and David.

Preface

This book's subject is managing in—not moralizing about—today's public service. It is written for professional managers in public agencies, where unprecedented demands for ethical judgment and decisive action resound at increasingly higher decibel levels.

Yet there is something about ethics that triggers nostalgia. It seems that people are not what they were. Except for classical music (the golden oldies of rock), ethics is the only subject I know of that sets off a yearning for the old days in young and old, public servants and private citizens alike.

Some argue that World War II was a watershed; after it, moral decay set in. Others single out the political activists and hippies of the 1960s who pointed disrespectfully at their parents and political leaders and today symbolize intergenerational conflict, lack of self-discipline, and rejection of community standards. Still others cite the baby boomers, yuppies by the 1980s (and in some instances the same beaded and bearded youths of the sixties), who drove Ivan Boesky's ethic "greed is good" to its limits and faxed us new national symbols of greed and corruption: insider trading on Wall Street and savings and loans ripe for the picking along Sunbelt freeways. Along Washington's Beltway, defense procurement attracted procurers, and federal housing programs fell to the fixers.

Common wisdom has it that a pervasive disillusionment and loss of confidence touch political, economic, and even religious leaders and institutions on America's Main Street. Bill Moyers captured the perceived change in *The Secret Government* (1988, pp. 81-82) by quoting two well-known sports ethics. The 1920s coached that it is "not that you won or lost, but how you played the game." By the 1960s the coaching had become "Winning isn't everything. . . . It's the only thing."

Is behavior today better or worse? Is there more corruption in government and society generally? Is moral character, that ingrained sense of right and wrong, a thing of the past? There really is no evidence either way, except through anecdotes, media images, and public opinion polls. More importantly and the reason these questions are not confronted with evidence and argument in this book is that the answers are intellectually interesting but practically irrelevant to managers in public service. First, we have no choice but to depend upon the moral character of public managers and employees. Our whole system is built on this. Second, to work at all, public managers work with what is here, now. Nostalgia contributes nothing to daily operations; it solves no ethical problems on the job.

I would argue that public service attracts a special breed and that the majority of practicing and aspiring public managers and employees (over seventeen million in government alone and many millions more in nonprofit and mixed agencies) are well intentioned and do bring good moral character to public service. It is the job itself—the ambiguous, complex, pressured world of public service—that presents special problems for ethical people who want to do the right thing. The job is a site that reinforces moral character and engages adults in a dialogue about ethics where it counts. And count it does, for supervisors, subordinates, colleagues, citizens, taxpayers, other peoples around the world, and generations to come.

Given my purpose of promoting ethical practice and assisting ethical managers in making ethical decisions, I opt for a managerial perspective. *The Ethics Challenge in Public Service* is designed for managers and meant to be a selective shortcut through a mass of information and alternatives. I chose issues according to my assessment of their current and future managerial impact rather than academic coinage or strictly philosophical import.

My method is, first, to link good character with the special values and principles that distinguish public from personal ethics. The spirit of informed individual judgment pervades my arguments, and the same rationalist approach obligates me to provide readers with some explanations of inclusions, omissions, emphases, and biases. I assume the following:

> Public ethics is different from personal ethics;
> The values and guiding principles are different;
> The burdens are heavier.

Second, my method is to provide practical tools and techniques for resolving workaday dilemmas on the individual and agency levels. Third, my method's purpose is to assist ethical managers to structure the work environment so that it fosters ethical behavior and eases the transition of good intentions into meaningful action in the agency.

The cases included here illustrate problems or are test runs in applied problem solving. They allow readers to practice in private (and at no public cost) until, following Aristotle, ethics becomes a habit. The cases exercise the two-step:

informed, systematic reasoning followed by (hypothetical) action. The open-ended questions encourage analysis, and the closed force decision making. Some resolutions depend on empathy and imagination; cases work best when readers alter decision premises and circumstances to double-check ethical judgments or reconcile different philosophical perspectives. The cases, like the book, are driven by democratic processes, for which accommodation is the vehicle and tolerance the grease.

Overview

This book offers some tools and techniques that professional public managers can use to meet the demands for ethical judgment and decisive action on the job. In sum, what counts? What is at stake? How can managers ensure ethical survival and professional success? Veterans and rookies alike may wonder now and then, "Are both possible?" The answer here is an emphatic *yes*. The argument is that ethics and genuine success march together.

   The Ethics Challenge in Public Service examines these questions in terms of managerial realities and their ethical dimensions, which together shape the book's structure. The introduction offers readers a look at ethical issues encountered on the job and in the profession. In Part One, public service ethics is rooted in moral character and anchored in ethical values and principle. Chapter One distinguishes public service ethics from personal morality and shows how contending values and many cross pressures translate into a personally demanding, ambiguous, complex context for everyday decision making. One of public service's special ethical claims on the manager is to implement and comply with the law, and an elementary decision-making model given in Chapter Two helps decision makers act on legal obligations without devaluing other considerations. The obligation of serving the public interest entails empathy as well as respect for future generations and spawns the public service standards regarding conflict of interest, impartiality, and the appearance of impropriety under public scrutiny (Chapter Three). Combined with the idea of individual responsibility, these obligations are converted into general guides to action for managers who work in an organizational context (Chapter Four): individual responsibility for decisions and behavior, for what is done and how, and for professional competence. The obligations and action guides are the ethical underpinnings for *doing public service*.

   The earlier chapters expose the problems, conflicts, and claims shouldered by the public manager. Now the task is to provide tools for reconciling and sorting them ethically. Part Two turns to individual managers who make ethical decisions and live with the consequences. Ethical reasoning is grounded in common sense and philosophical perspectives that lead to varying outlooks on what is important in particular decisions; experience and political tradition caution impartiality and open-mindedness over ethical extremism (Chapter Five). Using a decision-making model that allows for contending viewpoints and values, managers gear up for fact-finding, accommodation, and selective trade-offs that lead to the informed, principled choices managers must make (Chapter Six). The obligation to avoid doing harm is reconciled with collective action and selective action (Chapter Six). Practical tools and techniques for resolving workaday dilemmas help answer questions of *what* counts (obligations and responsibilities in Chapter Six) and *who* counts (stakeholders in Chapter Seven). Ethical managers are counted as well, and principled discrimination in responding to ethical offenses equips managers to discount trivialities and survive professionally—with integrity intact (Chapter Seven).

Moving from the individual to the organization, Part Three looks at ethics in the agency. Ethics codes—their functions, development, and management—in all their variety are a benchmark for the current record and a forecast of things to come (Chapter Eight). The supervisory function, a central managerial responsibility, turns the spotlight on organizational interaction. In a host of ways, including modeling, the manager shapes ethical conduct and the ethical organization. Supervising employee time is an ongoing stress point and demands special care. Work force diversity, alternate recruitment channels, mixed administrative settings, and collaborative relationships illustrated by the procurement function are among the current challenges (Chapter Nine). Routine agency operations set the organization's ethical tone, and those operations can be structured to support and promote ethical action. Prudential management overcomes specific objections to agencies' ethics programs, and feasible agency interventions allow managers to incorporate ethical concerns directly into daily routine. An ethics impact statement and process integrate ethics into agency decisions, and agency audit and risk assessment tools contribute to building an ethical agency (Chapter Ten). Throughout, *The Ethics Challenge in Public Service* pays special attention to what lies ahead on the manager's agenda and, with an eye on the future, the afterword draws together the book's major themes.

Storrs, Connecticut   Carol W. Lewis
August 1991

Acknowledgments

Now to the customary IOUs, which are heartfelt. A fitting start is to acknowledge the American Society for Public Administration (ASPA). This project was born in August 1989, when I received a telephone call from Bayard L. Catron, who was coordinating ASPA's first national thematic conference, "Ethics in Government: The Intricate Web," scheduled for November in Washington. He asked whether I would be willing to prepare a national version of *Scruples & Scandals*—in which I focused on my home state—as a conference report. From its genesis as a report of that conference through many permutations, the project evolved into a problem-solving guide for practicing public managers. The evolution is a tale of Bayard's inspiration, Shirley Wester's energy, Sheila McCormick's assistance, ASPA's conference resources and good offices, and a multitude of other supporters and contributors.

At the conference itself, practitioners, professors, and students joined forces as panel moderators, as rapporteurs organized by Kathryn Denhardt, and as working group facilitators coordinated by George Frederickson. The willing contribution of students Linda R. Woodhouse, Margreta K. Voskuilen, and Tatiana Strainic symbolizes what this book is all about. Apparently, enthusiastic magnanimity is not something one outgrows in public service. Practitioners and professorial volunteers included George Frederickson, Donald E. Eckhart, Kathryn Denhardt, Art Flesch, April Hejka-Ekins, Emerson Markham, Bill Richter, Ruth Schimel, Ed Twardy, Vera Vogelsang-Coombs, E. C. Wakham, and Mylan Winn.

My university and department supported this effort with words and resources, and I am grateful for both. The University of Connecticut's Graduate Research Foundation funded travel for research, and the Institute for Social Inquiry ran data base searches on public opinion for me.

An overview of practices and purposes cannot be written in glorious isolation, off in an ivory tower reputedly unaffected by deferred maintenance or other realities. Government offices from Philadelphia to Sacramento to Juneau, state and local ethics commissions, public interest groups, professional associations, private research groups, consulting firms, and individual authors responded to requests for information by contributing codes, cases, publications, and research materials. By their very nature, citations note only those contributions ultimately incorporated, but broad assistance nourished the project.

My appreciation is extended to managers and others from all over the country who responded generously to requests or volunteered assistance. Mentioning individuals' support in no way implies personal or agency endorsement or any association with the views expressed in this book but is just by way of noting my personal appreciation. Individuals who contributed ideas, cases, and research materials include John F. (Jack) Azzaretto, Gary Brumback, Joyce Bullock, Geoffrey Cowan, Lawrence D. (Larry) Fisher, Pat Keehley, John Larsen, John H. Larson, Edward W. Pratt, Harriet McCullough, Stephen Rolandi, David R. Simon, James D. Wells, and many others. The invited advisory group also contributed: Kathryn Denhardt and Rushworth Kidder scrutinized the original outline; Stuart Gilman and Bayard L. Catron commented in detail on the outline and draft materials.

After setting me off in the right direction, Alan Shrader of Jossey-Bass thankfully operated like a switching device on an old-time railroad—he kept me on track and licensed no detour. Eric McClure and Paul Potamianos, graduate students at the George Washington University and the University of Connecticut, respectively, provided reliable and timely research assistance.

By combining kindness with criticism, the colleagues, friends, and family who read the draft manuscript confirm what I long suspected: public service is part diplomacy. Bayard L. Catron, Vera Vogelsang-Coombs, James Bowman, Stuart Gilman, Morton J. Tenzer, E. C. Markham, Norman Kugelmass, Gloria Cooper, and others offered perceptive comments and valuable suggestions.

I conclude these acknowledgments with a paragraph lifted almost wholesale from another book of mine because it says what I want to say now. It is standard practice among authors who draw upon so many resources, contributors, and talents to close with a disclaimer on behalf of others and to take the responsibility for errors, omissions, and choices solely upon themselves. Doing so is an easy matter here, simply because it is not a formality but a statement of fact. And with a subject such as ethics, open to nuance, bias, opinion, and contention, there are not so many facts that such an important one should be discounted.

CWL

The Author

Carol W. Lewis is professor of political science at the University of Connecticut, where she teaches public administration. A Phi Beta Kappa graduate of Cornell, she received her B.A. (1967) degree in government. Her M.A. (1970) and Ph.D. (1975) degrees in politics are from Princeton University. Her teaching and research interests include public budgeting and financial management, urban politics and management, and ethics in public service.

Lewis has taught in colleges and universities in four states, lectured to scholars and practitioners nationally and internationally, and conducted training programs for public managers in many locales. As consultant or project member, she has worked with the International Institute of Administrative Sciences, the U.S. National Academy of Public Administration, cross-national projects with the U.S. Department of Housing and Urban Development, and government agencies at all levels.

Lewis has designed and delivered ethics programs for numerous government agencies, public interest organizations, and professional associations. Examples include the International Personnel Management Association, Government Finance Officers Association, National University Continuing Education Association (Region I), National Association of State Training and Development Directors (regional and state), and associations representing cities and towns in her home state. Lewis gave the keynote address to the Council on Governmental Ethics Laws' national conference in 1986.

Writing for professional managers, Lewis has published in the Council on Governmental Ethics Laws' *Guardian*, the Government Finance Officers Association's *Government Finance Review*, and the International City Management Association's *Municipal Year Book* and *Public Management*. Her numerous scholarly articles have appeared in *Public Administration Review, Publius,* and many other journals. She is coeditor of several books and handbooks for practitioners and the author of *Scruples & Scandals: A Handbook on Public Service Ethics for State and Local Government Officials and Employees in Connecticut* (1986).

As a state employee, elected union representative, consultant, trainer, writer, professor, and public official in elective office, Lewis confronts many issues in this book firsthand.

The ETHICS
CHALLENGE
in PUBLIC
SERVICE

Ethics in the
Public Service

Ethics and genuine professional success go together in the ethical enterprise called *public service*. This introduction examines ethics and the profession and then sets the stage for action with some hard questions from workaday experience and a few definitions so that we talk the same language. Professional public service's tradition, experience, and current agenda point toward fusing standard routes to public service ethics.

- You are nearing the end of a hard day when one of your case workers tells you how a client proudly described her new job. You realize that it puts the client a few dollars over the cutoff of the county's income assistance program. Losing that aid strikes you as an unfair return for the client's initiative. Looking at the employee, you think how easy it would be to make a mistake in arithmetic and slip a case under the allowable error rate.
- Your co-worker's personal troubles are affecting his work performance. You understand that his irritability and unreliability are temporary, stemming from a messy divorce. Staying late to finish his monthly reports, you feel your resentment build, and you wonder whether covering for him is good for the agency and fair to you.
- Town ordinance forbids more than four unrelated people to share common living quarters. Verifying a neighbor's complaint on a site visit, you discover a somewhat unorthodox domestic setup by otherwise law-abiding adults. Their life-style appears to offend the neighbor. After years in the health department, you know ordinances like these have not stood up in court. Do you start eviction proceedings?

What is the right thing to do? What makes a problem your responsibility, a resolution your obligation? What does the difference between helping someone

1

and not hurting someone mean on the job? What is the right thing to do when the rules push one way and reason or compassion another?

- The legislature is giving your agency its "fair share": an across-the-board budget cut. Because you have seen to it that your agency is very efficient, it is hard to absorb a cut like this. As the current fiscal year draws to a close, you confirm unexpended funds in an appropriation account. You remember how your first boss ran up the postage meter to buy some slack at the end of the fiscal year.

Where do loyalties lie? When good management is penalized, should a responsible manager circumvent shortsighted economies to protect the agency, its mission, its employees, and service recipients? If an action is legal, does that make it ethical?

- More than one-half of all local government employees and more than two-fifths of all state government employees work in elementary, secondary, and higher education. Over 5,000 public employees staff 110 Livingston Street, headquarters for the New York City Board of Education. They map school districts, supervise a transportation network, manage facilities maintenance, direct immigrant services and bilingual programs, verify compliance with federal regulations and state mandates, tabulate statistics, and in general keep New York in school. Themselves overseers and regulators, these employees are "trapped in the same bureaucratic labyrinth they are often accused of creating" (Berger, 1990, p. A1). A senior human resource manager describes her "most painful memory": In the fiscal crisis of the mid–1970s, her division ranked teachers by seniority in their licensed subject, prepared layoff letters, and listened to pleas and objections. Among the 16,000 laid off, there had to be personal tragedies and disrupted lives. The manager said, "I would not have the emotional stamina to live through that again" (Berger, 1990, p. B2).

If pain is not a good/bad meter, how do you know that what you are doing is right? "What am I doing, keeping my job and firing operational employees? What is the agency's purpose, after all?" What is the difference between what is right and what is easy? How do you cope when the job requires some dirty work? How do you survive budget-crunch pressures?

- In Idaho, public land managers can cross big business and the agency at the same time. Subsidizing ranching while protecting public land, the Forest Service and Bureau of Land Management manage several hundred million acres of public land and enforce grazing guidelines and land management practices. A quarter-century-plus veteran with the Forest Service advanced to district ranger and supervised 220,000 acres in the Sawtooth Forest. Defying the thirty ranchers with permits to run cattle, his campaign against allegedly abusive land practices went as far as an unannounced cattle count. His reason? "This land belongs to 250 million Americans, not just the guy with a cattle-grazing permit" (Egan, 1990b, p. 20). Even with threats on his life, he refused a transfer and blew the whistle to the Department of Agriculture's inspector general. According to a retired co-worker, "They may sacrifice him at the Forest Service, but what he's doing is right" (Egan, 1990b, p. 20).

If users' threats and supervisors' approval are no barometers, how do you know you are right? Who is the client? Why buck the system? How do you decide whether to blow the whistle or keep quiet?

Relentless pressures and quick decisions are routine in public service. Because the choices truly matter for everyone, including the public manager, this book examines dilemmas like these and offers some resolutions.

Working Definition

Public-sector managers do the job, solve the problem, even work some miracles—and practice ethics besides. Personal, professional, and public expectations converge to challenge managers who voice and resolve routine and emergency ethical problems. Ethical action is another part of the job.

Only a few definitions are needed for a meaningful, practical dialogue. *Ethics* involves thinking systematically about morals and conduct and making judgments about right and wrong. What makes ethics so important to public service is that it goes beyond thought and talk to performance and action. As a guideline for action, ethics draws on what is right and important, or "abstract standards that persist over time and that identify what is right and proper" (Boling and Dempsey, 1981, p. 14). Rooted in the idea of responsibility, ethics implies the willingness to accept the consequences of one's actions. Ethics also refers to principles of action that implement or promote moral values.

Moral character means having appropriate ethical values and is associated with attributes such as honesty and fidelity. It is a sort of internal gyroscope that distinguishes right from wrong and inhibits wrongdoing. Bringing their moral character to the job, ethical managers do a two-step: informed, systematic reasoning followed by action.

In sum, the subject of ethics is action based on judgments of right and wrong. Three questions summarize the subject's pragmatic underpinnings: What counts? What is at stake? How can managers ensure professional success and ethical survival? Finer distinctions and fancier terminology are available for conceptual clarification, but they threaten to bury the subject in semantics. That is a terminal exercise; it kills interest along with utility for practical managers more concerned with deeds than definitions.

The Scope of Public Service. Public service is *doing* and, for that reason, is better defined by public mission—what the manager is doing—than by legal statutes or other formal criteria. For our purposes, public service refers to agencies and activities *tending toward* the public side of the continuum shown in Figure I.1. In actuality, there is no clear division between public and private. Embracing more than government service alone, public service includes quasi-governmental agencies and the many nonprofit agencies devoted to community service (and often partially publicly funded). The many mixed activities and joint operations, such as public-private partnerships and even contractual relationships, turn on working with government and are, therefore, also oriented toward public service.

Actually, there is no autonomous isolated agency or activity that does *not* respond to, interact with, or affect those at the other end of the continuum. Consider, for example, the following: taxation and business decisions; corporate siting and land-use regulation; immigration, government hiring, and the labor pool; Social Security payments and consumer demand; and private producers and government procurement. Most activities, most institutions, and most resources fall between the polar extremes of purely governmental and purely private.

Because public service is broader than government service, it may be useful to take a moment to think over the status of your agency. Where is your agency on the continuum? Are you a public manager? Should public service standards and obligations apply to you?

A Special Calling. Given the action function, a savvy public manager logically asks what the point of all the noise about public service ethics really is. Ideally, the point is to promote ethical practice and support ethical practitioners in public service and, through that, in the larger society. Many people, including this author, unashamedly believe that this purpose underlies most public managers' choice of profession. Rational managers certainly are not in public service for the money; other inducements must be drawing them to the office.

That most public managers work to make a positive difference is a central tenet of public service lore. It is the earnest theme of the Public Employees

Figure I.1. The Public-Private Continuum.

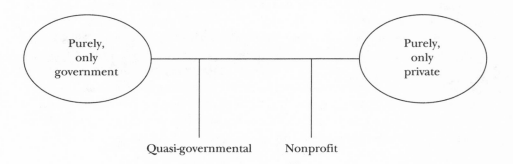

Purely, only government

Purely, only private

Quasi-governmental   Nonprofit

Roundtable's 1988 film entitled *The Difference You Make!* The goal is to have an impact on more than one's own pocketbook. It recalls President Kennedy's famous call in his 1961 inaugural address: "And so, my fellow Americans, ask not what your country can do for you—ask what you can do for your country." For great and small matters, "May I help you?" could be the public service mantra. Making a difference means that optimism underlies action and progress is a premier purpose.

The hard part about working for the best is knowing what it is and then doing it. This is what ethics is all about.

Disabling or Empowering. While belief in progress is a public service attribute, it does *not* cast public managers in the role of Don Quixote, tilting at imaginary windmills. It does *not* demand that managers butt futilely against a brick wall. It pays, then, to begin by assessing the situation.

The profession is animated by ethics' dual potential—for disabling and for empowering managers. The newfound concern with ethics has the potential for disabling managers if it is used as a coercive control device, an exploitative tool, a subtle motivational gimmick, or a public relations scheme. Alternatively, it can empower managers by promoting ethical practices, supporting ethical managers, and reinforcing accountability.

For many managers and this author, the first set of possibilities cries out "Stop!" while the second signals a careful "Go!" Either way, ethics is "the new political symbol to change controls over the bureaucracy," as Vera Vogelsang-Coombs, a state manager in the midwest, remarked to the author in August 1990. (Ethics is more accurately seen as a renewal rather than a radical departure from traditional practice. In its early years, professional public administration in the United States had a strongly moralistic dimension; it developed partly in revulsion against the partisan spoils system's blatant corruption.)

Cynics may downgrade ethics, dismissing the whole business as a public relations scheme or an alibi. For example, an open-ended question in a *City & State* survey (1989, p. 104) drew the reply, "The pay for governmental work is already lower than the private sector, without all the B.S. of these ethical standards." At the other extreme stand the idealists, who push too far, too fast. The impassioned go-ahead usually fails in American administration. Then there are the pragmatists, who back off and go slowly, aware that ethics proposals in public management open the door to misuse and abuse.

Public Administration's Track Record

The first step in figuring out how to get there from here is to pinpoint where we are now. A brief review of public service's experience with ethics helps us understand where we stand now, what it means, and how we arrived.

There are enough elements in management theory to support pragmatists' caution about administrative ethics. Going back to our theoretical roots, we see that both pre–World War I *scientific management* and the *human relations school* of the 1920s and 1930s treated ethical concerns as they did workers—instrumentally, to elicit more productivity. Image, not ethics, was one big difference between the two; the machine vied with the biological organism as the model of a social organization. Chester Barnard's *The Functions of the Executive,* published in 1938 on the eve of World War II, provides a much-cited argument for the instrumental approach to ethics for executives, who should "deal effectively with the moral complexities of organizations without being broken by the imposed problems of choice" (Stillman, 1984, p. 478).

The amoral machine won out in the dogma of public administration that dominates even today. A presidential committee's report issued in 1937 epitomized that view and also contributed the Executive Office of the President (itself to become a powerful institution and a source of ethical and legal problems). The report announced that "real efficiency . . . must be built into the structure of government just as it is built into a piece of machinery" (Brownlow Committee, [1937] 1987, p. 92). That same year, a core statement of classical public administrative theory enthroned a single, overriding value by proclaiming efficiency "axiom number one" in administration (Gulick, 1937). Having settled upon the primary value, public administration could ignore issues of choice, values, and ethics. This was simple and comfortably in line with the original posture that neatly divided amoral, technical administration from value-laden politics.

The developing social sciences such as sociology, anthropology, psychology, economics, and political science also contributed to the temporary triumph of amoral public management. Social science nurtured a dichotomy between facts and values and rejected the latter as unsuitable for scientific study. As a result, the positivists ignored ethics.

Business Backdrop. When ethics was not banished entirely, the instrumental view held sway. This is hardly surprising, considering the fact that business management was the primary source of theories and empirical research. Much was lifted wholesale; efficiency dominated. With respect to business ethics, "a critical ethical obligation . . . is to fulfill this basic business activity as efficiently as possible" (Rion, 1990, p. 46). The cardinal standard is getting the job done; all else is secondary. Initially, business served as the outright model for public administration, and the mantle of the generic *management expert* was bestowed upon business experts. (Max Weber, to whom we owe much of what we know or believe about bureaucracy, judged the distinction between public and private meaningless for understanding bureaucratic authority.)

A letter from Chester Barnard to Senator Paul Douglas hints at the consequences. Barnard declined for reasons of health and schedule to participate in the 1951 Senate hearings on establishing a governmental ethics commission. He wrote, "I have no consistent and worked-out ideas on this subject although it is one to which I have given a good deal of thought from time to time in connection with my experience both in the Federal Government and in that of New Jersey."

Measured by talk (codes, conferences, publications), ethics is a hot topic on today's corporate circuit. But its backseat status is built into an executive recruiter's observation: "A strong chief executive needs to stop and say, 'Wait a minute. We've got to think about the legal, social, and ethical ramifications of this decision'" (Ansberry, 1987, p. 35). Note that the implicit timing for raising these issues is directly contrary to public service custom.

Business management is not to be faulted for its influence on public management. We did it to ourselves. At the conception, Woodrow Wilson (practitioner-scholar *par excellence*, popularly credited with founding the field of public administration in the United States on his way to becoming president) firmly grounded professional public service in making government more "businesslike." Administration, as "government in action" (Wilson, [1887] 1987, p. 11), was formulated largely as a problem of science, technology, or businesslike management.

Rediscovery of the Ethical Enterprise. The private sector has standards, but that they diverge from public sector standards somehow was overlooked. (The difference is not in underlying ethical values and principles but in the number of standards, their emphasis and priority, and the degree of fastidious adherence to them.) Whether standards and aspirations are higher or lower is not the issue here, but rather that they are *different.* Perhaps this was forgotten in the rush to embrace the entrepreneurial spirit so prominent in American myth. Coming from a business background, public service would take decades to reorient and acknowledge that public and private management are alike "in all unimportant respects" (Allison, 1987). As President Jimmy Carter noted in *Why Not the Best?* (1976, p. 132), "Nowhere in the Constitution of the United States, or the Declaration of Independence, or the Bill of Rights, or the Emancipation Proclamation, or the Old Testament or the New Testament, do you find the words 'economy' or 'efficiency.' Not that these words are unimportant. But you discover other words like honesty, integrity, fairness, liberty, justice, patriotism, compassion, love—and many others which describe what human beings ought to be. These are the same words which describe what a government of human beings ought to be."

The profession had lost sight of government's fundamental purpose—making and enforcing normatively driven choices and pursuing selected social, political, and economic goals. Still, a few practitioners and educators expressed ethical concerns. Years ago, Paul Appleby (1951, p. 171) observed that "the genius of democracy is in politics, not in sterilization of politics."

Yet only now is the profession beginning to air the old philosophical proposition that, ideally, government *is* ethics institutionalized for pursuing the public good. (A senior federal manager quoted Rousseau's *Social Contract* on this point and the author hereby passes along his recommendation for required reading.)

Administrative ethics began to emerge as a concern in its own right only after catastrophic irrationalities such as two world wars, genocide, and atom bombs taught us the power of organization; groundbreaking analysis of decision making in organizations by Nobel Prize winner Herbert Simon (1947) and others taught us its limits; and administrative discretion prospered, thereby relegating the traditional dichotomy between politics and administration to the realm of delusion. At the same time, bureaucratic atrocities, misguided efficiencies, errors, and blind spots begged for explanation.

The sociological search led to the "organizational man," who is socialized and pressured by and for the organization and thus ethically benumbed. (Remember the Hollywood classic *The Man in the Grey Flannel Suit?*) The psychological search associated with names such as Skinner, Piaget, and Kohlberg took behavioralism well beyond the human relations school to learning theory and influential theories of cognitive development.

In public service, the search was not for an explanation but a solution. This led to more red tape instead of an ethical resurgence. Exploding responsibilities, growing staffs, and mounting budgets were transforming public agencies. Responses were keyed to classical public administration, with its emphasis on technical and organizational remedies, plus conventional institutional arrangements in the constitutional tradition. Many jurisdictions responded to new challenges by slapping on ever more numerous and sophisticated controls to ease the intensifying risk of fraud, waste, and abuse. The accent on controls and oversight diverted attention from people to dollars and from personnel to more readily controllable financial management. The 1982 Federal Manager's Financial Integrity Act (31 U.S.C. 3512) is a case in point.

Some would summarize the result for many agencies as a strangulating, dehumanizing, even less productive work environment. Some would emphasize how we tied ourselves and employees in knots and forced ourselves to look for ways around the rules. Few would argue that more controls led to more integrity among public employees.

Professional Legacy. Today's *ethics revival* in public service grows out of these intellectual roots and practical experiences. It also echoes concerns in the broader society. We acknowledge that legitimate government—meaning public management, too—is in fact an ethical enterprise.

What do managers do, then, with this professional legacy in terms of the ethical side of management? Do we just turn our backs, echoing the sentiment of a character in James Joyce's *Ulysses,* who remarks, "History . . . is a nightmare from which I am trying to awake"? Total rejection sets us up for self-contempt and the baby-with-the-bath-water syndrome. Sanctification is the polar extreme, but here we face the danger of mindlessly repeating old mistakes. That leaves a point in between, calibrated by picking and choosing in a pragmatic, reflective way.

Public service's track record counsels a "go" but "go-slow" attitude toward ethics in the workplace. Wariness, instead of paralyzing us, can short-circuit both excessive regulations and unbridled expectations. A cautious attitude now can prevent the later repudiation that is inevitable if we set ethics up as the single cure for all managerial ills.

Three Roads to the Future

Public management practice and theory offer two often opposing routes to the goal of encouraging ethical practice and ethical practitioners in public agencies. These routes encourage different behavior, make use of different vehicles, promote different purposes, and lead in different directions. A third path merges the other two and moves public service at slow speed in the direction of moderation and innovation.

The "Low Road" of Compliance. The path of compliance, in the words of the poet, means "dreaming of systems so perfect that no one needs to be good." A largely proscriptive, coercive, punitive, and even threatening route, this approach to ethics is designed to spur obedience to *minimum* standards and legal prohibitions. It is enforced by controls on the job that ordinarily aim at acceptable levels of risk, not flawless purity.

John Rohr (1989, p. 60) calls this the "low road." It features "adherence to formal rules" and a negative outlook. Along this road, Rohr argues (p. 63), "Ethical behavior is reduced to staying out of trouble" and the result is "meticulous attention to trivial questions." *How to Keep Out of Trouble*, the title of a publication from the U.S. Office of Government Ethics, makes good sense in this context.

A compliance perspective monopolizes thinking about ethical behavior in many quarters, including the federal government and many states and localities. The federal training course for deputy ethics officials deals with behavior exclusively in terms of legally enforceable standards and as legalistic problems to be solved (by reference, for example, to the U.S. Code and Code of Federal Regulations) rather than ethical dilemmas to be resolved (U.S. Office of Government Ethics, 1990c). Very much to the point is that more than three-quarters of the federal administrators responsible for ethics programs are in the *legal* offices of federal agencies (U.S. Office of Government Ethics, 1990a, p. 22).

Compliance seems to possess a magnetic charm; Congress, along with some state legislatures, is beginning to match the executive branch's ardor. Illustratively, the very first sentence of the first chapter in an ethics manual for members and staff of the U.S. House of Representatives (1987) reads, "Various penalties or consequences may arise for a violation of an ethical standard." The allure of compliance is both explained and mirrored in the words of a U.S. deputy attorney general in the U.S. Department of Justice: "In the minds of many Americans, public service, government officials, politicians, crooks, and criminal activity are inextricably mixed" (Burns, 1987, p. 46).

In managerial terms, compliance translates into oversight and controls.

When it comes to ensuring accountability, these are facts of life in the complex, highly structured, and very powerful organizations we label *bureaucracy*. Nikolai Gogol's play *The Inspector General* is a suggestive description of a response to compliance in the field. This nineteenth-century Russian drama opens with a governor, analogous to a political appointee, announcing the imminent arrival of an inspector! Feeling threatened by impending doom, the governor relates his dream of giant, peculiar rats that sniff and sniff at everything and everyone. Any manager who has undergone an audit probably can relate to his dream.

Realistically, public managers are not about to purge compliance from government operations. Nor should managers want to. Represented by administrative controls and legal sanctions, compliance is fundamental to the way the public business is conducted. As guardians of political relationships and political goals, *controls are accountability implemented*. For evidence, look on your desk. Controls are ingrained in budgeting and personnel, traditional managerial functions.

The American system has been preoccupied with accountability from its inception. Exhibit I.1 is probably the single most important travel reimbursement in American history. It shows that colonial controls were enforced even in revolution, when the founders actually were turning their backs on authority in "the first general crisis of authority in American history" (Lipset and Schneider, 1987, p. 2). Even so, Paul Revere duly submitted his bill for printing and "riding for the Committee of Safety" in 1775. The Massachusetts legislature approved payment "in full discharge of the written account"—but for less than the patriot requested. George Washington's detailed account of expenses incurred as commander-in-chief (Jotman, 1988) provides more and just as disillusioning historical evidence of using controls to implement accountability.

The "High Road" of Integrity. The path of integrity is ethics in the raw. Relying on moral character, this route counts on ethical managers individually to reflect, decide, and act. Integrity is a basic ethical value, not limited to public service by any means. Ethical behavior draws on appropriate values and principles, absorbed from upbringing, philosophy, or, in John Rohr's formulation, regime values as constitutionally derived ethical norms. Individual responsibility is both starting *and* end points on the integrity route in public service. Along it lie the normative, voluntary, prescriptive, persuasive, and positive—but no external—inducements or penalties.

Because the integrity route is noninstitutional by definition, public agencies show few signs of it. Examples from the field include the credos (mislabeled as *codes*) adopted by the Government Finance Officers Association, the International Personnel Management Association, and the American Society for Public Administration (GFOA, IPMA, and ASPA, respectively). Relying on persuasion, they cajole members to measure up.

An approach based solely on individual integrity, as upbeat as it sounds, brings its own difficulties. It bypasses unethical behavior entirely and preaches to the believers. When reduced to simplistic do-good exhortation, it overlooks the competing claims that perplex an ethical manager. By neglecting the decision-making environment and focusing exclusively on autonomous moral individuals, the integrity approach sweeps aside organizational and other influences that affect behavior. Given the fact that the organization is an important influence on an individual's behavior, an *exclusive* focus on the individual operates on an inappropriate level of analysis. Perhaps more to the point, the integrity route does not seem to have worked all that well, and abuse and corruption persist.

The Fusion Route. The low road of compliance does not care that most people want to make good decisions but only that most people meet minimum standards of conduct. Integrity's high road rejects administrative realities that stem from accountability. Both mistakenly reduce the world to two distinct categories of ethical and unethical, whereas managers actually cope in the gray areas of legitimate but competing values, principles, and responsibilities. Neither approach *alone* accomplishes the purpose of spurring ethical practice and practitioners in public service.

This purpose calls for fusing the two standard approaches and moving on both fronts at once. This is a bipartisan conclusion reached long ago, often repeated but rarely implemented. Now all we have to do is follow through.

To the extent that public service has moved on both fronts, it results more from default than strategy and is more a hodgepodge than a blending. In 1989, James Bowman (1989, 1990) surveyed a random sample of 750 practicing managers who were members of the American Society for Public Administration. (Usable responses were returned by 59 percent of the sample.) More than one-fifth of the respondents agreed with the statement, "Most organizations have a reactive, legalistic, blame-punishment approach that focuses on discouraging and detecting unethical behavior." Less than one-tenth answered, "Most organizations have [a] proactive, human-development, problem-solving approach that focuses on encouraging ethical behavior and deterring unethical behavior." Slightly more than two-thirds responded, "Most organizations have no consistent approach."

Public service and public employees would both be well served by management's selectively merging the best from the compliance and integrity routes. Such a merger fuses forces together to meet energetically the public service purpose stipulated at the start of this introduction. A purposefully modernistic symbol, fusion here implies no explosion. Its futuristic orientation has roots deep in Western (and other) culture, reaching back to Aristotle's golden mean defining virtue as the mean of excess and shortfall. In the familiar context of a balanced budget (less familiar, of course, in the federal context than others), the *good* outcome falls between surplus and deficit; any other outcome signals trouble.

This is the path of moderation, adaptation, and compromise; it works through phased innovation on both compliance and integrity fronts and at a slow pace. William L. Richter (1989) imparts its tone and direction in answer to the

Exhibit I.1. Paul Revere's Bill and Reimbursement.

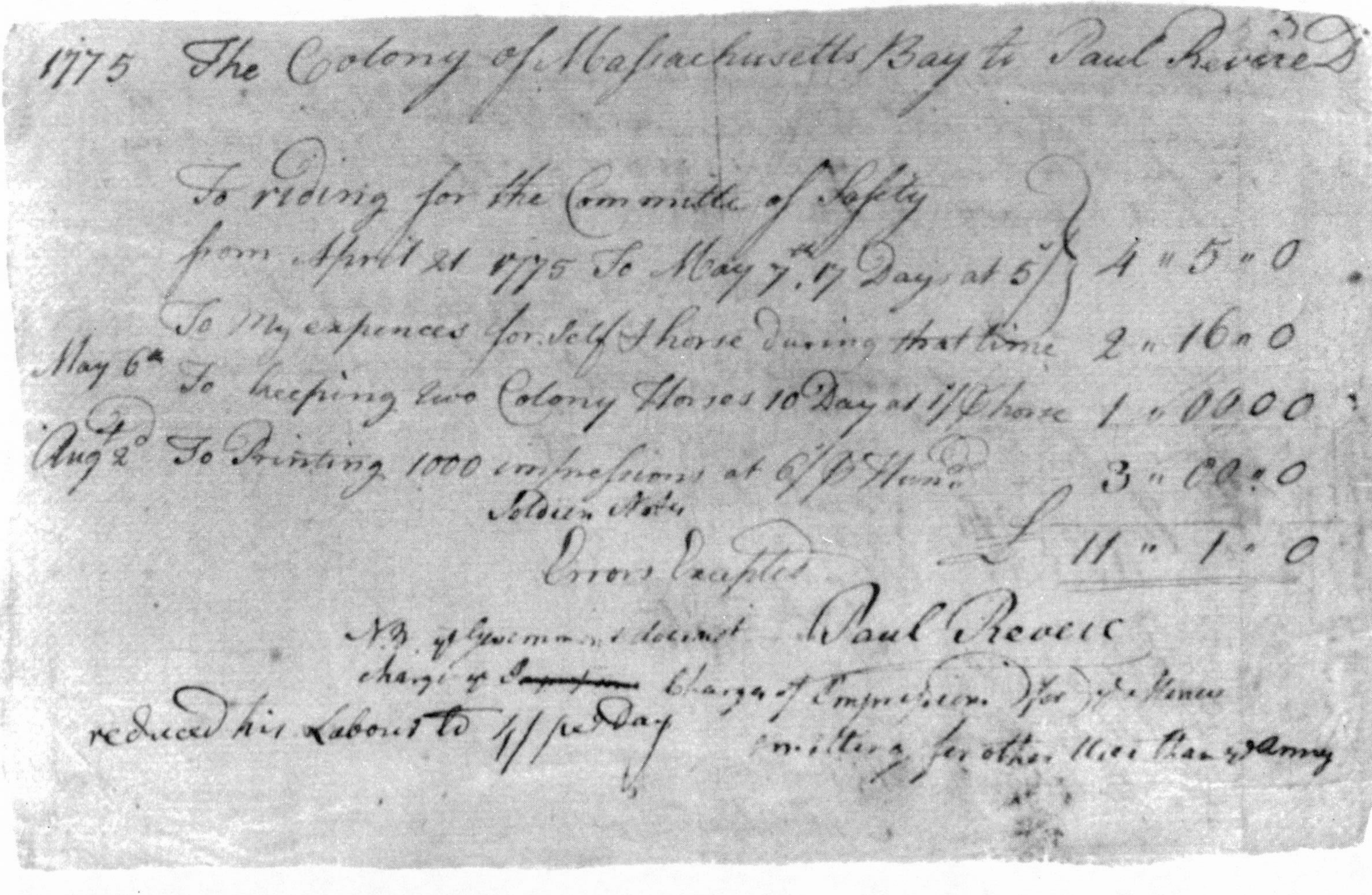

1775 The Colony of Massachusetts Bay to Paul Revere Dr

	To riding for the Committee of Safety from April 21 1775 To May 7th 17 Days at 5/	4 " 5 " 0
	To My expences for Self & horse during that time	2 " 16 " 0
May 6th	To keeping two Colony Horses 10 Day at 1/ horse	1 " 00 " 0
Aug 2d	To Printing 1000 impressions at 6/ pr Hund. Soldiers Notes	3 " 00 " 0
		£ 11 " 1 " 0

Errors Excepted

Paul Revere

N.B. the Government allowed [illegible] charge of [illegible] Charge of Impression for the Notes [illegible] other [illegible] the Army

reduced his Labour to 4/ per Day

Revere's Acct

In the House of Representatives August 22d 1775

Resolved that Mr Paul Revere be allowed & paid out of the publick Treasury of this Colony ten pounds Thirteen shillings in full Discharge of the within Account

Sent up for Concurrence

Jas Warren Speaker

In Council Aug 22d 1775

Read & Concurred Samll Adams Pres't

James Otis
Saml Adams
W Sever
Joseph Gerrish
John Winthrop
B Greenleaf
S. Holten
Jedh Foster
Eldad Taylor
Jabez Fisher
M Farley
W Spooner
T Cushing
Caleb Cushing
John Adams
J Palmer

£29.3

Received of Daniel Boardman £10.13
Aug 22. 1775

question of whether ethics regulations have gone too far. Calling for a different attitude, he says, "Positive ethics means concentrating a little less on what we must prevent—and a little more on what we want to accomplish." A two-pronged, systematic approach accomplishes that by incorporating both compliance with formal standards and the promotion of individual ethical responsibility.

There is no parade and no intoxicating drumbeat along this road. When public management jumps on the latest management bandwagon, the ancient virtue of temperance is heavily devalued. Ethics demands informed reflection and individual judgment; ethical managers are counted on to make sober decisions. Public service is too important to be swept up in the carnival atmosphere of the hottest fad, where reaching for the golden ring sabotages the golden mean.

Ethical Responsibilities of Public Managers

Chapter 1

What Is Important in Public Service?

Examining ethics and the profession, Part One asserts that ethics and genuine professional success go together in the ethical enterprise called *public service*. It is the job itself—the ambiguous, complex, pressured world of public service— that presents special problems for ethical people who want to do the right thing. Facing up to the ethical demands on public managers starts with biting the bullet: public service ethics is different from ethics in private life. The reason is that democracy is sustained by public trust, a link forged by stringent ethical standards. This chapter concludes with a diagnostic exercise that clarifies the contending values and cross pressures pressing on everyday judgment calls.

Public managers' morale, identity, and capacity for decision making and innovation are entangled in ethics, and rightly so because public service is our society's instrument for managing complexity. The National Commission on the Public Service, established in 1987 and chaired by Paul A. Volcker, concluded in its 1989 report, "If government is to be both responsive to the people's will and capable of meeting the challenges of the twenty-first century, it must have a public service of talent, of commitment, of dedication to the highest ethical standards" (Volcker Commission, 1989).

The concern with ethics and demands on managerial responsibility extend beyond academic halls to government corridors, public interest groups, and professional associations. Much of the recent action—for example, the race to adopt ethics codes in many jurisdictions—translates into new challenges for the public manager. New York State passed its Ethics in Government Act in 1987, and a year later the State Commission on Government Integrity proposed uniform, statewide standards for local jurisdictions. California and West Virginia subscribe to new or extended codes; Alaska is considering them. The Bush administration's executive orders and *Frontline,* the newsletter of the President's Council on Integrity and Efficiency, attest to federal interest emanating from the White House.

Public expectations and formal standards in increasing numbers of jurisdictions demand that managers undertake sophisticated ethical reasoning and practical application of ethical standards to decisions and behavior.

Several professional associations such as ASPA, GFOA, and the International City Management Association (ICMA) have adopted or updated their codes within the last decade. Canada's Institute of Public Administration embraced its "Statement of Principles Regarding the Conduct of Public Employees" in 1986. Common Cause, a public interest group, overhauled its original (1974) model ethics law in 1989. The Council on Governmental Ethics Laws (COGEL) drafted model legislation in 1990.

The guidelines of the National Association of Schools of Public Affairs and Administration incorporate ethics into curriculum standards aimed at aspiring public managers (Catron and Denhardt, 1988). Ethics training is today a conventional method for promoting ethical practices. It is required, for example, in California and for many specified federal appointees and employees. Typically, training exclusively targets compliance with minimum statutory or administrative standards written into codes of conduct. Some training programs focus on individual responsibility for ethical judgment but ignore or downplay the organizational context for decision making. Nonetheless, the fashionable trend toward ethics training testifies to the importance attached to the subject.

Why Me?

Ethical concerns target public service for two main reasons. One is that public power, authority, and accountability mean that a democracy depends on trust. That trust has declined. The second reason is the higher standards earmarked for public service and the public's perception of a pervasive shortfall.

Public Confidence. The relationship between ethics and trust is so widely presumed, it is written directly into professional codes, law, and regulations at all levels of government. The intuitive hunch is that public confidence in government is grounded in ethics. It carries with it broad acceptance of general activity. An openly instrumental approach cultivates ethics as politically useful because it makes collective action possible, desirable, and legitimate.

Public agencies are critical elements in our ability to govern effectively through the voluntary compliance we prefer over compulsory obedience. All mainstream segments of the political spectrum share this preference and assume that ethics, trust, and government power are linked. President Reagan affirmed his faith in his March 1987 response to the Tower Commission's report on the Iran-Contra investigation. He declared, "The power of the presidency is often thought to reside within this Oval Office, yet it doesn't rest here. It rests in you, the American people, and in your trust. Your trust is what gives a president his powers of leadership and his personal strength."

The "confidence gap" symbolizes a *pervasive* erosion of confidence in government and public trust of public institutions, paralleling attitudes toward all institutions (Lipset and Schneider, 1987). The public assessment: perceived wrongdoing plagues society; from Wall Street to evangelical tents, no segment is immune.

Public confidence started its downturn in the early 1960s. It continued its plunge through the 1970s and the events of Watergate that climaxed in August 1974, when for the first time an incumbent president resigned. The spirit was dubbed "moral malaise" in the Carter administration. The celebrated turnaround in the early years of the Reagan administration was so modest compared with the earlier, precipitous decline that it is more accurately interpreted as a decline in distrust rather than an increase in confidence. The Reagan record came to be shadowed by an ethics cloud under which many high-level officials left office.

The public attitude pervaded all types and levels of public service. In national Harris polls conducted between 1977 and 1985, less than one-quarter of the respondents expressed a great deal of confidence in those running state and local governments. The governor of West Virginia wrote in 1989, "At all levels of government, we have been faced with a seemingly endless erosion of ethical standards which has undermined public confidence in elected officials and belied the very premises on which public service is predicated" (Caperton, 1989, p. i).

Seasoned veterans habitually moderate their distress by allowing for the political mileage gained by bemoaning moral deterioration. It is a favorite pastime. Yet even the most cynical among us must admit that the nationwide, overall decline in trust in government is part and parcel of discussions of contemporary ethics. Low evaluations on ethical dimensions such as "honesty, dependability, and integrity" as well as on efficiency (the "ability to get things done") sound the alarm (Lipset and Schneider, 1987). Because public confidence is believed to be related to public perceptions of ethical practices, energies shift to improving the ethical posture and reputation of public service in order to increase public trust. Fundamentally, public service is and must be an ethical enterprise.

Higher Standards. Despite the ballyhoo, public opinion usually judges public service on the whole as no worse than other segments of society. Sparse data indicate that people in public service are usually seen as about average—no worse but also no better than others. Exhibit 1.1 lays out the details. The problem is that average is just not good enough.

In reality, average is not the public's, the profession's, or the public employee's expectation. Falling short of a higher expectation arouses a sense of ineptitude, even betrayal. Whatever the actual or perceived incidence of corruption or the fairness of it all, the simple fact is that public service is expected to operate on a higher ethical plane than other, garden-variety activities. Decades ago, an eminent practitioner-academic testified at Senate hearings (Appleby, 1951, p. 166): "It is significant, too, that the American people generally seek and expect from the Government of the United States higher standards than they expect elsewhere. . . . And on the whole they do receive from elected and ap-

Exhibit 1.1. Public Opinion: Only Average.

Most available data describe opinions about elected officials; data rarely refer specifically to career professionals.

- Ethical practices of federal, state and local officials, treated as an occupational group, were rated as fair or poor by a majority of respondents in three national surveys between 1981 and 1985; the practices of federal officials and those in state and local government were rated as excellent or good by *only* 23–33 percent and 31–37 percent, respectively (Lipset and Schneider, 1987, p. 433).
- In Gallup surveys conducted between 1977 and 1985, state and local political office-holders were judged by about one-half the respondents as *average* on ethics.
- A survey asking about the honesty and ethical standards of the people in different fields found that police ranked as average (41 percent) and high (40 percent), while state officeholders and local officeholders were ranked average by 55 percent and 56 percent, respectively (Gallup Organization, 1990).
- In answer to the question, "Do you think of the federal government overall as honest or not?" 50 percent of the respondents said no and 40 percent said yes (Associated Press/Media General, 1988).
- When Connecticut respondents were directed to think "not of high-ranking state officials, but of ordinary state employees" and to compare Connecticut state workers to their private-sector counterparts, more than three-quarters responded "about as honest" (University of Connecticut, 1989).

---

pointed officials generally a return of extraordinary devotion, even though the weighing of value questions is so complicated and difficult as to make the judgments reached highly controversial." Appleby's words ring true for all of public service.

The Latin word *virtu* means "excellence" and that summarizes the demands made on those in public service by public opinion, philosophical tradition, historical experience, and professional identity. In actuality, as a special endeavor, public service operates on distinctive standards that reflect particular values.

The proposition is this: public officials and employees truly are expected to meticulously conform to standards higher than those aligned with strictly personal morality. Almost nine-tenths of the respondents to a 1987 readership survey answered no to the question "Should ethics of the business world be different from personal ethics?" (Guy, 1990, p. 9). The nobility and burden of public service are that it cues a different answer.

The American political tradition resounds with that refrain. It is sounded in the well-known words of Thomas Jefferson, "Where a man assumes a public trust, he should consider himself a public property." Henry Clay echoed it: "Government is a trust, and the officers of the government are trustees; and both the trust and the trustees are created for the benefit of the people."

The interaction of trust, confidence, and governmental integrity is evident in law and regulation. It is conspicuous in governmental codes across the nation. For example, an ordinance from Austin, Texas announces, "It is the policy of the city that the proper operation of democratic government requires that public officials and employees be independent, impartial and responsible to the people;

... and that the public have confidence in the integrity of its government." ASPA's code forges an especially strong link: "Nothing is more important to public administrators than the public's opinion about their honesty, truthfulness, and personal integrity. It overshadows competence as the premier value sought in their public officials and employees."

Public Service Values. Ethical values are beliefs about right and wrong. These yardsticks for ethical behavior draw on feeling and thinking. Sentiment and reason combine into predispositions or inclinations to act (Cooper, 1987).

Not all values are the same or are associated with ethical behavior. Some muster *virtues*, the habits of ethical action imbedded in character. Virtues, the foundation of moral character that underlies ethical behavior, translate abstract, ethical values into customary, observable behavior. Many ancient traditions stress personal virtue, and Plato wrote of four: courage, wisdom, justice, and moderation. In Buddhist teachings, "Good men and bad men differ from each other in their natures. . . . Wise men are sensitive to right and wrong" (Bukkyo Dendo Kyokai, 1987, p. 264). In Exodus 18:21, when Moses sets about forming his administrative hierarchy for the tribes of Israel newly liberated from slavery, his father-in-law, Jethro, advises him to "provide out of all the people able men, such as fear God, men of truth, hating covetousness; and place such over them, to be rulers."

Because not all values are ethical values, contemporary observers of the managerial scene draw up their own lists of requisite values and virtues. Some relate to modern business management, others more directly to democratic ideals. Among those drawn upon in this book, Laura Nash (1981, 1990) and Michael Rion (1990) figure among the former; John Rohr (1989), Michael Josephson (1989; Josephson Institute, 1990), and Terry Cooper (1987, 1990) are among the latter. Also in the democratic mode, Stephen Bailey, an especially influential figure in public administration, selected optimism, courage, and "fairness tempered by charity" (1964, p. 236).

The point is, in public service, particular values are of special concern. They are part of the answer to the question "Why me?" asked earlier. These values support principles of action that distinguish public service from other endeavors.

Why not a select a single roster of ethical values? A list—plain dealing and direct—would be more compelling and maybe even more appealing. The answer lies in what ethics itself is all about.

- Ethical action is reflective; it is based on thought and reason.
- Ethical action is principled—based on sound values.
- Ethical action means making normative judgments—and that means choice.

For Adults Only

The hallmark of adulthood is tolerating ambiguity, uncertainty, and complexity. Not necessarily liking it, mind you, just tolerating it. That is the ethical context of public service, and it demands maturity, a solid sense of self, and a receptive frame of mind.

Competing Ethical Claims. Rival claims devour a public manager's time, attention, and loyalties. Competing obligations in modern life pull everyone in different directions while physical mobility disrupts ties that, once upon a time, lasted a lifetime. Ask the city manager or field agent whose career requires periodic relocation. The modem, fax, cellular phone, and other technological *comforts* let competing calls invade every arena. These pulls fragment thinking and can even shatter an undisciplined manager who exercises no selectivity.

Discriminating discipline is imposed by the manager's priorities that specify what is important and when. Choices among responsibilities are made with an eye to *roles—the sources of operative ethical responsibilities—*which define behavior expected by oneself and others in different circumstances. The demand to play multiple roles causes many of the pressures associated with contemporary public service.

Different perspectives stress different concepts and responsibilities, but all envelop numerous and varied roles and responsibilities. For example, Dwight Waldo (1981, pp. 104–106) seems to encompass them all in his unranked catalogue of twelve spheres of ethical claims on the public servant: the constitution; the law; nation, country, or people; democracy; organization-bureaucratic norms; profession and professionalism; family and friends; self; middle-range collectivities such as class, party, race, union, interest group, church; public interest or general welfare; humanity, world, or future; and religion or God.

This is a lot to absorb all at once, and an analytic handle may be useful. Michael Harmon's "theory of countervailing responsibility" organizes *opposing* aspects of administrative responsibility into three types: the political, professional, and personal. "Action that is deemed correct from the standpoint of one meaning might very well be incorrect or irresponsible from the standpoint of another" (1990, p. 154); therefore, tension is built into administrative life. Harmon (p. 157) defines each type:

> *Political Responsibility:* "Action that is accountable to or consistent with objectives or standards of conduct mandated by political or hierarchical authority."
>
> *Professional Responsibility:* "Action that is informed by professional expertise, standards of ethical conduct, and by experience rooted in agency history and traditions."
>
> *Personal Responsibility:* "Action that is informed by self-reflexive understanding; and emerges from a context of authentic relationships wherein personal commitments are regarded as valid bases for moral action."

Competing claims and interests are inevitable once the public service role is defined as distinct and different from other roles. The distinction, the separation itself, is what induces conflict. As the National Municipal League points out, "having a conflict of interest is not, in and of itself, evil, wrong or even unusual. Conflicts may be ethnic, cultural, emotional, nostalgic, regional, financial or philosophical" (Weimer, 1990, p. 16). This realistic perspective suggests that we also take just as realistic a look at multifaceted public managers who inhabit a rich, complex environment and enjoy job, family, friends, community, and other attachments.

Five Roles and Their Ethical Claims. Exhibit 1.2 shows the five primary clusters of roles with which managers cope. Each signals different bundles of concerns, values, and standards of behavior; each is marked by a mix of ethical claims. Some claims are *responsibilities,* meaning self-imposed, voluntary, and informal; others are *obligations:* formal, externally imposed, and legally or otherwise sanctioned. The fact that both types of claims confront managers cues the distinction between legality and ethicality explored in the next chapter. (By contrast, Cooper [1990, p. 60] distinguishes obligation as responsibility *for* a task or goal from accountability as responsibility *to* someone.) Responsibilities tend to be broad, even diffuse; obligations, if only for enforcement purposes, tend to be narrow and clearly defined.

Exhibit 1.2. Roles and Types of Competing Ethical Claims.

TYPE	Responsibility: Self-imposed, informal, voluntary		Obligation: Externally imposed, formal, sanctioned
ROLE		Personal: individual, family, religion, community	
		Humanity: human dignity, reciprocity, civilized society, globe (ecology), future, avoiding doing harm	
PUBLIC SERVICE		Professional: progress, optimism, competence, public trust, appearance, colleagues	
		Agency: regulations, procedures, accountability, mission, authority, hierarchy, supervisors, subordinates, peers, clients	
		Jurisdiction: constitution, law, citizenship, public interest, accountability, standards of conduct, residents, voters, taxpayers, officials	

The personal role, which involves self, family, personal beliefs, and community affinity, is the stuff of daily life and emotional bonds. While its ethical claims are self-imposed, they are still typically quite compelling. Sometimes this personal role is conceived as an arena protected from intrusion, regulation, or scrutiny and thereby is confused with the *private* and *privacy*. This confusion breeds misunderstandings about role boundaries (examined in Chapter Three.) Although many Americans value privacy and stress the informal responsibilities associated with the personal role, the equation of personal and private simply does not hold up historically or contemporarily. Individual, familial, and community obligations have long been on the books and backed by serious sanctions, from the ancient code of Hammurabi and the Book of Leviticus through today's inheritance, divorce, child abuse, right-to-die, and other laws. By comparison, the bundle of claims evoked by one's part in humanity is more abstract, by definition more inclusive, usually self-generated, and often less forceful.

This line of reasoning emphasizes the distinction between the formal obligations imposed by virtue of working in public service and the responsibilities customarily associated with roles outside the profession, agency, or jurisdiction. This emphasis is important because of the cross-pressures induced. Moreover, public service roles often invoke legal obligations in the sense that minimum claims are explicitly specified in written rules and enforced through legal provisions and penalties. Commonly formalized through accountability mechanisms, serving the public interest and legal compliance are central, recurring, but by no means the only ethical claims in public service. Some professional associations, such as the ICMA and American Institute of Certified Public Accountants, self-police members' adherence to formal obligations; other associations, such as ASPA and the GFOA, reject enforcement while articulating relatively broad obligations. The current trend in public service, as discussed in the introduction, is toward transforming responsibilities into obligations and obligations into legal requirements through the adoption of enforceable standards of conduct.

Given the differences between public service and other roles, as well as among ethical claims, conflicts are bound to provoke pressure every so often. Each of the five primary role clusters has numerous facets, and all five are interrelated, sometimes directly, and at other times filtered or mediated through intervening claims. Following the trail to its primary source is an instructive exercise for understanding and meeting different claims. For example, accountability as a formal obligation imposed by the jurisdiction is related to the appearance standard of professional public service; asking whether a manager would be comfortable explaining a decision to family members (see end of Chapter Three) calls on family claims as a support.

Getting It Together

Evidence of the inevitable strains caused by vying, often incongruent claims is all around us, especially when it comes to family. Sura IV of the Koran (iv. 1–

14) opens with an appeal to the unity of mankind and respect for mutual rights; it goes on to speak of sacred family relationships and their implications for rights, property, and inheritance. The Universal Declaration of Human Rights, adopted by the General Assembly of the United Nations on December 10, 1948, as "a common standard of achievement for all peoples and all nations" identifies rights and responsibilities on many levels, including the individual, family, community, society, state, and humanity. According to Article 16(3), "The family is the natural and fundamental group unit of society and is entitled to protection by society and the State." Clashes are predictable with Article 29(1), which declares, "Everyone has duties to the community in which alone the free and full development of his personality is possible."

Almost forty years ago, Kenneth Boulding (quoted in Boling and Dempsey, 1981, p. 13) charged that our ethical thinking lags behind social realities. "We are still . . . thinking in terms of a society in which organizations are rather small and weak, and in which the family is the dominant institution." While the family remains a forceful institution in the United States, extended families, tribes, and even nuclear families are no longer the sole or even dominant relationship in which one lives one's full life. The market economy, physical mobility, geriatric medicine, and many other developments have seen to that. Other institutions, relationships, and roles exert a strong pull on the modern manager, who must find a way through the maze of competing claims and loyalties or be immobilized.

Override. Fixing exclusively on a single value or role-generated ethical claim is a simple way out but may do serious damage to excluded contenders. "It is unusual that one value or duty obviously 'trumps' another" (Kernaghan and Langford, 1990, p. 30).

The tragic story of Pavlik Morozov, onetime hero of Soviet communism, illustrates the friction between family and public service obligations and between abstract justice and personal compassion. As a youth, Pavlik denounced his father for aiding kulaks when the Stalinist regime of the early 1930s considered it treason to help these rich peasants. They were blamed for Pavlik's murder after he informed on his father and testified against him in court. Pavlik's example became a fable by which to teach children an overriding devotion to law and society. However, over time, the moral changed and the assault on family allegiance lessened.

Although Pavlik is now more a model of ordinary virtues unobjectionable even to a Boy Scout, the original version had betrayal distorting relationships and loyalties. Sacrificing individuals to overriding abstract concepts and *all* values to the "public good" contributed to developments like the infamous gulags (labor camps) and, according to a Soviet historian, to "deep psychological and moral deformation" (Barringer, 1988, p. A1).

This story warns of the danger of justifying an action *in the name of* a greater good or higher authority rather than taking action *for the sake of* that purpose. The first invokes authority in order to empower the doer and fails to distinguish the deed done from the *good* being sought. The second pursues the good by exercising its spirit. Doing your duty with public power behind you is heady enough.

Personal Integrity. The tensions aroused by competing ethical claims jeopardize *personal integrity*—keeping oneself integrated and whole, in balance, and *ethically* sincere. The cartoon shown in Figure 1.1 makes the point that the core of personal integrity is ethical values, not self-indulgence.

Tom Peters, the business management expert, turns to self-knowledge to explain how a leader deals with competing roles (and therefore competing claims). He says, "First, you have to deal with all the roles but that doesn't keep you from paying attention to your own vision, your own agenda" (Peters, 1987a, p. 243). A state budget director defines integrity as "personal adherence to one's own moral principles and values" (Mensen, 1990, p. 96). The problem is that these views discount obligations imposed specifically by public service.

Supporting authentic, unbiased convictions—holding the high ground— is a measure of a manager's administrative skill (Appleby, quoted in Bailey, 1964, p. 237). In President Kennedy's pointed formulation, people of integrity "never ran out on either the principles in which they believed or the people who believed in them . . . whom neither financial gain nor political ambition could ever divert from the fulfillment of our sacred trust" (quoted in Richter, Burke, and Doig, 1990, p. 291).

J. Patrick Dobel (1990, p. 355) offers an inclusive view of ethical integrity that suits managerial realities in public service. "The ideal of personal integrity describes a condition where individuals can hold multiple realms of judgment in tension while keeping some coherence in their actions and lives." Integrity is more like a web than a hierarchical structure, which is "too static and rigid to account for the way individuals live their lives and keep moral coherence" (Dobel, 1990, p. 355). Finally, we are left with ambiguity and choice, which is precisely the point of ethics. *Ethics is founded on normative choice that allows and demands the exercise of judgment.*

Mapping Ethical Obligations (Diagnostic)

Professional public administration is more than a century old in the United States, and over that time it has adapted to new demands, adjusted to new truths (social, economic, organizational, and technological), and absorbed new values. By way of example, turn to the U.S. Constitution and compare the dissonant definitions of what is *fair* in the Fourteenth Amendment (equal protection clause) and the Sixteenth Amendment (income tax). In the former, *fair* means treating everyone identically, but in the latter, it came to mean treating people in different circumstances differently.

Today public service is an amalgam of discordant values and the action principles they underwrite. All operate at the same time and in tension with one

Figure 1.1. Ethical Values Are the Core of Personal Integrity.

BLOOM COUNTY   by Berke Breathed

another. Because managers—and services and policies—cannot and should not swing like a pendulum from one to the other, managers daily find themselves reconciling the values and balancing the claims.

A road map of sorts arrays the numerous, often competing values, standards, and obligations cluttering modern public service and tugging at its members. Exhibits 1.2 and 1.3 impart a sense of what is right and important to us and how that fits into public service generally. Obviously, oversimplification here is risked for the sake of clarification.

These values and obligations are classified in Exhibit 1.3 into four multidimensional arenas. Each is illustrated by a selected, single dimension depicted as a continuum with the extremes identified. Overlaid on an ambiguous and untidy world, this map is not a universal taxonomy. (The author takes this opportunity to be the first to observe that the categories are not discrete or comprehensive; classification in particular applications may be problematic.) The arenas include (1) types of values and standards, capturing the manager's and government's goals and illustrated by a democracy-productivity continuum; (2) the manager's worldview or units of analysis, with an illustrative continuum running from the general to the individual; (3) a justice-compassion continuum that illustrates the arena focusing on how people are treated and the manager's preferred means; and (4) the manager's own conduct as shown on a public service-personal continuum that identifies the primary role that generates dominant obligations.

The map points to many different issues and values—that is its purpose. Efficiency is an enduring core value in public administration. Social equity was added relatively recently. After suffering some depreciation, values associated with compassion were condoned rhetorically by President George Bush in his inaugural address on January 20, 1989: "America is never wholly herself unless she is engaged in high moral principle. We as a people have such a purpose

Exhibit 1.3. Values and Standards in Public Service.

Each of the four arenas listed below is multidimensional and illustrated by a single selected dimension depicted as a continuum with extremes identified.

What counts?	Types of Values and Standards

PRODUCTIVITY ——————————————————— DEMOCRACY	
"Hard," economy, efficiency, competence, expertise, merit, Hamiltonian bureaucracy, technical implementation	"Soft," accountability, representativeness, citizen access, policy advocacy, Jeffersonian bureaucracy, volunteerism, public demand

Counting others?	How Individuals Are Treated

JUSTICE ————————————————————————— COMPASSION	
Uniformity, standardization, rules, neutrality, stability, precedent, 14th Amendment to U.S. Constitution	Responsiveness, equity, circumstance, flexibility, 16th Amendment

Who counts?	Unit of Analysis for Identifying and Ranking Interests/Stakes

GENERAL ————————————————————————— INDIVIDUAL	
Rights, overarching public good, cost-benefit analysis, allocational issues, future generations, global ecology	Liberty, client claims, majority interest, distributional issues, private property, privacy

Counting source?	Primary Role–Generating Obligations

PUBLIC SERVICE ————————————————————— PERSONAL	
Law, public interest, regulations, chain of command	Self-interest, career, family

today. It is to make kinder the face of the Nation and gentler the face of the world."

Used to organize and make sense of the many different managerial and democratic values mentioned earlier in this chapter, these exhibits help us translate abstractions into meaningful, realistic guidelines for public management. For example, Rion's "avoid harm" principle emerges from humanity as a source of ethical claims in Exhibit 1.2; Josephson's "excellence" relates to Exhibit 1.3's first category. These exhibits can be used to probe any proposed litany of public service values and standards.

In this way we accept public administration's messy inclusiveness and the sundry values that push and pull on public managers. The end point on each continuum represents legitimate, authoritative positions, but each derives its meaning in actual practice from its position in tension with the other end point on the continuum. Practical conflicts—between rights and liberties, freedom and justice—are familiar examples built directly into our political system. "The questions that now urgently confront us are as old as the Republic itself. How can we maintain a government structure and administrative system that reconcile liberty with justice and institutional and personal freedom with the general welfare?'' (Seidman and Gilmour, 1986, p. 29).

The many values are modified by contending values on the same continuum. "Only from the clash of opposites, contraries, extremes, and poles can come the accommodations that are themselves American public service ethics" (Chandler, 1989a, p. 613). The four arenas in Exhibit 1.3 depict not an either-or choice but efforts to moderate the extremes and reconcile different value dimensions. This reconciliation is at the heart of ethical decision making in public service because a complete rejection of other values on the continuum distorts the American polity. Pavlik's story warns against a pathological goal displacement that exaggerates solitary values and excludes all other points on the continuum.

Figure 1.2 uses the four selected continua in Exhibit 1.3 for a quick diagnosis of strengths, weaknesses, deficiencies, and excesses. (Dwight Waldo called for mapping public service values in 1981 in *The Enterprise of Public Administration*.) The method here begins with laying out the four continua on a circle. The next step is to identify the approximate location on each continuum that best describes the actual or preferred position as we see it. The third and last step is to connect the points and show the diamond pattern.

Figure 1.2 asks managers to describe their agency as it is, but it is also interesting—and challenging—to plot two other maps: the manager's preferred pattern for public service generally and the pattern predicted for the next generation of managers. A mismatch between the two sounds an alarm. Over the years, public service paradigms have shifted or absorbed new values; moreover, public outrage and countless ethics initiatives hint that another shift is in the wind. That is the reason for displaying the " 'new' public administration."

This is an exploratory device, with public service rather than personal values as the object of exploration. A radical, ungainly shape is a warning signal that something is wrong, and an exercise in ethical fitness—*shaping up*—may be in order. That is up to the manager. Despite the kite shape and the fact that managers do not operate at a single discrete point but move along the continua, the intent of the exercise is to survey the present and anticipate the future with both feet firmly on the ground.

Of course, the shape of public service is molded by the larger society, and career professionals in public service are not a group apart. They inevitably reflect the moral tone of the society in which they live and the institutional contexts in which they work. The problems and challenges are neither light nor likely to disappear. On the contrary, the "quiet crisis" in public service identified by the Volcker Commission is being institutionalized in several ways. The widely perceived downturn in reputation and related job satisfaction undercuts recruitment and retention of talented people *both dedicated to public service and sensitive to its meaning and commitments*. Demoralization among senior federal executives is already a serious managerial problem (Posner and Schmidt, 1988). A suggestive tidbit: "Most states have found their early retirement plans—no

Figure 1.2. Diagnostic: What Shape Are We In?

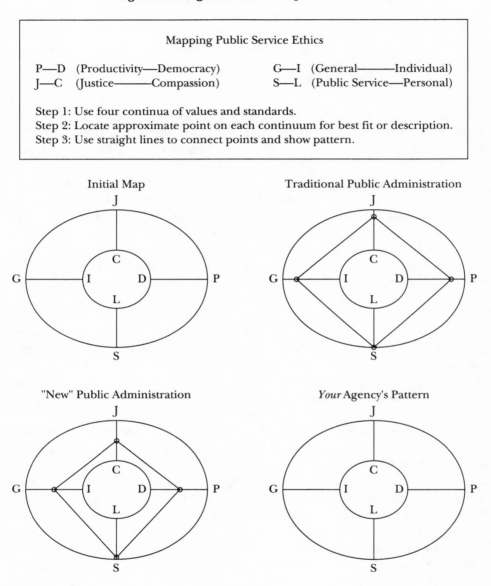

Mapping Public Service Ethics

P—D   (Productivity—Democracy)   G—I   (General———Individual)
J—C   (Justice———Compassion)   S—L   (Public Service—Personal)

Step 1: Use four continua of values and standards.
Step 2: Locate approximate point on each continuum for best fit or description.
Step 3: Use straight lines to connect points and show pattern.

Initial Map

Traditional Public Administration

"New" Public Administration

Your Agency's Pattern

matter how they are structured—to be more popular than anticipated" (Enos, 1990, p. 2).

Public accountability is being reshaped as new public disclosure standards accept and even encourage media revelations of once private realms, subjects to which we turn in later chapters. Scandal customarily triggers new or tighter ethics codes and compliance elements, and the scandal glut in every branch and at every level of government threatens to reduce public concern to restrictive rules that minimize individual responsibility and managerial integrity. That this would be shameful and counterproductive is suggested in President John F. Kennedy's message to Congress on April 27, 1961. "The ultimate answer to ethical problems in government is honest people in a good ethical environment." He called on government leaders "to develop in all government employees an increasing sensitivity to the ethical and moral conditions imposed by public service."

Chapter 2

To Obey and Implement
the Law

Wielding power and public authority entails special ethical obligations. In this chapter, the obligation of legal compliance derives from the mix of power, public trust, and promise keeping. Its knotty spin-offs include differentiating among legal obligations, disobeying illegal orders, and engaging in personal dissent. A fundamental decision model that concludes the chapter centers on legal obligations without devaluing other core managerial concerns.

Public managers work with public power at their backs. Managers actually implement decisions through the compulsory powers of legitimate government authority. The public relies on law to tame arbitrary power. The rule of law effects justice and produces predictability and reliability in public programs and in society more generally. Otherwise unfettered discretion is tied by law to authorized, permissible public purpose and procedure.

Government authority gives public servants power over ordinary citizens. Citizens are dependent upon government services, including the administration of justice. Citizens are vulnerable to public servants' decisions, from program eligibility to arrest, taxation, and more. In *The Peloponnesian War,* Thucydides wrote, "You know as well as we do that right, as the world goes, is only in question between equals in power, while the strong do what they can and the weak suffer what they must." Democracy depends upon law to equalize power so that *right* dominates decisions and interactions.

The whole political system turns on this: trust, public confidence, a faith in public servants and institutions. Democracy relies on public trust to accomplish civic purposes through voluntary compliance. The reciprocal is that *public managers are obligated to implement and comply with the law*. Failure to do so is a legal and ethical violation. The law draws boundaries around public power. It curbs commitments to mission, client, or personal claims. Two broad boundaries are compelling public servants to take action (*mandamus*) and forbidding action beyond legal authority (*ultra vires*).

Taking the Job and the Pledge

The ethical values of truth telling and promise keeping underlie citizens' faith. They place their trust in public servants who have sworn to uphold the law. Like so many ideas in public service, the idea of oath can be traced to the roots of Western civilization, and the Oath of the Athenian City-State (Exhibit 2.1) reveals the idea's durability.

By taking the job, you have given your word. The promise to obey and implement the law is part of taking a public position. The promise may be unspoken, but it is still understood. Many public service employees, such as those in nongovernmental agencies, do not take an oath in actuality. Yet, the implicit promise underlies the public's grant of trust. Reinforcing the commitment to special ethical principles, the promise functions as a symbol of conferring public power on the one hand and, on the other, agreeing to exercise it within permissible boundaries. This function is obvious in ceremonial oaths, of which the presidential oath of office set forth in the Constitution is an outstanding example: "I do solemnly swear (or affirm) that I will faithfully execute the Office of President of the United States, and will, to the best of my ability, preserve, protect, and defend the Constitution of the United States."

Many government employees do take a formal oath. In 1989, more than 400,000 newly appointed civilian federal executive employees (plus additional legislative and judicial appointees) swore "true faith and allegiance" to the Constitution by taking the oath of office. Each federal civilian employee completes the Appointment Affidavits (Exhibit 2.2) when first appointed and for each new

Exhibit 2.1. Oath of the Athenian City-State.

We will never bring disgrace to this our city
by any act of dishonesty or cowardice,
nor ever desert our suffering comrades in the ranks;

We will ever strive for the ideals and sacred things
of the city, both alone and with many;

We will revere and obey the city's laws
and do our best to incite to a like respect and reverence
those who are prone to annul or set them at naught;

We will unceasingly seek to quicken the sense
of public duty;

That thus, in all these ways, we will transmit this city
not only not less, but greater, better and more beautiful
than it was transmitted to us.

Exhibit 2.2. Federal Appointment Affidavits.

STANDARD FORM 61
Revised June 1986
U.S. Office of Personnel Management
FPM Chapter 296
61-108

APPOINTMENT AFFIDAVITS

_____

(Position to which appointed)

_____

(Date of appointment)

_____   _____   _____

(Department or agency)   *(Bureau or Division)*   *(Place of employment)*

I, _____ , do solemnly swear (or affirm) that—

A. OATH OF OFFICE

I will support and defend the Constitution of the United States against all enemies, foreign and domestic; that I will bear true faith and allegiance to the same; that I take this obligation freely, without any mental reservation or purpose of evasion; and that I will well and faithfully discharge the duties of the office on which I am about to enter. So help me God.

B. AFFIDAVIT AS TO STRIKING AGAINST THE FEDERAL GOVERNMENT

I am not participating in any strike against the Government of the United States or any agency thereof, and I will not so participate while an employee of the Government of the United States or any agency thereof.

C. AFFIDAVIT AS TO PURCHASE AND SALE OF OFFICE

I have not, nor has anyone acting in my behalf, given, transferred, promised or paid any consideration for or in expectation or hope of receiving assistance in securing this appointment.

_____

(Signature of appointee)

Subscribed and sworn (or affirmed) before me this _____ day of _____ , 19_____ ,

at _____   _____

(City)   *(State)*

[SEAL]

_____

(Signature of officer)

Commission expires _____

(If by a Notary Public, the date of expiration of his/her Commission should be shown)

_____

(Title)

NOTE.—*The oath of office must be administered by a person specified in 5 U.S.C. 2903. The words "So help me God" in the oath and the word "swear" wherever it appears above should be stricken out when the appointee elects to affirm rather than swear to the affidavits; only these words may be stricken and only when the appointee elects to affirm the affidavits.*

NSN 7540-00-634-4015   U.S. GOVERNMENT PRINTING OFFICE : 1990 O - 273-878 (20164)   Prior Edition Usable appointment. The oath is required by Title 5, Section 3331 of the United States Code (hereafter, U.S.C.) for all individuals except the president "elected or appointed to an office of honor or profit in the civil service or uniformed services."

By taking the military oath of office, military personnel swear (or affirm) to defend the Constitution and "bear true faith and allegiance to the same." When the president commissions an officer in the U.S. military, he charges the officer to follow orders by superiors "acting in accordance with the laws of the United States." Accepting the commission means accepting its terms. This promise induces the ethical obligation for military personnel to abide by civilian authority.

These oaths spell out the foundation of duty in public service. By taking the job, office, or position, the public servant promises legal compliance. The federal ethics code (P.A. 96-303, unanimously passed by Congress and signed into law by the president on July 3, 1980) spells out a simple standard: "Uphold the Constitution, laws, and regulations of the United States and of all governments therein and never be a party to their evasion."

The principle sounds simple, but it raises practical (and philosophical) questions that managers are bound to face. Laws and regulations with the force of law may push managers to personally objectionable behavior. Sometimes laws or regulations conflict. At other times, the spirit and purpose of public service is undercut by to-the-letter or by-the-book legal obedience.

Two questions in particular have hounded public service for centuries: What are a manager's obligations in the face of an illegal directive? What if the manager dissents and sincerely believes a law is unjust, wrong, immoral?

The Force of Law

Not all legal formulations are of equal weight. The oaths noted above reflect the primary position of the Constitution. Public service is both rooted in and bound by the Constitution's provisions. They are the ethical manager's framework for action and the citizen's basis for trust.

The responsibility for seeing that lesser laws conform with the Constitution lies with the Supreme Court. An individual manager who renders a legal opinion on unconstitutionality to justify his or her own noncompliance goes far beyond official competence and legal boundaries. In a real sense, usurping the Supreme Court's role is abuse of office. When, who, and how the law is tested against the Constitution is a matter for negotiation in the agency and litigation in the courts. Yet in the face of a conflict between the Constitution and a statute, a regulation, or a supervisor's command, the ethical public manager is committed to the Constitution. This double bind is part of public service reality.

Reading the Rules. An agency's *rule* has the force of law, but it should not be confused with law itself. Further, there are rules and *rules*. According to the federal Administrative Procedure Act, Section 551(4), *rule* "means the whole or part of any agency statement of general or particular applicability and future effect designed to implement, interpret, or prescribe law or policy or describing the organization, procedure, or practice requirements of any agency."

A document submitted to a hearing before the House Employment and Housing Subcommittee (U.S. House of Representatives, 1990b) describes the Supreme Court's formulation governing review of an agency's deviation from its own regulations. A reviewer should "determine whether the regulation was intended (1) to require the agency to exercise its independent discretion, or (2) to confer a procedural benefit to a class to which complainant belongs, or (3) to be a 'mere aid' to guide the exercise of agency discretion. If the first or second, invalidate the action; if the third, a further determination must be made whether the complainant has been substantially prejudiced. If he has, invalidate the action; if not, affirm." Thus, justice for a potential casualty of government discretion leads to the differential weighting of rules.

How does one read the rules? It depends. While existing agency rules entail legal liability, the ethical obligation based on the oath to uphold the Constitution is of a different order altogether. With that obligation in mind, rules are narrowly or broadly interpreted, loosely followed or scrupulously obeyed. With effort, rules can be waived or changed.

A discriminating manager distinguishes the standard way of doing business in an agency from formal procedure, regulations, and law. The obligation is legal compliance, not the manager's or client's slavery to routine. The distinction between organizational habits and substantive regulation is important if managers are to retain their capacity for adaptability, innovation, and leadership.

Disobedience Before Illegality. Legal compliance imposes on managers the heavy burden of refusing to obey a superior's illegal order or directive. For each manager empowered to guard the legal basis of citizen trust, disobedience is preferred over illegality. Admittedly, the disobedient manager "practices civil *obedience* under particularly stressful conditions because he upholds the rule of law against his lawless superior" (Rohr, 1989, p. 12). The principle extends to military service. During the nationally televised Iran-Contra hearings, Senator Daniel K. Inouye (D-Hawaii), himself a wounded veteran, asserted for the nation to hear that even military orders do not take priority over law.

What about disobeying lawful orders? An unqualified no is overly formalistic and uselessly simplistic, given what public managers know. Managers cannot afford the self-indulgence of sentimentality or sanctimoniousness. Realistically, in the field and in the central office, we know managers bend, twist, curve, and break laws and regulations. This is what selective enforcement is all about: facing an ethical dilemma and blinking. It may be for pragmatic reasons, to accomplish the mission and get the larger job done. There may be an imperfect fit between by-the-book and public purpose. Sometimes judgment rests on rival values or contradictory laws or regulations. At other times, faulty judgment or even downright ignorance is at work. Managers understand this, but they should not celebrate it.

Judgment, it often is argued, rests on fulfilling a superior's underlying intention and purpose, the spirit rather than the letter of the order. This leeway enables flexible, instant response to changing circumstances. One view on disobeying lawful orders is expressed in the military context in Exhibit 2.3. A civilian version is the first case that opens this book. The same reasoning—spirit and purpose over knee-jerk obedience—lies behind determining legislative intent. Different from discretion, intent really narrows wiggle room because it calls on managers to abide more fully by the law.

Good Reason. This author is not about to tell public managers that it is *ethically* defensible to break a law. Given the prior promise of legal compliance, it is not. Moreover, those who do break the law may be personally liable. This is not to say managers do not and will not do it; they do and will. Their reason is usually a "good" one, but it cannot serve as an excuse.

Exhibit 2.3. On Disobeying Lawful Orders.

The following is excerpted from M. D. Taylor's "A Do-It-Yourself Professional Code for the Military," *Parameters: Journal of the U.S. Army War College*, 1980, 10, 10–15. (General Taylor was chief of staff of the U.S. Army, 1955–1959; chairman of the Joint Chiefs of Staff 1962–1964; then ambassador to South Vietnam.)

[T]here is the dilemma which may arise if an officer receives a lawful order to undertake an impossible or prohibitively costly mission, or one likely to produce dire consequences apparently ignored by his superiors. Our model, recognizing that obedience to orders is one of the highest military virtues, one without which armies are worse than useless, will be instinctively inclined to obey any legal order. He would consider making an exception only in the rare circumstances when all the following conditions are met:

- He is sure that he understands the purpose of the order and the results desired by the issuing authority.
- He is equally sure that this authority does not understand the local situation and the disastrous consequences that would ensue from compliance.
- There is no time to appeal the order or a prior appeal has been rejected.
- He is disobeying on sound military grounds, not in compliance with the voice of a disapproving conscience, and is fully prepared to accept the legal and professional consequences.

As for his attitude toward the voice of conscience as a guide to military behavior, he has serious doubts as to its reliability. He is aware that wise men over the ages have disagreed as to the source, nature, and authority of conscience. Is it, as some think, the voice of God or at least a God-given moral sense with which we are endowed to serve as a source of higher guidance? There are skeptics who maintain that it is little more than the voice of conventional morality, or ingrained habit resisting a departure from past practice, or of self-interest in a pious guise. Then there are the cynical words of H. L. Mencken: "Conscience is the inner voice that warns us that somebody may be looking."

When other ethical claims push in the direction of illegality, the manager confronts a true ethical dilemma. Any decision in this situation stirs controversy. People of good character and strong principles will disagree. The argument here is that the law is the center of gravity in public service, and the Constitution is the touchstone.

Abusing Public Office for Personal Dissent

If a public manager believes a law is unjust or immoral, is he or she ethically obligated to comply? Or does another, higher law prevail? Managers today know there exists the possibility of an unconstitutional order, an evil empire. It is symbolized historically by Nazi Germany or futuristically by *Star Wars*. This argument is a red herring. It changes the subject from legitimate government to illegitimate regime. It changes the question from *what now?* to *what if?* It is irrelevant to the contemporary constitutional system of American public service.

Then there is the likelihood of unjust human law to consider. When ethical judgment conflicts with legal compliance in major matters, conscientious dissent or civil disobedience substitutes a standard from outside the administrative system. Religion or philosophy may provide standards for judging whether a human law is just or not. "Civil disobedience rests its case on a higher *moral or natural law*, not on positive law" (Rohr, 1989, p. 12). Current politics is well versed in peaceful and not-so-peaceful civil disobedience, thanks to Gandhi's struggle against colonialism, the sit-ins and freedom rides of the civil rights movement, and the antiapartheid and antinuclear campaigns.

In his renowned "Letter from Birmingham City Jail" (1963, p. 6; reprinted by permission of Joan Daves, copyright 1963, 1964 by Martin Luther King, Jr.) Martin Luther King, Jr., explained:

> You express a great deal of anxiety over our willingness to break laws. This is certainly a legitimate concern. Since we so diligently urge people to obey the Supreme Court's decision of 1954 outlawing segregation in the public schools, it is rather strange and paradoxical to find us consciously breaking laws. One may well ask, "How can you advocate breaking some laws and obeying others?" The answer is found in the fact that there are two types of laws: There are *just* laws and there are *unjust* laws. . . . [O]ne has a moral responsibility to disobey unjust laws. I would agree with Saint Augustine that "An unjust law is no law at all." . . . A just law is a man-made code that squares with the moral law of the law of God.

King (p. 7) goes on to state a central tenet of ethical civil disobedience, taking responsibility for one's actions. "One who breaks an unjust law must do it openly, lovingly . . . and with a willingness to accept the penalty."

Dissent as Citizen. May a public servant ethically engage in conscientious dissent *outside* his or her office? This question accents professional and organizational roles, but they are not the only ones (see Exhibit 1.2). How should a city manager respond to an urban planner who takes part in a peaceful demonstration opposing abortion? How should a state finance analyst decide to participate in an antiwar protest? There are two issues when the action is not related to official duties: responsible citizenship and the legality of the mode of dissent.

When the actions are legal, a *yes* underwrites important citizenship obligations and reserves rights already limited by ethical standards, laws, and regulations discussed throughout this book. In practice, the answer is often modified by the appearance standard discussed in the next chapter. Unwelcome professional consequences will likely vary according to the visibility of the administrator and the action. Part of ethical action is a willingness to take responsibility for it.

Not all modes of dissent are legal. Respect for democratic processes, public trust, and the promise of legal compliance ethically constrain the public servant. As a result, the ethicality of dissent outside of office turns on the action's legality. A county hospital administrator who challenges nuclear weapons by refusing to pay personal income taxes is breaking the law and shrugging off the ethical value of promise keeping. Bear in mind that a sincere ethical argument can be made—the dissenter may believe that public interest is paramount in this case.

Dissent Using Office. It may be ethically permissible or even imperative for a citizen to break a law. Yet that does *not* extend to public servants the privilege of using government authority and public position to do so. *The ethical manager may not use public office to dissent as a citizen.* By definition, *civil* dissent or disobedience is not possible through a public position that draws on government authority. Nor is it an option for an ethical public manager, who would thereby violate an important value and break the prior promise of legal compliance. Pursuing conscientious dissent through public office—for whatever reason—makes a liar of the public servant and a lie of public service. Were managers to use public office to break the law at will, public trust would be broken as well. (Again, we are speaking of routine circumstances, not an evil empire but a constitutional system with implemented safeguards and exercised rights.)

What does an ethical public manager do when faced with a choice between legal compliance and violation of a central, personal, ethical belief? (Granted, a choice this clear-cut is rare.) The answer lies *outside* public position. Because no organization or law should dictate central ethical choices, if the choice is truly that momentous and stark, then the preferred option may be to resign.

If some misguided public servants try to have it both ways—justified illegality and use of public authority—they are operating under the delusion of moral superiority and disguising it as legal authority. Having it both ways is inherently antidemocratic and unethical, and such individuals will find themselves caught in a vise of unethical behavior and public censure as a result.

Grabbing for power under cover of public position undercuts the very foundations of constitutional democracy. (A pragmatic note: managers also open themselves to legal action.)

Events in the Iran-Contra affair and the HUD scandal have revealed public servants disobeying the law on grounds of religion, conscience, or superior knowledge. They have been sobering experiences for the public and for the players. That dissent through public position is abuse of office is one lesson of "Robin Hood in Public Service," the case that concludes this chapter. The expressed remorse speaks to the ethical cost and practical price of abusing public office for personal dissent.

Go/No-Go Decision Model

In public service, the law prevails. From the Athenian oath's "we will revere and obey the city's laws" (Exhibit 2.1) to contemporary standards and professional codes, additional ethical questions arise only after the legality of the action is settled. For example, GFOA's code identifies legal compliance as an ethical responsibility.

Accepting the law's priority is the first step in making routine decisions in public service. The obligation to make a legal decision is hardly enough justification; the scope is still too broad. A narrowly legalistic perspective may pervert rather than implement the law's purpose. This is what is offensive about legal manipulations to circumvent the appropriations process in the postage meter case at the beginning of the introduction. Ethical decision makers, sensitive to ethical concerns, aim at "good" decision making. Action should be both legal and ethical.

There is also a third consideration: the job to be done. There is, after all, a service component to public service. Rational and busy managers take action not for its own sake but for the purposes they are trying to accomplish. There should be a logical link between the objective and the decision. While management without ethics is purposeless or worse, impractical public management is doomed to failure. *Useful* action adds the element of pragmatism to decision making: action should be legal, ethical, and effective.

Simply giving up on an ethical, legal, but ineffective course of action can stifle creativity or justify immobility. Therefore, not all matters should stop here. The next step is to innovatively redesign the proposed action so that it meets all three criteria. Likewise, if action is ethical and effective but illegal, it may warrant a place in the agency's legislative package.

The three questions asked in sequence in Figure 2.1 function as a first cut for decision making. The go/no-go decision-making model is elementary but hardly simplistic; it helps decision makers act on legal obligations without devaluing other core concerns. Is the decision legal? Ethical? Effective? Because only a *yes* response leads to the next question, while a *no* ends the matter (pending

Figure 2.1. Go/No-Go Decision Model.

Three judgment calls on immediate action:
1. Is it legal?
2. Is it ethical?
3. Is it effective?

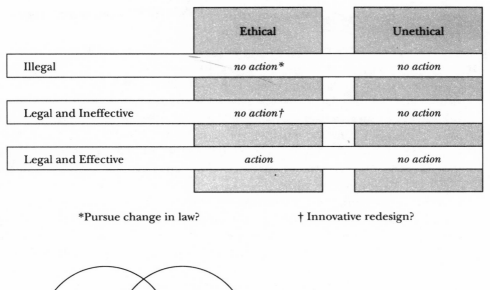

	Ethical	Unethical
Illegal	*no action**	*no action*
Legal and Ineffective	*no action†*	*no action*
Legal and Effective	*action*	*no action*

*Pursue change in law?   † Innovative redesign?

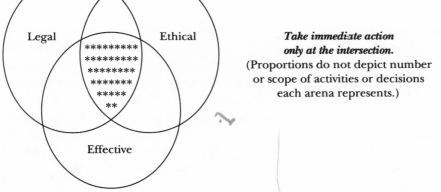

***Take immediate action
only at the intersection.***
(Proportions do not depict number
or scope of activities or decisions
each arena represents.)

alterations), this approach is efficient and managerial. Immediate action is taken only if the answer is yes to all three questions in turn.

The model is useful in thinking through falsification of public documents. Undeniably, this is illegal. It is also unethical—deception is the purpose and method. Although there may be situations in which a "small deception" seems an acceptable price for a greater good, the point of this venture is to undercut accountability, avoid taking responsibility, and evade the test of publicity (described in Chapter Four). The cumulative impact of each instance is unknowable because the record is, in fact, bogus.

Leaving a false trail via protective communication may become habitual or abused for personal purposes. A classic example is the defensive report, an informal mechanism for reconstructing reality for purposes of self-protection. Perhaps a police officer files charges of resisting arrest because the suspect sustained injury during a botched arrest. Perhaps a performance appraisal reflects spurned sexual overtures. While fiction may be effective, it is neither legal nor ethical.

A related twist is passing bad news up the hierarchy, an unenviable task. It tests courage by pitting self-protection against misrepresentation. (By contrast, the issue is competence, not courage, when an analyst or subordinate fails to scrutinize and evaluate data carefully, systematically, and in accord with rigorous standards.) A former assistant to President Carter describes "the government's version of the law of gravity, that bad news never flows up. The only times I saw anyone struggle to warn his superior of impending trouble . . . were on those occasions when the superior was sure to find out anyway" (quoted in Patterson, 1988, p. 47). Of course, the silent subordinate is not performing the job, despite the promise implicit in taking it. Therefore, while the behavior may be legal and personally expedient (although risky, if discovered), it is not ethical. Presuming discovery, how would *you* handle a silent subordinate? What is it about the behavior that offends you—its being unethical or organizationally ineffective?

Case: Robin Hood in Public Service

In a song popular during the Depression, the down-and-out asked for a dime. A half-century later, inflation raised the pitch on city streets to a quarter. Homelessness became a publicly recognized problem. At the U.S. Department of Housing and Urban Development (HUD), some political appointees, career professionals, contractors, and consultants upped the ante even higher.

The 101st Congress grappled with a huge problem the Bush administration had inherited: fraud, embezzlement, favoritism, lack of documentation and accountability, and other abuses in HUD that had gone undetected for years. Attorney General Richard Thornburgh announced on June 15, 1989 that all HUD local offices across the country would be investigated. At a hearing the next day before the Employment and Housing Subcommittee of the Committee on Government Operations of the U.S. House of Representatives, Chairman Tom Lantos characterized this step as a "very dramatic, almost unprecedented action."

At the same hearing, HUD's inspector general, Paul A. Adams, listed over two dozen HUD employees who already had been charged with various offenses. Then there was Marilyn Louise Harrell, former settlement agent under contract to HUD and dubbed "Robin HUD" by the media. She admitted to theft of more than $5 million in HUD funds, which she claimed to have used to help the homeless and poor. Her explanation? At the June 16, 1989, House hearing, she said the following:

> I, in no way, justify what I have done as being anything less than sin. I have come forward, as one who loves the Lord, in an attempt to confess to the world that I am a sinner, and I am sorry that I diverted government funds. I am prepared to give everything that I have or will ever have to restore to the government that which was taken. . . . Gentlemen, it was through love and compassion that I diverted the money and tried to help others. I did not keep any for myself. . . .
>
> Suffice it to say, I humbly apologize for becoming part of a scandal and diverting funds without the authority to do so. I justified my actions inwardly only by reminding myself that I followed a higher law in an attempt to ease suffering. My only explanation lies in John 15:12–14. . . . [In regard to a $37,000 shortfall in her escrow account] I felt that the government isn't personal, if you'll forgive me for saying so, that if I have to hurt someone because of an error, I would prefer that it would be the government rather than a private individual.

At this point, Chairman Lantos said, "Well, you know it was poor judgment on your part, of course you do." Harrell responded, "Yes. Of either of the choices, I was in trouble either way. At least this way someone wasn't in trouble with me."

According to the U.S. Constitution, Article I, Section 9, "No money shall be drawn from the Treasury but in consequence of appropriations made by law." What Harrell did was illegal.

> In your opinion and assuming that all the *diverted* funds were donated to charitable purposes, was what Harrell did *ethically* justified? The right thing to do? Why or why not?

"Government employees are about as likely as private citizens to belong to fundamentalist churches, to attend church weekly, to consider themselves 'strong' members of their religions, and to pray daily" (Lewis, 1990, p. 223).

> In your view, is it ethical for a public employee or contractor to use public office or funds to answer to an authority higher than the U.S. Constitution?
> - Is it ethical for a public official or employee to use public office and resources to pursue a personal agenda, however laudable?
> - Is a private contractor such as Harrell also bound by your answer?
> - Does your answer change if that agenda is based on basic religious beliefs? Family loyalties? Policy preferences? As you answer, think about

the possibility that high public officials' personal religious convictions contradict your religious beliefs. Consider that they have the power and made the promise of legal compliance.

What does civil disobedience through public position do to public accountability?

What would happen if everyone acted as Harrell did? What would be the consequences for public policy? For public trust? For a government under law?

At the October 12, 1989, hearing before the House Subcommittee on Housing and Community Development, Secretary Jack Kemp said, "She [Harrell] was no Robin HUD. She was not stealing from the rich and helping the poor. She was stealing from the rich to enrich herself. So she should not be considered a Robin HUD."

Is the ethical offense—theft—defined by the use of the resources? (See Chapter Seven.)

– Does it matter whether personal gain or charity was the purpose? Why or why not?

Is it ethical to use immoral means to accomplish moral ends? Why or why not? (See Chapter Four.)

The part played by greedy and misguided individuals was compounded by mismanagement. For over three years, from July 1985 through September 1988, no one at HUD noticed anything about Harrell's accounts. The public record (from congressional hearings) reads: "shockingly lax and inept management"; "HUD lost and lost track of millions of dollars"; "HUD did not have a system in place to monitor these payments"; "getting control of the money flow was ignored." Corruption and mismanagement often walk together, hand-in-hand.

Representative Henry B. Gonzalez, chairman of the House Subcommittee on Housing and Community Development, stated at a hearing on October 12, 1989: "As I look at the so-called scandals that have been revealed at HUD, it is my view that we have seen a people's problem and not so much a program problem. What we have had in the last 8 years at HUD are ambitious and rather self-seeking people who betrayed public trust. I make the distinction between scandalous mismanagement and the integrity of the HUD programs. Let me be clear. These programs work when people of good will are there to administer them. There is no way we can pass laws to make people good or to make administrators honest and efficient."

Do you agree with Representative Gonzalez's assessment? Explain.

In your view, what contributed to HUD's problems: individual greed, careless recruitment, lax oversight, and/or weak management and controls? How?

Former congressional colleagues praised Secretary Kemp throughout the 1989 hearings for decisively facing up to the problems that preceded him at HUD and for taking responsibility for the clean-up and overhaul. At the October 12 hearing, Kemp unveiled a full-scale reform of departmental procedures. The blueprint, "Clearing the Decks," called for ethics, management and finance, and Federal Housing Administration overhaul. Compliance-oriented proposals included the following: sunshine all funding decisions, eliminate discretionary funding, require registration of consultants and disclosure of fees, mandate documented accountability for regulatory waivers, and increase the powers of the inspector general.

What would you have recommended Secretary Kemp do to attend to integrity issues in the agency?

Chapter 3

To Serve
the Public Interest

Another public service obligation is championing the public interest. Invoked by empathy and respect for future generations, this obligation generates three standards: maintaining impartiality, avoiding conflict of interest, and avoiding the appearance of impropriety. After confronting the realities of public scrutiny, this chapter offers practical guidelines for working with the media and concludes with a case study of the tension between public duty and private life.

Use of public position to pursue any personal agenda is unacceptable ethically (and politically) in public service. Public managers wield power and authority. This is simply a fact of life in public service. Managers do much of the choosing in the "authoritative allocation of values" that is the standard definition of what government is all about. To keep the citizens' trust, public managers are bade to pursue the public interest.

Trade-offs and paradox top today's political agenda: the environment competes with economic interests; public health programs and insurance proposals face off against AIDS, medical technology, and an aging population; deficits challenge tax preferences; and so on. Resolution carries with it considerable ethical content and fallout.

The paradox is that private self-interest—selfish, greedy, and unrestrained or, more technically, maximizing short-term, individual utility—plunders the common pot. Selfish self-interest threatens shared resources, often the very source of the prize. Bounty becomes booty, and the whole community is at risk. Mere mention of the savings and loan crisis drives the point home.

Protecting common assets is a governmental purpose. In the conventional contractual view, we voluntarily submit to coercion and establish government to restrain liberty from destroying us all. Public service obligations derive from this creation myth. Public servants ideally mold and sustain the links to our future and to the whole, without unduly curbing liberty.

46

The problems on the public service agenda call for "a fundamental extension in morality" (Hardin, 1972, p. 250). These problems have no technical solution. Public interest cannot be laid out on a spreadsheet or figured on a calculator. Public interest mandates the forging of a link between the short term and the long term and between individually rational self-interest and the aggregate, common good. The agency's mission statement is a sensible place to start in understanding what public interest entails.

The buzz words *the public interest* encode the obligation to search for the common ground, to find the common threads that bind us together. The word *us* is broadly defined to include future generations for whom public service is a trustee. Public service in its finest sense demands looking at the long-term implications of today's decision. This obligation is expressed with elegant simplicity in the oath of ancient Athens (Exhibit 2.1): "we will transmit this city not only not less, but greater, better and more beautiful than it was transmitted to us."

The public interest idea urges public managers to live in a dynamic time warp, with a foot in the future. *One simple test of public interest is respect for future generations.* It is simple to understand but not necessarily simple to do. In a democracy, managers *must* remain responsive to citizens or the public interest idea degenerates into irresponsible justification of antidemocratic action. Wrapping oneself in the public interest or alleged future interests incites concern (and Pavlik Morozov's story in Chapter One reveals that it should). The key is the context and accommodating rather than spurning the important values, principles, or interests at stake.

Exhibiting this outlook, federal budget director Richard G. Darmon blasted America's taste for consuming our future by debt-financing current consumption, which he sees as a moral problem reflecting "cultural now-now-ism." Darmon cited the "massive Backward Robin Hood transaction—robbing the future to give to the present. . . . In its private form, it may be understood as shortsighted selfishness. In the public domain, however, this self-indulgent theft from the future borders on public wilding" (quoted in Haas, 1989, p. 2014).

Public interest mandates that the public manager take an empathic leap across time *and* across condition. *Empathy is another test of public interest* and decrees open-mindedness and participation. The latter is an important part of ethical public service (and built directly into the agency ethics process presented in Chapter Ten). Even Attila the Hun, "a dubious character upon whom to base a metaphor on leadership," is credited with this: "Chieftains must develop empathy—an appreciation for and an understanding of the values of others, a sensitivity for other cultures, beliefs and traditions" (Roberts, 1987, pp. xiii, 19).

The obligation of empathy relates to stewardship, the fiduciary relationship inherent in exercising government authority. This means that public managers are trustees for the vulnerable, dependent, and politically inarticulate, those most likely to be overlooked in formulations of the public interest. As trustees of the public interest, public managers are expected "to search imaginatively for a public-will-to-be. In this search, the public servant is often a leader in the creation of a new public will" (Bailey, 1964, p. 235). Empathy may demand inventive resolution needed to overcome an "ethical impasse" (Hart, 1974) that can otherwise paralyze decision makers.

The "new public administration" of the 1970s (Frederickson, 1987; Hart, 1974; Marini, 1971) activated the value of benevolence which, in light of traditional Christian values, is not as radical as was thought at the time. It established social equity as a "third pillar" in public administration (Frederickson, 1990), right alongside efficiency and economy and was elevated to another "basic operational guideline" (Hart, 1974, p. 3).

This move was heavily influenced by John Rawls's *A Theory of Justice* (1971), in which the philosopher provides an idealized method for arriving at the public interest or general welfare. By abstracting oneself from one's own class, status, and social circumstances, one discusses and reflects behind a "veil of ignorance"; because decision makers do not know how they would be affected by decisions, they are persuaded to minimize their own (and descendants') risk by choosing truly just arrangements and institutions.

The voluntary assumption of social conscience by professional public managers was also heavily influenced by the racial, economic, and intergenerational turmoil of the 1960s. President Lyndon B. Johnson captured the ethical content in his War on Poverty and Great Society speeches. In calling for economic and racial justice—a new social order—he declared a war on poverty on March 16, 1964: "Because it is right, because it is wise, and because, for the first time in our history, it is possible to conquer poverty."

An unrealistic timetable and other factors bred disillusionment and a turnabout in public and especially government programs and duties. The reversal in little more than a decade saw the realists (cynics, some would say) among us reject public service's competence and therefore its legitimate intervention in the pursuit of social justice. Inescapably, however, present-day interactions and modern interdependencies speak for coexistence. They beg for an inclusive, empathic stance.

Is the notion of empathy idealistic? Yes, intentionally so. Idealism, too, is a public service trait mirrored in the Athenian oath (Exhibit 2.1). It has been said that the notion of ethics itself "derives from man's imaginative power, from his tendency to idealize, to envision perfection, to extend his selfhood in identification with humanity as a whole" (Berkson, quoted in Boling and Dempsey, 1981, p.14).

Is the principle of public interest antipragmatic? No, because *ethical public service rejects both naïveté and cynicism.* Surely, the "essential moral qualities of the ethical public servant" include optimism, the faith that things can be improved, and the courage to act on that faith (Bailey, 1964, p. 236). Optimism—pragmatic, realistic, confident—combines "can do" with "should do." Public service is privileged to retain an old-fashioned and hard-headed belief in the possibility and desirability of progress.

Avoiding Conflict of Interest

Public interest, like law, draws a boundary between public and personal life. As a result, conflicts among competing roles and claims are predictable in public service. The very separation of public from personal roles induces the potential for conflicts of interest. It is the logical and practical by-product of the multiple roles shown in Exhibit 1.2.

Managers are ethically obligated to act through public position on behalf of the public interest. This standard is a public service rudder by which public managers are expected to steer. They are expected to have personal interests but are ethically constrained from using public office to pursue them. Public managers should anticipate conflicts and temptations but *not* indulge them at public expense.

In practice, the separation of public from personal translates into an ethical (and legal) prohibition against sale of office, as illustrated by Exhibit 2.2. The formulation depends on the legitimacy of property and ownership. The fact is that "no public official or administrator, high or low, owns the government, his organization, or his office. The government belongs to the public, and the administrator's role is that of a trustee, not a proprietor, in the use of his authority" (Graham, 1974, p. 92).

Article 17 of the Universal Declaration of Human Rights formalizes a universal right to own property privately and collectively. This right has meaning only if theft is prohibited. Because use of office for personal gain—whether by bribery, extortion, or otherwise—is theft, this posture effectively enthones a prohibition against sale of office to a global standard. It is outright abuse of office.

The avoidance of conflict of interest by public servants is so widely accepted in our society that it ranks as orthodoxy. It persists as a standard precisely because violations continue and typify conflicts between public and personal claims. At its most minimal, the standard is this: use of office for personal gain for oneself or others is unethical. (Usually, it is also illegal; see Exhibit 8.1).

Outright bribery, a form of sale of office, is usually prohibited outright. According to one government definition, "A bribe is an offer to employees of something of value to (a) do something they should not do or (b) fail to do something they should do, in their official duties. The something of value need not be money; it can be anything of value" (U.S. Department of Defense, 1984, p. 40). Bribery competes for the title of most unambiguous ethical offense.

What to do when the opportunity strikes—or threatens—is less obvious. The following advice comes from a federal ethics handbook (U.S. Department of Health and Human Services, 1989, p. 15) and is offered here as something to think about. "A bribery attempt usually begins with a subtle suggestion rather than a specific offer. If you are approached by someone who mentions an exchange of money or anything of value for a special favor, you should not cut the person off abruptly. This will discourage the attempt to bribe you, but will leave the person free to make an offer to someone else. Investigators recommend equivocating by letting them know you need time to think about it. Then immediately contact the Office of Inspector General." The Defense Department seconded the use of noncommittal responses such as "I have to think about that carefully." The ethicality of the intended hoax is ignored.

Some temptations do not—and will not—disappear. Individuals succumb, no matter how widely accepted the ethical standard. One specimen is nepotism, meaning favoritism shown to relatives. The word's derivation reflects its longevity and persistence; it comes from the old Italian word for nephew and refers to special favors in job placement shown church dignitaries' relatives in Europe centuries ago. Contemporary examples are all too easy to name (Exhibit 6.3, on friendship). A case in point is the late Mayor Richard J. Daley of Chicago. Asked about awarding a contract to his son, Daley reputedly said, "If you can't help your family, who can you help?" (ChicagoMetro Ethics Coalition, 1989, p. 4). Today, nepotism is prohibited outright by at least twenty-three states (Council of State Governments, 1990, pp. 144–145). In public service, preferential treatment for personal gain, even if not one's own immediate gain, is unacceptable.

Impartiality

The impartiality standard, which is closely tied to avoiding conflict of interest, speaks to the possibility, even the likelihood, of bias. Public managers are ethically obligated to promote the public interest, which means to be impartial. Because competing claims make impartiality problematic, ethical public managers bend over backward to retain objectivity and reduce bias in action and decision making. This can be done by steering away from any avoidable influence that may cloud vision, bias decision, or appear as if it may. Exhibit 3.1 illustrates this routinely frustrating, yet invariably tough, standard. West Virginia's Governmental Ethics Act of 1989 (Chapter 6B, Section B1.2) speaks directly on this matter: "Independence and impartiality of public officials and public employees are essential for the maintenance of the confidence of our citizens in the operation of a democratic government." Similarly, a county council expresses this sentiment in its code (Section 19A-2[a]): "The county council of Montgomery County, recognizing that our system of representative government is dependent in part upon the people maintaining the highest trust in their public officials and employees, finds and declares that the people have a right to be assured that the impartiality and independent judgment of public officials and employees will be maintained."

That the impartiality standard, like so many other things, is easier said than done does not diminish the obligation. This is widely recognized among senior managers. In a survey of members of the National Association of State Budget Officers, impartiality was the most frequently cited ethical concern (Mensen, 1990). "While some acts are clearly wrong (where the individual uses his or her office for private gain, or for the benefit of someone with whom he

Exhibit 3.1. Insider Trading on the Public Trust.

The following is adapted from a training case on ethics and supervision from the Department of Employee Relations, State of Minnesota. Provided by courtesy of Linda W. Harder.

You are a newly promoted parole agency supervisor who is serving a six-month probationary period. One of your responsibilities is writing presentence investigation (PSI) reports, used by the district court judges in sentencing convicted felons. Another is supervising parole agents who also write PSIs. Right now, the prisons are overcrowded and the county jails are full. Consequently, the number of PSIs you are required to write each month is increasing.

One new type of sentence for nonviolent offenders is electronic monitoring, in which an electronic sensor is attached to the felon's leg and a monitor alerts the police if the felon exceeds a specified range. You and your fellow parole agents increasingly have been recommending the electronic anklet as a way to prevent overcrowding in prisons and jails.

Some of your parole agents realize that electronic home arrest devices are a growing industry. Several agents have purchased stock in the one company doing business in your state. You have the opportunity to do the same because the stock is publicly traded at less than $5 per share. It looks like an attractive investment; a national brokerage firm's recent newsletter rates it undervalued, a "buy."

You are particularly interested because you have begun to think about your children's college education but have been unable to save money on a salary that barely meets your current needs.

What would you do personally?
What are your responsibilities as a supervisor?
Should parental responsibilities influence this decision? Why?
How does your state code of conduct apply?
What factors influenced your decision?

	Yes	No
–Law?	——	——
–Avoiding conflict of interest?	——	——
–Avoiding appearance of impropriety?	——	——
–Opportunity for financial gain?	——	——
–Inadequate public sector salary?	——	——
–Other?		
_____	——	——
_____	——	——

---

or she has a private relationship), others are not so easy to characterize, such as those occasions when the official believes he is acting in the public interest *despite* a private relationship" (Cowan Commission, 1989a, p. 145). The argument holds for personal policy preferences as well.

Bias stemming from political party affiliation has had a long and altogether infamous career in American public service. President Grant's administration even today epitomizes the problems: ineptitude, preferential treatment, and public contempt. Terms such as *party boss* and *machine politics* conjure up the old images of public employees being required to toe the party line and donate time, money, and even votes to partisan campaigns. Spearheading the professionalization of public service over a century ago, the move to civil service began the divorce of public administration from partisanship by interposing merit.

The federal Hatch acts, enacted on the eve of World War II, sought to protect the public interest by forbidding partisan political activities by federal employees and, by extension, all government employees whose jobs touch federal programs or money. Many state and local jurisdictions followed suit. "Hatched" employees today are forbidden to be candidates for public office in partisan elections, campaign for or against candidates in partisan elections, engage in campaign activities to elect partisan candidates, collect contributions or raise funds for partisan functions, organize or manage partisan political meetings, hold office in political clubs or parties, circulate nominating petitions, and register voters for only one party. An election is defined as partisan "if any candidate for an elected public office is running as a representative of a political party whose presidential candidate received electoral votes in the last presidential election" (U.S. Office of Government Ethics, 1986, p. 12).

Keyed to nonpartisanship, these prohibitions were initially aimed at *protecting* public employees from unwilling participation in political party campaigns, fundraising, and the like. What began as a move to protect public service and public employees from partisan predators metamorphosed, first, into insulation from partisan political directives and, second, into severe limits on public servants' rights as citizens.

Proposals to amend the Hatch acts devolved in 1990 into a presidential-congressional tussle in which citizen rights of public employees were arrayed against ensuring nonpartisanship. With or without the Hatch acts, the generally recognized public service standard of impartiality rejects bias in action or decision making for reasons of political party affiliation or preference.

Avoiding the Appearance of Impropriety

Publicity is an evaluative test regularly applied to ethical choices in all spheres of life (Rawls, 1971, p. 133). It is particularly meaningful in public service, where obligations are linked to public confidence and trust. Public servants are expected to attend to public perception of the way their activities and decisions look and the public's response. It is not enough for managers just to uphold the law and be ethical. Public service must look right, smell right, feel right; in short, it must avoid the appearance of impropriety.

On the one hand, the appearance standard is rarely, if ever, defined. On the other hand, it operationalizes public confidence and public scrutiny at the level of community standards. While appearance is often defined as *what a reasonable person could reasonably believe,* this definition leaves a good deal to the imagination. What is an impropriety? As it appears to whom? Do facts count? In its best form, this standard reciprocally obligates the public to be informed, which is not always the case.

Some managers interpret this standard to imply that looking good is as important as doing good. They see it as offensive, intellectually barren, or practically bankrupt. For some, it recalls the old quip about obscenity, "I can't define it but I know it when I see it," and represents an unjust basis for civil or even administrative sanctions. Peter Drucker (1981, p. 28) questions whether the standard involves leadership or hypocrisy. The American Bar Association (1980, p. 47) cautions against subordinating duty to potential misunderstanding or criticism, and Ralph Elliot, past president of the Connecticut Bar Association, suggests that appearance "sets up the standard of the most suspicious person, a very difficult standard" (Lewis, 1986, pp. 11–12).

Despite criticisms and cautions, the standard that calls for avoiding the appearance of impropriety drives public service. In no small measure, it even defines it. This standard is geared to maintaining public confidence in public service and therefore voluntary compliance. It is written into many state statutes, local ordinances, and professional codes of conduct. In the Chicago City Council's formal explanation of why it added an ethics ordinance to the municipal code in 1987, the council pointed to the importance of public confidence that "can best be engendered and preserved by the avoidance of conflicts of interest, impropriety, or the appearance of them" (Section 26.2-1).

This standard is not intended to substitute for ethical action. Instead and ideally, it points to the public manager's obligation to reinforce public perception of legitimate authority exercised on behalf of the public interest.

Concerned managers may be persuaded to borrow a question from former New York mayor Edward Koch: "How am I doin'?" The answer: not nearly good enough. A Roper Organization survey (1981) asked respondents whether they thought most government officials "tend to act more in their own self-interest, or more in the public interest"; 45 percent indicated the former, 44 percent the latter (11 percent said they didn't know).

It is not just that more needs to be done in this area but that avoiding the appearance of impropriety is an ongoing and never-ending standard. Three decades ago, in his 1961 message to Congress on codifying standards in federal service, President Kennedy noted, "There can be no dissent from the principle that all officials must act with unwavering integrity, absolute impartiality, and complete devotion to the public interest. This principle must be followed not only in reality but in appearance."

Public Duties, Private Lives

In November 1987, Judge Douglas H. Ginsburg withdrew from consideration for a seat on the U.S. Supreme Court in response to the furor over his admission that he had smoked marijuana in the 1960s and 1970s. His admission raised issues of judgment, character, and illegal behavior. Then two Democratic candidates for president, Senator Albert Gore, Jr. (then age thirty-nine), and former governor Bruce Babbitt (then age forty-six) admitted having smoked marijuana. Senator

Joseph R. Biden, Jr., had already weathered a storm over plagiarism, and Gary Hart had endured public scrutiny of an adulterous liaison.

These events swept up elected officials, but many city managers, police chiefs, and state commissioners can testify that the spotlight shines on appointed officials and career professionals as well (see the case at the end of this chapter). So could the late John Tower, President Bush's initial nominee for secretary of defense, whose drinking and extramarital entertainments were disclosed at Senate confirmation hearings where questions of character eclipsed policy and beliefs. The impact of public scrutiny was aptly summarized almost a half-century ago: "[E]very governmental executive lives and moves and has his being in the presence of public dynamite" (Appleby, [1945] 1987, p. 162).

Recent events trigger thoughtful but still inconclusive probing into the distinction between public roles and private lives, a subject that has sparked debate since the days of ancient Athens. Does the public's right to know mean there is *no* realm of wholly private behavior unrelated to job performance and, more broadly, public trust? In that light, consider the case of a second-shift maintenance worker with several years of service with the county; the employee is convicted on a minor gambling charge. Are you *ethically* justified in dismissing the worker?

There really is no consensus here. Frequently, standards are limited to *official* action or public activities. Federal administrative standards and the American Institute of Certified Public Accountants' 1973 Code of Professional Conduct fall in this category. Alternatively, standards may extend to personal realms as well. The International Association of Chiefs of Police takes an uncompromising position in its 1989 code, which states, "A police officer's character and conduct while off duty must always be exemplary, thus maintaining a position of respect in the community in which he or she lives and serves. The officer's personal behavior must be beyond reproach." Similarly, the ICMA's 1987 code would have members be "dedicated to the highest ideals of honor and integrity in all public and personal relationships in order that the member may merit the respect and confidence of the elected officials, or other officials and employees, and of the public."

Article 12 of the United Nations' Universal Declaration of Human Rights offers a suggestive standard aimed at the general population: "No one shall be subjected to *arbitrary* interference with his privacy, family, home or correspondence, nor to attacks upon his honour and reputation. Everyone has the right to the protection of the law against such interference or attacks" (emphasis added).

In 1974, Washington State's supreme court articulated a standard that is readily extended beyond elected officials to appointees and employees. In some respects, it amounts to the *compelling interest* justification: "The right of the electorate to know most certainly is no less fundamental than the right of privacy. When the right of the people to be informed does not intrude upon intimate personal matters which are unrelated to fitness for public office, the candidate or officeholder may not complain that his own privacy is paramount to the interests of the people" (quoted in Weimer, 1990, p. 15). Some of these issues are illustrated in an administrative setting described in Exhibit 3.2.

The Press Pass. What makes a person fit for public service is a consideration for the media no less than for the public person who works under the glare of the spotlight or the threat of disclosure. A panel of journalists and elected officials recently tapped issues such as public and private, youth and adult, community standards, public record, and character indicators. The discussion revealed that while the press exercises selectivity, nothing is inherently excluded. Visibility cues vulnerability—exposure increases the higher one climbs in government. (Panel participants in the discussion at ASPA's 1989 ethics conference included former members of the U.S. House of Representatives, Geraldine Ferraro and Richard Bolling; Tom Fiedler of the *Miami Herald*; Martin Tolchin of the *New York Times*; Rushworth Kidder of the *Christian Science Monitor*; and Michael Josephson, moderator, of the Josephson Institute.) Press standards are shown in Exhibit 3.3.

For the press, self-censorship means filtering the public's right to know. The competition over news, to break a story or at least not be caught napping, is also compelling. People make a better "story angle" for television viewing than abstract ethical or technical issues. Hypocrisy, greed, sexual exploits, and the like give events a "personal touch." They help an exposé "reach a critical mass,"

Exhibit 3.2. *Public* Works.

Joe has lived in this city of 25,000 residents most of his life, and now he is a civil engineer and the public works director. He's invited several neighbors and friends, some of whom work with him at city hall, to his home for cocktails to mark the holiday season. He agrees cordially when a neighbor asks whether she may bring along her dinner guest, a reporter for the local newspaper. Unfortunately, Joe succumbs to too much holiday spirit and drunkenly collapses in the kitchen before the guests depart.

> Has Joe done anything unethical, or has he just been stupid?
> Should the reporter print the story?
> Is Joe's home a protected reserve?

Changing the circumstances clarifies the mode of reasoning and pinpoints critical factors in making judgments. Closed questions force decision making; open-ended questions encourage analysis.

> Would your answers to the three preceding questions change if
> –Joe's drinking were habitual, perhaps affecting his performance on the job?
> –Joe had made several racist remarks during the party?
> –Joe were chief administrative officer in a city of 300,000?
> Would your answers to the first two questions change if it had been an office party in a local restaurant?
> Do the public opinion polls affect your answers? Should public opinion affect a manager's ethical choices?

Note: For federal law, see 5 U.S.C. 7352 on excessive and habitual use of intoxicants and 7362 on alcohol abuse and alcoholism.

Exhibit 3.3. Press Standards on Fair Play.

The following excerpt is from the Code of Ethics of the Society of Professional Journalists, revised 1987.

V.   FAIR PLAY

Journalists at all times will show respect for the dignity, privacy, rights, and well-being of people encountered in the course of gathering and presenting the news.

1. The news media should not communicate unofficial charges affecting reputation or moral character without giving the accused a chance to reply.
2. The news media must guard against invading a person's right to privacy.
3. The media should not pander to morbid curiosity about details of vice and crime.
4. It is the duty of news media to make prompt and complete correction of their errors.
5. Journalists should be accountable to the public for their reports and the public should be encouraged to voice its grievances against the media. Open dialogue with our readers, viewers, and listeners should be fostered.

---

allowing that the "ability to reduce complicated events to colorful drama is the key to a scandal's market value" (Kurtz, 1989, p. D5). As a result, the civics conversation tends to be "conceptually narrow and impoverished" (Jennings, 1989b, p. 23). "The quality of deliberation in a democracy is debased when sensationalist exposés of private activities displace discussions of questions of public policy" (Thompson, 1981, p. 225).

There is no consensus among public managers on the proper role of the media. At the 1989 ASPA conference, survey responses differed widely on a question about the media being too intrusive in investigating ethical behavior of public servants (Keehley, 1990). Not surprisingly, practitioner conferees responded significantly differently from academics, who expressed a desire for more attention to policy issues in the legislature and media.

Do public servants have a right to any privacy? Balancing individual privacy and the public's right to know becomes more troublesome as the speed, capacity, and standards of disclosure change. Today so much *is* public record that it is hard to distinguish privacy from anonymity. (Computer systems, public information, and freedom of information join together to create new problems.) The functional equivalent of puritan New England's public pillory is the nightly news, but with at least one big difference. Not too long ago, private peccadilloes were isolated from public responsibilities. Public scrutiny (and public voyeurism) was limited by technology and convention. Once, living a lifetime in a small town, our friends and neighbors knew all the secrets, but anonymity was within a few days' ride on horseback. Today, our neighbors may not know our names, but personal matters are headlines for all the world to see. In some respects, modern life has turned the public and private domains inside out.

Drawing a Line. While it is squarely in the American political tradition to apply one set of standards of behavior to the private citizen and another to a public figure, we have not yet developed selective *material* criteria. In that regard, Ralph Chandler (1989b, p. 1) notes with due sarcasm, "If Martin Luther King really slept with a variety of women other than his wife, as Ralph David Abernathy says in *And the Walls Came Tumbling Down,* he does not deserve to be called a great man, does he? Someone else must have written the 'Letter from Birmingham City Jail' and given the 'I Had a Dream' speech." Chandler goes on to mention presidents Washington, Jefferson, Roosevelt, Eisenhower, and Kennedy, all of whose great public contributions are more significant historically than their private mischief, including their love lives. Chandler calls for "moral grandeur" in making judgments rather than in making grand demands upon someone else's behavior.

The case that concludes this chapter suggests that we have more questions than answers. Is *appearance of impropriety* a code term (pun intended; see Chapter Eight) for higher standards or double standards? Is it an excuse for titillation at the expense of public officials and employees? Can we separate what is trivial or irrelevant from what is meaningful? Should we distinguish a youngster's misstep from a character defect in the mature manager? Governor Bruce Babbitt and others have suggested that we apply a statute of limitations or proclaim an amnesty (Raspberry, 1987, p. A27). The court uses a "least restrictive means" test for curbs on individual liberties. Cannot a comparable standard be developed for public appointees and employees? Should a line be drawn between pertinent public and private behavior? If so, where? And by whom?

When ethics is politically—and cynically—abused for partisan purposes, public managers and employees, their morale, and the image of government get hit in the crossfire. July 1990 headlines in the *Wall Street Journal* on the savings and loan scandal illustrate the point: "Thrift Scandal, Viewed as Political Dynamite, Is Slow to Detonate" and then "Democrats Are Being Hurt as Much as Republicans; Public Blames the S&Ls." An analyst of political ethics summarizes the current stew, heavily spiced with partisan ingredients (Jennings, 1989a, p. 175): "In the present climate of ethical charge and countercharge, accusation and defense, wherein the hit men of each party are devouring their victims and one another, it is very difficult for other public officials, journalists and citizens alike to exercise their political judgment on these matters [public purpose] because the very language of political judgment has become suspect and subsequently debunked."

Public opinion reflects the quandaries and inconsistencies. A national survey asked whether certain actions should disqualify someone from holding a high-level government position (Yankelovich, Skelly and White, 1989). A majority's response that cheating on income taxes (86 percent) and being drunk in public (68 percent) should disqualify one from office may help resolve the case in Exhibit 3.2. That a majority (64 percent) of the respondents rejected having an extramarital affair as grounds for disqualification is especially provocative because it is among the wrongdoings prohibited by the Ten Commandments.

A poll conducted by the University of Connecticut's Institute for Social Inquiry (1987) was confined to opinion about elected officials in Connecticut, but it turned up intriguing evidence on public opinion. Fully 70 percent of the respondents agreed that "what a politician does in his private life, so long as he doesn't actually break the law, is nobody's business but his own." Testifying to public opinion's mixed signals, a strong majority (73 percent) agreed that "in judging candidates, it makes sense to look at their character and integrity, and that includes what kind of family life they have." Of course, a look is not necessarily a rejection, and the look empowers the citizen.

If the test of competence includes perfection, then we are doomed to disillusionment and to the loss of public confidence. Therefore, the obligation to maintain the public trust must not degenerate into sanctimonious platitudes or feeding vulgar curiosity. The genuine obligation depends on meeting meaningful standards and intelligible guidelines. According to columnist William Safire (1989, p. A31), "That's why the current hollering about ethics in Washington is sensitizing and good. Pretending the troubling subject is trivial or discourages good people from serving is numbing and bad."

Pressing Business. There are at least five lessons for the public manager in all this: use common sense, go on record, establish ethical credibility, tell it as it is, and tell it as it should be. Let us take them one at a time.

   Use common sense. First, be realistic. Learn what to expect from the media—nothing; that is its calling and professional duty. Be prepared for special scrutiny, not special treatment.
   Go on record. Second, professional survival skills include making it difficult to be misinterpreted, misunderstood, or misquoted. Giving good interviews and writing good press releases are useful professional skills. Although professional standards for city managers and Canadian public servants urge anonymity, a public manager may not always have a choice in the matter.
   Establish ethical credibility. Third, take a hand in training; help break in media novices to establish a good working relationship and personal rapport and to expose them to the legal and professional standards operating in the jurisdiction. (An ethics component is included when Connecticut's statewide city managers' association annually briefs rookie reporters along with editors.) This exposure can include workaday ethical choices and even a crisis or two.
   Tell it as it is. Fourth, tell the truth. Let the media know they are dealing with a person they can trust. Lying is both unethical and impractical. Bill Donaldson, whose managerial career took him from Arizona to Ohio and then to Philadelphia, cautioned a student aspiring to public service that "any attempt to conceal anything is more trouble than it is worth and the more open and public you are, the better off for everyone" (Tinkham, 1990). Surely, we all make mistakes; the key is to

admit them and not repeat them. Ethics restrains deception but does not prevent error.

Tell it as it should be. The fifth and final proposal shifts from self-protection to plea bargaining. It invokes a senior manager's responsibility to protect a blameless subordinate who is unjustly accused. It also invokes the value of compassion, which is more compelling when not self-serving. If an otherwise promising subordinate with a valid excuse (meaning a reason to be treated as if innocent) is threatened, a manager can call out the artillery—reason. One forceful argument is that only hypocrites will respond to a call for perfection. Another is the need to allow for human error and personal growth. The public manager can also urge caution along with compassion by suggesting that even when moral judgments are wrong, the personal damage persists. The senior manager's purpose here is to speak up, not cover up, and keeping subordinates' trust demands both charity and courage.

When operating under public scrutiny, the manager's acid test is whether he or she would like to read all about it on the front page of the local newspaper. Imagine, too, explaining the behavior or decision to family and friends. To safeguard personal integrity in the face of public disclosure, a no less important test consists of answering two questions: What kind of person would do this? Do I want to be and be known as this kind of person?

Case: Public Jeopardy

The Fedders tragedy progressed from a 1985 newspaper exposé to a 1990 television drama. The cast of characters included John M. Fedders, director of the Securities and Exchange Commission's (SEC) enforcement division from 1981 to 1985. Disreputable, reprehensible personal conduct coexisted with exemplary job performance. His divorce proceedings in Montgomery County's circuit court exposed to public record both admitted wife beating and financial pressures associated with government pay lower than private law practice income. A front page article in the *Wall Street Journal* launched the publicity about his personal affairs, and other newspapers soon followed.

According to press accounts, the SEC chairman affirmed Fedders's fine job and that his work had not been harmed. As chief enforcer in the securities market, Fedders supervised a staff of about 200, including lawyers and accountants, and substantially increased the number of enforcement actions.

White House spokesman Larry Speakes initially responded to the question of resignation by explaining that it is "standard practice to accept the recommendation of the head of an agency when dealing with a problem of that type" (Nash, 1985a, p. D1). A senior administration official conceded the delicacy of the case because "it's something between a man and his wife" and there was no evidence that he had not performed well on the job (Taylor, 1985, p. A16).

The managing editor of the *Wall Street Journal* said, "As a general rule,

I don't think we should be writing about the private lives of public officials when there is no indication that the behavior in private is affecting their public performance." The executive editor of the *New York Times* noted that marital problems can't be ignored if they become public record, affect the job, or "when laws are broken or when an obvious scandal is taking place" (Taylor, 1985, p. A16).

Fedders was an important, visible law enforcement official, admitted the wife-beating charges, and tested the White House's announced condemnation of family violence. On the other hand, he was not accused of official illegality, nor do personal problems such as marital disputes generally require dismissal from government service. Section 101 of Executive Order 11222 (issued in 1965 by President Lyndon Johnson and in effect in 1985) limited vulnerability to official duties: "Where government is based on the consent of the governed, every citizen is entitled to have complete confidence in the integrity of his government. Each individual officer, employee, or advisor of government must help to earn and must honor that trust by his own integrity and conduct in all *official* actions" (emphasis added).

On February 26, 1985, Fedders resigned his government position because "the glare of publicity on my private life threatens to undermine the effectiveness of the division of enforcement and of the commission." In his resignation letter, Fedders described the seven instances of marital violence as "isolated events" in more than eighteen years of marriage and argued that press reports "exaggerated allegations in the divorce trial" (Fedders, 1985, p. D5). The SEC chairman accepted his resignation "with regret."

What are the ethical issues here? Should Fedders have resigned? Been asked to resign? Should the press have printed the story? Would your answers change if a civil servant rather than an appointed official were involved? Are the standards different? Should they be? What do *you* think is more important in thinking about this case, the nature of the wrong or the official's rank?

For a local version, consider an actual case of a firefighter convicted of child molestation after almost two decades of service in a southwestern city. A deal struck between the fire department and city used a leave of absence to cover the prison term; with accumulated sick leave added, the firefighter became legally eligible for a lifetime pension (Bergsman, 1991, p. 63).

As a member of the pension board, would you be *ethically* justified in denying the pension? (Before answering, anticipate the public controversy that ensued in this community.)

As a manager with the city, would you have negotiated the agreement?

– What if the off-duty offense were petty, harmed no one, and the city job involved no public contact?

Chapter 4

To Take
Individual Responsibility

This chapter converts public service obligations into general guides to ethical action in public agencies by drawing on the idea of individual responsibility and everyday and extreme bureaucratic experiences. The chapter confronts central facts of managerial life: individuals work in organizational settings, exercise discretion, and ply their expertise. Starting by warning against substituting scapegoating for problem solving, the argument moves from individual responsibility to responsibility for means and ends and, finally, to professional competence. A concluding case puts the action guides to work.

Ethical principles are guides to action; they operationalize values and cue behavior befitting public service. Three clusters of action-driving principles stem directly from legal compliance and public interest—core ethical obligations in public service—and the definition of ethics. These action guides point to individual responsibility, substantive responsibility, and competence. The level of generality thwarts a formula-like application, which is all to the good. Ethical decision making requires individual judgment, and workaday problems are so diverse and so complex that even an encyclopedic compilation would not cover all possibilities. The goal is to guide action, not stymie or dictate it.

Searching for Demons

Most principles, in their exaggerated or absolutist versions, are shaky, even suspect. Thus, avowing individual responsibility can decline into preoccupation with allocating blame, ferreting out the guilty, finding the one at fault. This is encouraged by the fact that individual wrongdoing is easy to understand, or at least easier than legalistic abstractions or systemwide flaws. As a result, we occasionally try to dodge difficult issues by finger pointing. Sometimes we "use" a person as an example or escape hatch: victor, villain, or victim. Diversionary tactics and scapegoating are ethically unsound. Often they are not even very useful in the long run and are trivial subplots in national dramas over fundamental ethical issues.

Two incidents corroborate the generic quality of the diversion-scapegoat proposition. In 1968, almost 600 largely unarmed and unresisting civilians were massacred at My Lai in Vietnam. U.S. soldiers in Charlie Company under platoon leader Lieutenant William L. Calley were directly responsible. The exserviceman whose letter originally provoked the investigation, Ron Ridenhour, said in an interview two decades later (Cockburn, 1988, p. 403), "The important thing is, this was an act of policy, not an individual aberration. My Lai didn't happen because Lieutenant Calley went berserk. There were similar acts of policy all over the country. I mean, every once in a while they decided they would make an example." Note that Ridenhour's letter begins the ethics chapter in West Point's textbook on leadership (United States Military Academy, 1985, p. 21-1).

In time, the army charged about two dozen officers and enlisted men with direct involvement in the massacre but convicted only Calley, who wound up serving three years under house arrest. William Wilson, the army colonel in the inspector general's office who handled the investigation, recently wrote about it and quoted General Peers: "The failure to bring justice to those who inflicted the atrocity casts grave doubts upon the efficacy of our justice system." Wilson concludes, "I do remember being startled when the public seemed to make a hero out of Rusty Calley, or at the least a victim. It sure didn't look that way from up close" (Wilson, 1990, p. 53).

The American response to the massacre at My Lai is worth comparing to the Soviet's response to the disaster at Chernobyl. *Pravda*, the Soviet Communist Party's newspaper, blamed plant managers for ignoring safety measures in "cleaning up" after the nuclear accident at Chernobyl in April 1986. While charges ran the gamut from nepotism and drunkenness to management abuses, the main point is that blaming plant managers for stressing power production "at any cost," including repair and maintenance, obscures the realities of pressure from Moscow to increase energy output (Keller, 1988). Undoubtedly, that pressure was linked to the accident in the first place. While many acts of personal courage marked the events, the irresponsibility and ineptitude of scientists, senior officials, and government workers in planning, construction, and operational phases contributed to the tragedy to which Soviet physicist and dissident Andrei Sakharov attributed universal significance (Sakharov, 1991, p. viii).

The purpose behind the storytelling is not to defend the indefensible but to emphasize that *individual responsibility is by no means identical to sole responsibility*. In fact, some individual administrators and soldiers did commit reprehensible deeds. Both stories have a perverse ending: a search for demons functions as a sorry substitute for solving systemic shortcomings or organizational flaws. According to the United States Military Academy text (1985, p. 21-23), "Whether the My Lai incident . . . is interpreted as simply the fault of a few weak or flawed characters who happened to hold key leadership roles or is seen instead as symptomatic of a complex organizational phenomenon, moral failure on such a scale . . . illustrates the awesome importance of the ethical dimensions of organizational leadership."

Accountability is not just a military or government problem but a bureaucratic one. The spacecraft *Challenger* disaster in January 1986, in which corporate executives played a crucial role, testifies to its immediacy and magnitude. *A public manager's first task is to fix the problem and only secondarily to fix the blame.* These incidents demonstrate the need for both ethically supportive organizations and ethically responsible individuals.

We Are Individually Responsible for Our Decisions and Behavior

Ethics rests on voluntary moral judgment, with the individual as ethical player. Rephrased, this idea means individual responsibility for judgments and choices. Logically, decision making turns on selecting and accepting responsibility. Individual responsibility is *not* obliterated by collective decision making in organizations and agencies. Because most of us work in organizations most of the time, arguing otherwise would put ethics (along with contemporary civilization) on the endangered species list.

The dilemma often referred to as the problem of many hands is reflected in a study of senior federal executives (Posner and Schmidt, 1988). All aspects of working conditions were felt to have deteriorated over the preceding two decades. "To what extent do [did] you have the influence necessary to do your job well?" a question touching on organizational decision making, fared no better. In a 1979 survey of 20,000 federal employees, fewer than half of the respondents agreed with the statement, "My supervisor encourages subordinates to participate in important decisions" (Goodsell, 1985, p. 102). The principle appears in its negative cast in a government report on factors that increase the risk of unethical behavior: "Employees lack opportunities to participate in decision making and creative planning, especially with respect to their own work" (General Accounting Office, 1981, p. 21).

The organizational habitat of public managers affects decision making, action, *and* ethical analysis. The ecology features implicit norms, predominant values, established routines, underlying decision premises, and pressures for obedience and loyalty (for example, rewarding the team player). To these are added explicit policies, procedures, and routines. Public administrators are attuned to the organizational context of decision making. A 1989 survey of the ASPA's members prompted almost four-fifths of the respondents to "agree" or "strongly agree" with the comment, "While each individual is ultimately responsible for his/her ethical behavior, organizations define and control the situations in which decisions are made" (Bowman, 1989, p. 107).

Through selective recruitment and the imbibing of organizational habits and group norms (socialization processes), many but not all organizational members come to identify strongly with the organization and absorb its standards as their own. This is not just a classroom theory. Almost half (47 percent) of the ASPA survey respondents agreed or strongly agreed with the statement, "Public managers feel under pressure to compromise personal standards to achieve organizational goals" (Bowman, 1989, p. 107). A government analysis identified "peer and hierarchical pressures to compromise personal standards and/or be successful" and overwhelming zeal among managers for organizational goal achievement as factors contributing to potential misconduct (General Accounting Office, 1981, p. 19).

In some cases, the identification becomes extreme. "Their job contract with bureaucracy soon becomes a psychological contract" (Hummel, 1987, p. 7). As a result, "what is likely to be *substituted* for ethical deliberation is an application of the individual's understanding of the norms and values of the organization" (Denhardt, 1988, p. 91).

The bureaucratic mentality (or, in Heclo's more accurate phrase, *bureaucratic dispositions*) applies to large-scale corporate cultures and private organizations, along with governmental ones. Bureaucracy is not a governmental trait (see Figure I.1) but the way contemporary society organizes joint action to perform complex tasks. Some experts view bureaucracy as inherently constricting, pathological, amoral, or even immoral. Others, such as Charles Goodsell in *The Case for Bureaucracy* (1985) and James Q. Wilson in *Bureaucracy* (1990), counter with contrary evidence and arguments. Beneath these broad generalizations lies a mix of cultures, missions, procedures, and other characteristics. Bureaucracy is neither uniform nor monolithic, and bureaucrats are not of one face or one mind.

While artificial stereotypes do injustice to all employees, organizations *do* exert pressures on members to conform. *The pressures can be for better or for worse.* Peter Drucker (1989, p. 229) explains. "Management is about human beings. Its task is to make people capable of joint performance, to make their strengths effective and their weaknesses irrelevant." Mutually restraining interaction between the individual and organization is an institution's danger and its promise, and it is precisely the point of building ethically supportive agencies. At any rate, while organizational demands may challenge individual responsibility, they do not erase it.

The ethical benchmarks of the twentieth century teach us that bureaucracy is powerful, but power is neutral—it can be used for great good as well as great evil. The very fact that these benchmarks are extreme cases helps crystallize issues and clarify thinking. By definition, they do *not* reflect daily routine in public service. The distance and magnitude of awesome events sometimes make them useful learning devices. Both heroic behavior and heinous behavior direct our attention to the interplay between individuals and organizations and their capacity for good and evil.

In this light, consider the Nuremberg Charter. It specified the procedures and principles underlying the trial of the major Nazi war criminals by the victorious allies (the United States, France, Great Britain, and the Soviet Union) after World War II. On making decisions and giving orders, Part II, Article 7 of the charter states, "The official position of defendants, whether as Heads of State or responsible officials in Government departments, shall not be considered as freeing them from responsibility or mitigating punishment" (Nuremberg Charter, 1947, p. 12).

So It Follows That We Cannot Hide Behind Our Boss or Our Desk to Escape Responsibility. In the organizational habitat, the manager's niche is defined as a particular spot in the chain of command, the hierarchy of legitimate authority. Here deference to superior-subordinate relations generally and routinely prevails. It is supposed to do so. But neither discipline nor obedience defines the boundaries of subordinates' ethical responsibility.

Moral outrage, incomprehension, or both are usual responses to the notorious words of Adolf Eichmann, the Nazi official kidnapped to Israel, tried by an Israeli court, then hanged in 1962. Denying legal culpability and ignoring ethical responsibility, his defense is popularly rendered as "I was only following orders." On taking orders, Part II, Article 8 of the Nuremberg Charter (1947) states, "The fact that the defendant acted pursuant to order of his Government or of a superior shall not free him from responsibility, but may be considered in mitigation of punishment."

The former prison psychologist at Nuremberg notes the *"psychologically aberrant nature of an adult person who defines good and evil merely as synonyms for obedience and disobedience to one's superiors"* (Miale and Selzer, 1975, p. 6). Hannah Arendt's thesis in *Eichmann in Jerusalem: A Report on the Banality of Evil* (1964) is that ordinary people are capable of doing evil. Stanley Milgram's well-known psychological experiments on obedience required subjects in the United States to inflict painful electric shocks that were, unknown to them, counterfeit. Arendt's and Milgram's works are often marshaled as evidence of how easy it is to unthinkingly obey authority and ignore questions of right and wrong, good and evil. Maybe so on both counts, but that does not justify the behaviors or make them ethical.

While few indulge themselves in outright evil and fewer still in righteousness, people are evidently influenced by authority, by apathy, by thoughtlessness, and by their environment. Take a moment to think about the results of ceding responsibility for moral reasoning. Think about the willingness of many—though not all—of Milgram's subjects to inflict sham shocks on human subjects feigning pain. As a counterbalance, keep in mind that a member of Calley's platoon refused to shoot. The individual and the setting interact. But whether that setting is help or hurdle, the individual is still the responsible agent.

Blaming one's own unscrupulous behavior on circumstance or other people is a well-worn excuse, summarized by Machiavelli in *The Prince:* "A man who wishes to make a profession of goodness in everything must necessarily come to grief among so many who are not good. Therefore it is necessary for a prince, who wishes to maintain himself, to learn how not to be good, and to use this knowledge and not use it, according to the necessity of the case." Even if one accepts the personal utility argument, being coerced into it by rogues, villains, or one's boss does not make the behavior any more ethical.

To act as ethical agents and retain personal integrity, public managers must avoid the trap of what Dennis Thompson (1985) calls the "ethic of structure." Here responsibility is defined by the job description, and "it is not my job" lamely justifies irresponsibility. Inaction or looking the other way is a choice but not necessarily an ethically neutral one. Invalidating moral reasoning and responsibility altogether, the claims are (1) "not administrators but the organization (and its formal officers) should be held responsible for its decisions and policies" and (2) "personal moral responsibility extends only to the specific duties of their own office for which they are legally liable" (Thompson, 1985, pp. 555, 559). By shedding the burden and possibly the onus of organizational outcomes, this argument denies individual responsibility, efficacy, and ethics. Even were these claims valid, the manager could not duck responsibility: what is one doing working in that agency?

Responsibilities and loyalties to the boss complicate the cross currents of obligations. One pitfall is exaggerated personal allegiance. Aaron Wildavsky (1989, p. 779) puts it this way: "What is the temptation of administrators? By confusing their patron with their God, they mistake serving their superior with helping their people."

Despite the boss's relative power, successful managers are fully aware that the boss does in fact depend on them. Management pundit Peter Drucker (1986, p. 16) defines a manager as "someone who is responsible for the performance of all the people on whom his own performance depends. The first person on whom a manager's performance depends is the boss, and the boss is thus the first person for whose performance a manager has to take responsibility. . . . Managing the boss means, above all, creating a relationship of trust." While Drucker is speaking of business managers and has rejected the notion of distinctive business ethics (1981), the implication for public managers is that mindlessly following orders serves neither ethical nor managerial purposes.

So It Follows That We Cannot Hide Behind Our Subordinates. Ronald Reagan dramatized the principle that we cannot hide behind our subordinates in his response to the critical report issued by the Tower Commission he appointed to investigate the Iran-Contra affair. In a nationally televised address on March 4, 1987, Reagan said, "First, let me say I take full responsibility for my own actions and for those of my administration. As angry as I may be about activities undertaken without my knowledge, I am still accountable for those activities. . . . [T]his happened on my watch." By publicly and personally taking responsibility and despite his disengaged management style that abetted the activities, the president went a long way in the minds of many toward separating this affair from Watergate. The principle guiding action is echoed in Senator Howard Baker's famous question asked during Watergate: "What did the president know and when did he know it?"

The idea is far older and broader than American public administration, however. The biblical advice Jethro gives Moses about designing an administrative structure in Exodus 18 concedes Moses's responsibility for recruiting subordinates of good character and for retaining the hard cases for himself. In a change of venue, consider that *negative responsibility* in the Tokyo war trials (after World War II, in 1946–1948) held that a superior can be guilty for failing to prevent subordinates' actions that were preventable. The results of two national surveys shown in Exhibit 4.1 provide a more workaday example of managerial responsibility.

Reasonably, a city manager is not directly answerable for a road crew's unauthorized coffee break any more than is the president answerable for what goes on deep in the innards of a cabinet-level department. Federal executive branch employees number more than three million civilian employees and more than two million uniformed military. Commonsense yardsticks such as proximity, saliency, and gravity rightly affect our assessment of managerial responsibilities. A key in the question posed by the *New York Times* surveys is the word *widespread*. Although managers may not know what is going on, shouldn't they?

What about managerial responsibility for oversight? On the casual attitude toward exercising managerial controls, Senator Bob Graham of Florida said on October 31, 1989, in a Senate hearing on HUD abuses, "It would not be acceptable in a state government for the chief executive officer, who had been found to have presided over an agency so swept with fraud as HUD appears to have been, to have said that it was the responsibility of persons at lower levels to see that these matters were attended to" (U.S. Senate, 1990). The senator went on to ask William M. Diefenderfer, III, then deputy director of the Office of Management and Budget (who chairs the President's Council on Integrity and Efficiency), "Could you review for me what management controls were in effect from the president through the Office of Management and Budget to determine that,

Exhibit 4.1. Should the Agency Head Resign?

The following question and responses come from *New York Times* surveys conducted in 1985 and 1986.

Question: "If an investigation reveals widespread corruption at low and middle levels of a government agency, but it is clear that the head of the agency was not corrupt and did not know about it, should the head of the agency resign, or not?"

Responses	December 1985	April 1986
Should resign	16%	19%
Should not	75	75
Depends	4	2
Don't know/No answer	5	4

Do you agree with the majority response?
Managers may not know what is going on, but shouldn't they?
While the agency head may not be corrupt, is he or she acting responsibly?

at each step of the process . . . those below were carrying out their proper responsibilities?" In response, Diefenderfer said, "Well, the answer to that question is
a short answer. There weren't many, sir" (U.S. Senate, 1990).

The principle of responsibility for subordinates' actions is tied to the principles introduced next, which involve knowledge and competence. For example,
in the July 1987 congressional hearings on the Iran-Contra affair, John M. Poindexter, former national security adviser to President Reagan, testified that the
president was misled or lied to by omission to protect him: "I made a very
deliberate decision not to ask the president so that I could insulate him from the
decision and provide some future deniability." At joint Senate and House hearings in July 1987, Poindexter said, "I think it's always the responsibility of a staff
to protect their leader and certainly in this case where the leader is the commander
in chief . . . to make sure that he's not put in a position that can be politically
embarrassing." He also remarked, "I was convinced that the president would, in
the end, think it was a good idea." Poindexter explained, "The president never
indicated in any way to me that he did not want to be responsible for his decisions
or that I should have provided deniability to him. . . . This was an integration
of a lot of experience that I had that made me conclude that this was the way
we should go." The end result is that *plausible deniability* is usually implausible,
and its costs are figured in terms of credibility.

So It Follows That We Cannot Hide Behind Our Ignorance. Because serving the
public interest means, in part, identifying the public interest, getting the facts is
an important and often first step in thinking through ethical problems. Usually,
there is not enough information or time to guarantee one of being absolutely
certain of all spin-offs and side effects. Yet public managers cannot be paralyzed;
they must make decisions as best as they can. Unanticipated or unintended results, if by-products of indifference, thoughtlessness, or carelessness, point to
inexcusable ignorance. Here the rule of reason applies, and ethical people *can*
make mistakes. There is an obvious kinship between this principle and competence. "Where the welfare of so many is at stake, officials must make exceptional efforts to anticipate consequences of their actions" (Thompson, 1985
p. 560).

The most elementary standard of required knowledge springs from the
obligation of legal compliance: know the law. This standard is summarized in
three questions (Mertins and Hennigan, 1982, p. 5): "Do I know the laws governing my activities? . . . When faced with inequalities, omissions, and contradictions in laws affecting my work, what do I do? . . . Are there *any* conditions under
which I think the law should be compromised?"

A profession is defined largely by its specialized knowledge, on which its
privileges rest. Ignorance here undercuts all members. Many professional codes
incorporate standards that require the continuing professional training and tu-
toring of junior colleagues. By way of example, ASPA's code of ethics exhorts
members to "strive for personal professional excellence and encourage the pro-

fessional development of our associates and those seeking to enter the field of public administration.''

Even more to the point is the fact that specialized knowledge is a source of substantial power in today's information society, and its manipulation increases the handler's exploitative potential. The Law Enforcement Code of Ethics stresses confidentiality and notes the public's "right to security and privacy." The *danger zones* in information handling are outright deception; prejudicial distortion; inaccuracy; spurious accuracy and false certainty; proprietary, privileged, and confidential information; disclosure, public access, freedom of information, and privacy; and data integrity and computer security. Accordingly, the Government Finance Officers Association's code targets information as a central concern and obligates members to "demonstrate professional integrity in the issuance and management of information." In that regard, New York City's fiscal crisis of the mid 1970s (see Paul, 1990) is a first-rate negative example of how defective disclosure degenerates into abuse of information and deception.

Public managers are responsible for actions undertaken under the umbrella of their authority or in their name. Expert advice, professional judgments, and policy recommendations—all part of the daily routine—ideally rest on up-to-date information and assessment techniques. Getting the facts is logically part of many ethical decision-making models. In direct contrast to the nonchalance exhibited in Figure 4.1, responsible information management demands honoring basic standards. Checking against the seven questions in Exhibit 4.2 should help minimize bias and error.

This kind of approach has already been adopted in some jurisdictions. The 1988 budget forecast in California included statements of margin of error and uncertainties and emphasized accuracy, disclosure, reliability, and information users (Shkurti, 1990, pp. 90, 92–93). Federal regulations for environmental impact

Figure 4.1. Ethical Decision Making Demands *Getting the Facts* and Handling Them Responsibly.

Exhibit 4.2. Getting the Facts.

Yes

____ 1. Are underlying analytic assumptions known and open?

____ 2. Are significant omissions disclosed?

____ 3. Are reliability or error estimates provided?

____ 4. Are factual disagreements declared?

____ 5. Is information appropriate for the intended use and user?

____ 6. Are available, consequential data or views included?

____ 7. Are data sources credible? Independently corroborated?

Checking yes to all seven questions conforms to basic standards.

statements require disclosure of all major opinions, points of controversy, and incomplete or unavailable information.

We Are Responsible for What Is Done Along with How It Is Done

With the traditional boundary between politics and administration routinely breached by discretion (decisions made) and expertise (decisive influence), responsibility extends to both meaning and method, to substance as well as technique. Most managers perceive some scope and clout. A 1979 survey of federal employees found 84 percent agreeing with the statement, "My job gives me the opportunity to use my own judgment and initiative" (Goodsell, 1985, p. 102).

At hearings on establishing a commission on ethics in government before a Senate subcommittee on June 27, 1951, Paul H. Appleby related the cross-pressures to hide behind impotence and to duck managerial responsibility for building an ethical work environment.

> Public officials dealing with public programs struggle with problems . . . constantly in the business of drawing the line between desirable considerations of citizen concerns in a somewhat flexible and sympathetic way and carrying on systematically in pursuit of the general public interest without discrimination and without favoritism. In one sense these problems are most acute for low-ranking officials engaged in operational dealing with the citizens and groups most directly concerned. They often feel weak and insecure as minor cogs in a great machine, and may on that account bend too easily to importunities from groups which seem to them powerful; they may feel unable to guess what backing they will get at higher levels if they hold firmly what would appear to them to be the general public-interest line. They may also be so closely associated functionally with such groups as to mistake them for the

public. These subordinates can act reasonably well only with institutional patterns of responsibility laid down and constantly supported and developed by officials at higher levels.

Discretion and expertise obviously operate in policy analysis and at the
higher administrative ranks, where broad policy decisions are made (Tong, 1986).
Legal, budget, and personnel staffs' decisions affect everything that goes out the
door. But think of the many daily decisions made at the operational level, especially by those line employees who are direct service providers, or "street-level
bureaucrats" in Michael Lipsky's (1980) term. They are the building and health
inspectors, zoning enforcement officers, lifeguards at county parks, police officers, emergency dispatchers, air traffic controllers, park rangers, and even teachers. Away from the central office and often unsupervised, they meet the citizen,
treat the citizen, and teach the citizen about government on the justice-
compassion continuum shown in Exhibit 1.3. Each transaction shows the human
face of government through *individual but not arbitrary treatment.*

Discretion. Line employees dispense services by making choices every day. These
choices are constrained to a limited range of responses by standard operating
procedures (SOPs) dictated by the agency or supervisor, intergovernmental mandate, judicial directive, legislative oversight, professional association, and other
sources, including informal culture. As a result, operational employees interact
with people by *case management,* according to categories assigned by that public
employee but defined by procedure.

The categories themselves, the assignment of them, and interactions based
on them have profound ethical content, often dramatized by triage in medical
services (see Egan, 1990a, for an example from Oregon). Consider a general order
(public document provided to author by Michael D. Breen, spring 1990) adapted
from one jurisdiction, that informs all sworn law enforcement personnel about
arrest discretion.

> In most cases, it is not the role of a police officer to decide whether
> an offense should be prosecuted; that is the responsibility of the
> court prosecutor. . . . A police office may consider not making an
> arrest when
>
> 1. the incident is minor in nature, and
> 2. arrest would only result in harm and embarrassment to the
>   offender rather than address a public safety issue, and
> 3. the situation did not pose a threat to any person or property,
>   or
> 4. arrest would cause a greater risk of harm to the general public
>   than the offending conduct did, or the offender's remaining free
>   from custody would. For example, in a crowd situation, a po-

lice officer's decision to arrest may aggravate tension and lead to a riot. . . . A decision not to arrest when there are grounds for an arrest is considered good police practice only in the special circumstances given. Consequently, if there is doubt that these circumstances exist, a police officer should make the arrest.

The professional police standards shown in Exhibit 4.3 recognize the power inherent in police discretion and the responsibility that power entails. Note, too, that discretion has been called "a structural invitation to corruption" (Chambliss, 1988, p. 96).

Discretion is all about rationing—resources, time, attention—with serious ethical content and grave practical outcomes. In March 1990, a fire at the Happy Land Social Club in New York City killed eighty-seven people. The previous year, after building violations had been reported, the facility was ordered closed and summonses were issued. When the owner failed to appear in court to answer safety complaints, an arrest warrant was issued and filed in criminal court and with the New York City Police Department. Nothing happened; building violations have low priority among the 100,000 and more warrants issued yearly in New York City. A police lieutenant explained, "We are interested in all warrants but we are more interested in going after the guy who has committed a murder over a guy who has violations in a building" (Barbanel, 1990, p. B1). Rules and resources must be selectively, sensibly, and sensitively applied in day-to-day operations.

Means and Ends. Martin Luther King, Jr., (1963, p. 13) argued that "it is wrong to use immoral means to attain moral ends [and] it is just as wrong, or even more so, to use moral means to preserve immoral ends." (Reprinted by permis-

---

Exhibit 4.3. Professional Standards for Law Enforcement.

Commission on Accreditation for Law Enforcement Agencies (CALEA)
Standard 1.1.5: "A written directive requires all sworn officers to abide by a code or canon of ethics adopted by the agency." (Commentary accepts the code adopted by the International Association of Chiefs of Police. This standard is mandatory for all accredited agencies.)

Law Enforcement Code of Ethics, International Association of Chiefs of Police
From the code of ethics adopted in 1957: "There must be a moral philosophy and a strong appreciation of the need for service in any profession. . . . Unwavering adherence to such a moral philosophy will earn for police officers the respect and support of the public."

From the code of ethics adopted in 1989: "A police officer will use responsibly the discretion vested in the position and exercise it within the law. The principle of reasonableness will guide the officer's determinations. . . .

"Consistent and wise use of discretion, based on professional policing competence, will do much to preserve good relationships and retain the confidence of the public."

---

sion of Joan Daves. Copyright © 1963, 1964 by Martin Luther King, Jr.) ASPA bids its members to "exercise whatever discretionary authority we have under law to promote the public interest." This requires Aristotle's *practical wisdom,* meaning "the ability not only to know the means to certain desired ends, but also to know what ends are desirable (worthy of desire)" (Tong, 1986, p. 88). As Aaron Wildavsky (1989, p. 787) sees it, "For public administrators, the second question is how well you accomplish objectives; the first is which objectives it is right to try to accomplish. Answers to the second question matter, but only after the first is settled."

Both public purposes and managerial practices have ethical dimensions. Often, managers do what they can rather than what is best according to some objective standard. Contemporary thinking about decision making views connection between ends and means as part of the routine decision-making process. According to Charles Lindblom (1959), goals and actions are intertwined, not distinct.

A 1988 administrative decision illustrates how ethical considerations about method can temper an otherwise single-minded commitment to meeting goals and getting the job done. A protest letter from scientists at the Environmental Protection Agency (EPA) prompted the agency's chief to ban data from Nazi experiments on humans from an EPA report. The use of data on phosgene, a toxic gas, provoked a debate about benefiting from unethically obtained information, along with questions about its reliability. One toxicologist argued that use of the data threatened to "condone taking some lives in order to save others," while an opposing opinion argued that "when data is [*sic*] collected in an unethical fashion, if it is important in protecting public health and is not available in any other way, I would use it" (Shabecoff, 1988, p. A17).

Ethical neutrality is different from policy impartiality, unbiased treatment, and nonpartisanship. The "ethic of neutrality" denies that morality is possible in public bureaucracies by asserting that public managers "should follow not their own moral principles but the decisions and policies of the organization" (Thompson, 1985, p. 555). Ethical neutrality takes bureaucracy and transforms it into an assembly line. It means working in one's own little cubicle or with blinders on. It is akin to senior corporate managers at Morton Thiokol refusing to admit or act on the implications of, for example, a defective booster joint on the *Challenger.* This posture attempts to transform human beings into technical problems of transport, timetables, case quotas, check processing, and so on. *Ethical neutrality strips the humanity from both the manager and service recipients. Dehumanizing the players serves to deny the ethical element.* Blaming the victim generally accomplishes the same thing.

By ousting the individual ethical agent who thinks through ethical problems and makes judgments, this reasoning also jettisons ethics. A famous quotation from the great American nineteenth-century essayist Ralph Waldo Emerson sums it up perfectly: "We must hold a man amenable to reason for the choice of his daily craft or profession. It is not an excuse any longer for his deeds that they are the custom of his trade. What business has he with an evil trade?"

Incompetence Is an Abuse of Office

Today's professional public service is based on competence in contrast to the old patronage and citizen-volunteer methods of staffing. According to President George Bush (Volcker Commission, 1989, p. 2), "How well the tasks of government are done affects the quality of the lives of all our people. Moreover, the success of any political leadership in implementing its policies and objectives depends heavily upon the expertise, quality, and commitment of the professional career employees of government." Mary Ellen Guy (1990, p. 15) asserts, "The pursuit of excellence means striving to be as good as one can be. . . . It is not enough to be content with mediocrity," and puts that pursuit on her list of essential ethical values. A posture of competence ("we can do it") implies a commitment to needed change and demands a good-faith effort.

Competence is an ongoing aspiration, a moving and therefore always unmet goal, and a professionally decreed ethical obligation. General Maxwell D. Taylor (1980, p. 12) argued that an admirable officer must know his current job and mission and prepare for the next one. "Thus, continuous self-improvement will be a conspicuous characteristic of an ideal officer." Applying to public service generally, this standard is a heavy payload because it means by definition that managers permanently fall short.

Professional public service is rooted in making government more *business-like* (as discussed in the introduction), and productivity and efficiency remain pivotal (see Chapter One). The general standard in federal service from 1965 to 1989 specified that employees avoid any action or appearance of "impeding government efficiency or economy." Its successors, signed by President Bush in 1989 and 1990, stipulate: "Employees shall put forth honest effort in the performance of duties."

Competence in public service turns on more than just these values, however. APSA's code commits members to "accept as a personal duty the responsibility to keep up to date on emerging issues and to administer the public's business with professional competence, fairness, impartiality, efficiency, and effectiveness." The standard is related logically to responsibility for the specialized knowledge associated with a profession. Professional competence is obligatory in many professional codes, including those of ASPA, GFOA, IPMA, and ICMA.

Perfecting, Not Perfection. Incompetence is an intolerable condition, a breakpoint or floor below which an action is unacceptable. For professionals pledged to strive for competence, operating below the floor delineates unethical action (or inaction). "Incompetence can lead to such catastrophes as the failure of a bridge, the spreading of epidemic or endemic disease, the growth of narcotics addiction, playground accidents and fatalities, and the 'blighting' of urban areas" (Graham,

1952, p. 262). The problem is that outcome, over which managers may have little control, is part of the public's competence test.

Within the agency, fairness demands that due consideration be given employee performance. Expectations of infallibility serve no good purpose and do no one any good. Being wrong for the right reasons is quite different from behaving unethically; allowance for error is imperative. Perhaps it is fitting here to cite Murphy's Law: "If anything can go wrong, it will." Fortune may play a role in outcomes, but in public service, competence plays the lead.

The competence standard demands from public managers not perfection but perfecting, that is, an effort to do the best that can be done given the state of the art and within reasonable limits. Expert judgment is, after all, still judgment. In a world of scarce resources, uncertainties, and unknowns, performance as well as product and effort as well as outcome define competence.

The California earthquake in October 1989 reveals how the competence standard is bounded by realistic limits. Part of an interstate freeway collapsed and killed forty-two people, and another person died on a crumbled section of the Oakland–San Francisco Bay Bridge. According to the federal General Accounting Office's (GAO) report (1990, pp. 50–51),

> GAO examined what the California Department of Transportation (CALTRANS) knew about the vulnerability of the two structures to earthquake damage; levels of federal and state spending to strengthen bridge and viaduct structures vulnerable to earthquakes; and funding needed to complete California's seismic retrofit program. GAO found that the retrofit program, initiated 18 years ago to correct deficiencies in structures designed before 1971, has been a lower priority project than other highway safety projects. Only the first phase of a three-phase program has been completed. Had the retrofit program progressed to the third phase—which calls for reinforcement of all multicolumn structures like the Cypress Viaduct—before the October . . . earthquake, CALTRANS engineers believe they would have identified a structural flaw in the viaduct's support columns that they think contributed to its collapse. CALTRANS officials thought the Bay Bridge had been retrofitted sufficiently before the earthquake. Since the earthquake, the state has focused more attention on completing its retrofit program, creating a separate budget and staff for the project.

In a June 1990 referendum, California voters approved additional funds.

A fair standard of performance distinguishes incompetence from a professional, good-faith effort that proves to be erroneous by subsequent events. The standard allows that being wrong or falling short does not necessarily translate into being unethical. There are four parts, then, to a fair competence standard:

perfecting, not perfection; performance and product; effort and outcome; and doing the best that can be done given the state of the art and reasonable limits.

Self-Victimization. Bureaucrat bashing is an all-American spectator sport. Yet it is unjust and demoralizing for public managers and employees to accept bureaucracy's *inaccurate* street image. Three well-known maxims about bureaucrat's alleged incompetence communicate the image: slouch, bumbler, bungler. The Peter Principle (Peter and Hull, 1969) couples eventual inadequacy with promotions until a bureaucratic organization is inherently inept. Parkinson's Law sights inefficiency: "Work expands so as to fill the time available for its completion" (Parkinson, 1957). Boren's testimony (1971), a parody presented as irreverent testimony to a House subcommittee, counsels, "When in charge, ponder; when in trouble, delegate; when in doubt, mumble." A can-do attitude of competence rejects that image; there is no reason for managers to disparage public employees by accepting satire as gospel.

There also is no excuse for managers' tolerating incompetence as business as usual. Perhaps a good start is owning up to the pressures pushing against it: a manager who swallows employee incompetence to protect the agency in the short run ends up embroiled in cover-up and deception; a supervisor's easygoing leniency is misread as a go-ahead. Here the manager is letting compassion or caring block other values.

Forbearance and leeway make daily routines flexible, bearable, and humanistic, but the point is to enable public employees to do their job, not dodge it. Providing some maneuvering room should coincide with communicating the message that competence is the standard of performance. Organizational competence and individual competence are directly supported by "responsible communication habits" (Brown, 1990, p. 168).

Impossible Promises. Incompetence may be organizationally induced by managers' own exaggerated promises and underestimated costs, manipulative deceits designed to bypass full disclosure. (Padding budget requests may be a commonplace practice, but it is deception nonetheless.) Substituting strategy for neutrality and accuracy, managers are then forced to follow through on the proverbial shoestring. Cutting corners is an illusory response to cutting budgets when making do slides into gross negligence, as well as when planning is shortchanged, corrective steps are not taken, or testing goes undone. A retired air force general leading a shuttle safety inquiry after the *Challenger* tragedy said, "Good managers drop things they might otherwise do" (Broad, 1990, p. 32). This and the switch from engineering to contract monitoring describe the erosion of competence at the National Aeronautics and Space Administration (NASA).

Nothing symbolizes public service's competence more than the phrase "the eagle has landed," radioed back from the first manned lunar landing. It took about two decades to descend from that to the flawed mirror in the $1.5 billion

Hubble telescope. An agency commitment to competence as an ethical standard is needed as much as the routine remedies of staff and budget increases.

In actual practice and public perception, public management operates— or should operate—in a "culture of performance" (Volcker Commission, 1989, pp. 13, 47). An all-too-frequent scramble to *prove* competence rather than *improve* it, individually or organizationally, revives the issue of blame raised at the beginning of this chapter.

Leave Responsibility Where It Belongs

Responsibility for ethical decision making belongs in the hands of individual managers. Detailed, hard and fast rules preempt individual responsibility and may chain, rather than empower, public service. In the spirit of individual responsibility, the choice between guidelines and rules is left up to each manager. Ralph Chandler (1989a, p. 605) notes that "certain ethical precepts have guided American public administrators from the earliest days of the republic. Some are implicit, some are explicit, several are contradictory to each other, and all are subject to differing interpretations." It is hardly surprising, then, that many alternative game plans for ethical behavior have been spelled out over the years. Knowing this, some managers ask for more direction, for definite rules based on duty or law. Some professional codes of conduct supply just that; GFOA's purpose in revising its code was to provide more guidance and direction. There is also the Josephson Institute's (1990) elaborate list of behavioral rules derived from a public trust theory of government.

George Graham's "rules of the game" for professional administrators strikes a middle ground. Relatively clear-cut and concrete, this formulation demands impartial open-mindedness. Graham divides "the hard questions" into three categories: participation, compromise, and implementation. Each is related to "accepting the melding process as a necessity in organized representative government in a democratic society, and guided by the principles of due process which are embedded in the public law of the land" (Graham, 1974, p. 91). Accordingly, the administrator's role summons three sets of standards and obligations.

Participation. Inform participants of significant information relevant to their role. Interpret and explain data and policy impact, while ensuring no personal conflict of interest and revealing personal values. Advocacy is guided by the issue's importance and the administrator's cognizance and competence. "Accept decisions made within the 'rules of the game' . . . made rationally by informed persons, acting within their authority, and attempting to be fair and reasonable" (p. 91). Defend such a decision, but remember that one is "not required under any circumstances to testify falsely" on facts or personal judgment.

Compromise. Contest provisional decisions outside routine channels only when assured the mistake is significant, judgment is unbiased, and the issue's gravity justifies personal risk and potential contributions. Sign only documents one approves. Obey and enforce the law. Resign if controlling orders cannot be accepted.

Correlates. Administrators are forbidden to order a subordinate to take illegal action; suppress significant information, distort facts, or deceive; take responsibility for an opposed decision for which the superior can take responsibility; sign unapproved documents.

Implementation. Implement a legal, final decision whether agreed with or not. If legality is in doubt, " 'go slow' until legality is determined" (p. 92). Alternatives are to request a transfer or to resign.

Like this book's, Graham's formulation calls for legal compliance and action in the public interest.

Many managers prefer guidelines over rules because they equip managers to make decisions in varied, everyday situations and keep responsibility in the managers' hands. Many may agree with one manager's appeal: "I want guidelines—not rules—and I want them to say, 'Here's how we do business around here' " (Rice and Dreilinger, 1990, p. 103). This author prefers guidance as key to the fusion route because it bridges compliance and integrity.

The action guides in this chapter are geared to summarizing and sorting public service obligations and responsibilities so that they are linked logically and practically, retain their intellectual content while broadly guiding behavior, and can be mustered from memory. In this author's view, they represent consensual ethical guidelines developed over more than a century of professional public administration in the American democratic context. Their practical ramifications are explored and refined time and again in the cases and discussions in this book. The case that immediately follows depicts this chapter's principles at work.

Case: Accountable Counting

The following material is reprinted by permission from *Washington Post*. Rene Sanchez, "Enrollment Figures Purposely Withheld, D.C. Audit Alleges," the *Washington Post*, June 12, 1990, pp. B1, B8.

Top officials in the D.C. school system deliberately withheld from the D.C. Council statistics that showed a steep drop in student enrollment, an internal school system audit reveals.

The confidential audit, obtained yesterday by The Washington Post, contradicts remarks School Superintendent Andrew E. Jenkins and school board members made about the system's enrollment discrepancies earlier this year. Jenkins and the board have said their failure to give the council accurate enrollment figures during a February hearing on the school budget was an accident.

Overall, the auditors draw a portrait of widespread incompetence, along with the concealing of information, in what is one of the school system's fundamental tasks: counting students. The count plays a large role in council deliberations over how much money the schools should have.

According to the audit, Arthur G. Hawkins, one of the school system's three deputy superintendents, told the system's budget director, Linden E. DeJoseph, to "pull out" the lower enrollment figure from documents the council had requested.

Hawkins told school auditors he thought the lower enrollment figures—about 6,500 fewer students—were not supposed to be released. The report does not say why he felt that way. Neither Hawkins or DeJoseph could be reached yesterday to comment on the audit.

Jenkins, in an interview late yesterday, said he did not know why the top officials failed to include the accurate enrollment. "Certainly I directed no one to take such an action," he said. "Absolutely not."

Jenkins said the audit, which criticizes school officials for bungling enrollment procedures for the past four years, is credible. "I think the findings are pretty hard," he said. "But I think the system needs to know this and start rebuilding."

The auditors say that enrollment in D.C. schools, now 81,300 students, dropped an average of about 2,000 students a year between 1980 and 1990. In recent years, school system officials have been saying publicly that enrollment was stable and that the system's budget had to increase.

The rate of decline means "budget reductions of $10 million per year should have been expected during the decade," the audit states. It contains documents that show the school system's budget—now $512 million annually—nearly doubled between 1980 and 1990.

By fall 1986, the audit concludes, the system should have known its counting methods were wrecked because there were large discrepancies in the enrollment numbers given to the city and to the U.S. Department of Education.

The audit also lists several other times—both long before the numbers controversy with the council this spring—when the system knew its population had dwindled. In January and June 1989, school system researchers discovered errors in the count that they did not report to the superintendent or the school board. In each case, enrollment was found to be thousands of students lower than the count the school system handed the council and mayor in December.

According to the audit, many errors occurred when the

school officials were asked to tabulate enrollment by computer. "The change was too abrupt for many principals to comprehend," the audit states.

It adds that attendance records at many schools are poorly kept, and that responsibility for enrollment has been scattered in too many parts of schools' bureaucracy.

Jenkins, who has conceded in other interviews that the enrollment confusion has hurt the system's credibility, said yesterday that a private accounting firm soon will begin another audit of student population.

That audit was scheduled to begin three months ago but has been mired in delays. Meanwhile, Jenkins and school board members have not yet said what is causing the enrollment decline— which, according to the internal audit, has been most severe in the past two years.

Parents United, the city's leading school advocate group, contends that drug-related violence is prompting many families to remove their children from city schools.

Jenkins said he is still reviewing the audit and has not decided if he will reprimand Hawkins, DeJoseph, or any other administrator. "We're in very serious deliberations about that right now," he said.

School board member R. David Hall (Ward 2), who lobbied Jenkins to hire Hawkins last year as a deputy superintendent, said reprimands would not be wise because so much of the system is to blame for enrollment errors.

"There have been systematic shortcomings," Hall said. "People have been relying on computer systems more than common sense and hard work."

Hall said he had implored the board and Jenkins not to release enrollment figures until they were certain what was correct, but did not tell Hawkins to withhold the numbers from the council.

"I don't think this was a cover-up. There were just many sets of numbers, and Hawkins did what good managers do: He made a decision," Hall said.

What circumstances or statements relate to the fundamental ethical principles in public service?
- Legal compliance?
- Serving the public interest?
What circumstances or statements relate to the five guides to action in public service?

- Individual responsibility? (a) Boss or job? (b) Subordinates? (c) Ignorance?
- Meaning and method?
- Competence?

Are enrollment figures and computer systems solely management issues, or are ethical issues raised? Why?

School enrollment figures—accurate or not—drive billions of aid dollars throughout the country. What danger zones of information are illustrated in this case?

- How does this case illustrate the standards in Exhibit 4.2?

Did management know or have reason to know what was going on?

- How does management responsibility for subordinates' behavior come into play in this case?
- How do the factors of proximity, saliency, and gravity affect your assessment of managerial responsibilities in this case?

By this account, senior managers failed to take preventative or immediate corrective action. Does this constitute intentional manipulation or incompetence?

- Does the answer matter? Does the ethical offense affect your reaction or response?

According to this account, did anyone commit an ethical offense? Which? Why?

- Is fraud for public purposes more acceptable than fraud for personal gain?
- How does bypassing the dollars-per-student standard for distributing aid affect accountability?

Is anyone described as taking individual responsibility in this case? How?

- Responsibility for what?

Tools for
Personal Decision Making

Chapter 5

Finding Solid Ground: Ethical Standards and Reasoning

Earlier chapters expose the problems, conflicts, and claims shouldered by public managers. Here the task is to reconcile and sort them ethically. Part Two provides the techniques and tools by turning to how individual managers make ethical decisions.

This chapter looks at how ethical reasoning is grounded in common sense and two broad philosophical perspectives, one centered on duty or principle and the other on results. Overlaid with the clash between the delegate versus the trustee roles for public servants, these perspectives lead to very different outlooks on what is ethically important in a given decision. The ethical public manager draws on impartial open-mindedness to overcome an ethical impasse or resolve an ethical dilemma. Political traditions and practical experience counsel moderation and reconciliation in preference to ethical extremism. In the case at the chapter's end, different ethical postures lead to different stands on an everyday problem.

The public manager must act quickly in a gray, marginal area where laws are silent or confusing, circumstances are ambiguous and complex, and the manager is responsible, well-meaning, and perplexed. Consider an example from John F. (Jack) Azzaretto, director of the Institute of Public Service at the University of Connecticut (unpublished cases provided to author, May 1990): "In order to avoid dealing with an almost certain grievance and a probable law suit, are you [ethically] correct in taking your superior's advice to overlook the marginal to poor performance of a minority employee?" This example summons honesty, justice, impartiality, loyalty, and prudence, which pull the manager in different directions.

Where does the manager turn? Ethics commissions or designated agency ethics officers are not available in all jurisdictions; where they do exist, their emphasis on compliance means that the legal staff may not be able to help, and they take time to respond. What other resources are there? A friend? The boss? Religion? Philosophy? A survey conducted by the *Wall Street Journal* (1988) asked 1,000 corporate executives to name their most trusted confidant when faced with an ethical situation. The single largest category, 44 percent of all responses, was "myself." Although this kind of self-sufficiency may be popularly admired and what ethical integrity boils down to, it is inadequate in a head-on collision over contending ethical values and principles. Accountability precludes public managers from playing cowboy, shooting from the hip and roaming where they please. Ethical benchmarks and philosophical sounding boards keep managers in tune with public service.

Common Sense

The manager may prefer to rely on character and upbringing for a commonsense, visceral choice between right and wrong. In fact, we make most of our ethical choices this way: in the pit of the stomach, automatically, reflexively, intuitively in the popular sense, by common sense, and in tune with the first category in Exhibit 5.1. We must do this, or contemplative demands would bring the office to a standstill and suspend our daily lives.

A good start, going with how it "feels" is a suitable and efficient method for making relatively straightforward, routine choices. Having faced these predicaments before, we reliably use our experience again. The best-seller *All I Really*

Exhibit 5.1. How Do I Make Ethical Choices?

If I believe
    I learned to tell right from wrong as a child and that does not change
    an itch, warning bell, or uncomfortable feeling tells me it is wrong
    What is there to think about? I have to live with myself and my conscience
    sophisticated arguments are used to justify unethical behavior
then I may be using a commonsense approach.

If I believe
    some principles like the sanctity of human life must not be compromised
    fundamental right and wrong never change, only excuses change
    the way we do something is more important than what we do
    there are certain things I would never do or condone, for any reason
    it is my responsibility and no other reason is needed; it is that simple
then I may be using a principle-based approach.

If I believe
    it is not fair to treat people in different circumstances the same
    rules are rigid; we need flexibility to respond to changing situations
    what matters is people; we do not agree on principles anyway
    government should be efficient and effective; it is results that count
    noble principles are fine, but I have to be practical when I spend taxpayers' money
then I may be using a results-oriented approach.

Need to Know I Learned in Kindergarten (Fulghum, 1988) resolves life's muddles with childhood lessons. Of course, this problem-solving approach can only be as good as the character and common sense of the decision maker.

A commonsense approach works well on routine problems. These are the ones amenable to President Bush's advice, "It's not really very complicated. It's a question of knowing right from wrong, avoiding conflicts of interest, bending over backwards to see that there's not even a perception of conflict of interest" (Volcker Commission, 1989, p. 14). This is the approach presumed in the report of the President's Commission on Federal Ethics Law Reform (the Volcker Commission), which argues, "Ethical government means much more than laws. It is a spirit, an imbued code of conduct. It is a climate in which, from the highest to the lowest ranks of policy and decision-making officials, some conduct is *instinctively sensed* as correct and other conduct as being beyond acceptance" (1989, p. 1; emphasis added).

Philosophical Perspectives at Work

Well-meaning managers sometimes find themselves sincerely baffled and needing to bounce decisions off someone or something else. The philosophical concepts that have penetrated our society and culture over thousands of years are rich resources. An unfashionable topic? Yes. An annual survey conducted since 1966 by the American Council on Education shows a decline in the proportion of college freshmen for whom developing "a meaningful philosophy of life" is essential or very important ("Fact File," 1990, pp. A33–A34). With the proportion falling from three-fifths in 1976 to two-fifths in 1989, new recruits into public service are unlikely to bring philosophical proficiency with them. Granted, a busy manager may dismiss philosophy as artificial, impractical—as an abuser's guide to reality. Then, too, agency problems do not fit neatly into predrawn ethical categories.

Sometimes the administrative world is complex, circumstances ambiguous, the situation new, and thoughtful reflection is needed for an ethically sound decision. Then, bumping against a true dilemma, we need expert advice. Philosophy is the expert in ethics, a "systematic attempt to understand, establish, or defend basic moral principles or rules of conduct, judgments about what is right and wrong" (American Society for Public Administration, 1989, p. 101). Our thinking about right and wrong rests on two broad philosophical traditions, one based on duty or principle underlying action (deontological) and the other on consequences of action (teleological). A brief review serves as a reminder of their main features. There is no need to repeat at length what is readily available in many philosophy and ethics texts. (For further exploration, see Bok, 1978; French, 1983; and Strauss and Cropsey, 1987.)

Duty or Principle. According to deontological frameworks based on duty or principle, some types of behavior or acts are either good or bad in themselves, and the outcome is irrelevant to moral judgment. As its name implies, this approach uses duties or moral rules or principles as guides to action. The Golden Rule is a familiar example. Another comes from Le Chambon, France, whose residents, community leaders, and public officials defied Nazi orders and saved thousands of people. According to the pastor's wife (recorded in Johnson, 1989–1990, p. 19), "Sometimes people ask me, 'How did you make a decision?' There was no decision to make. The issue was: 'Do you think we are all brothers or not?'"

Immanuel Kant (1724–1804) provides the categorical imperative, a rational rather than a religious formulation whereby one should only act as if one were legislating a universal law for everyone to follow in a preferred world; people are never treated instrumentally, as a means, but only as ends in themselves. An insistence on human beings' dignity and worth is central to Kant's ethical perspective.

Deontological reasoning comes in many shades, depending upon whether the rules of behavior are seen as permanent and universal; knowable or unknowable; derived from revelation, human law, or community norms; and so on. All permutations dictate that there are certain underlying rules according to which behavior is judged, and no matter how desirable the consequences, there are certain things the manager (and government) may not do.

Results. The results-based or teleological approach judges ethical worth by an action's consequences. Because this standard is frequently applied to international affairs, U.S. power on a global scale makes it especially important to understand. An illustration comes from Lieutenant Colonel Oliver North, who played a leading role in the Iran-Contra affair during the second Reagan administration; North explained his lying to Congress this way: "Lying does not come easily to me. But we all had to weigh in the balance the difference between lies and lives."

In results-based reasoning's most familiar form, *utilitarianism*, ethical action means utility maximization, defined as society's net benefit over harm. An excessively simplistic formulation would have it that the ends justify the means, but Figure 5.1 sounds the necessary warning against this caricature. More sophisticated formulations speak on behalf of impartiality and benefiting all concerned. John Stuart Mill argued, "As between his own happiness and that of others, utilitarianism requires him to be strictly impartial as a disinterested and benevolent spectator." Variations within the results-based approach stem from the good to maximize (happiness? pleasure?) and other factors.

Accommodating the Two Traditions. Our democratic society has been unable or unwilling to reconcile the deontological and teleological traditions or choose between them. So our ideology accommodates both. The American political system operates according to two different ethical standards within constitutional and legal limits. Teleology's utilitarian principle is deeply imbedded in Amer-

Figure 5.1. Self-Centered Rationalization Is a Sorry Substitute for Ethical Reasoning.

ican culture and politics, as illustrated by the widespread use of formal and informal cost-benefit analysis. The Bill of Rights represents deontology's alternative of underlying rules. Their joint role in political discourse is invoked by the remark of Representative Lee H. Hamilton of Indiana at the congressional hearings on Iran-Contra: "A great power cannot base its policy on an untruth, without a loss of credibility." Over a quarter-century earlier, President Kennedy appealed to both duty and results in his 1961 inaugural address: "To those peoples in the huts and villages of half the globe struggling to break the bonds of mass misery, we pledge our best efforts to help them help themselves, for whatever period is required—not because the communists may be doing it, not because we seek their votes, but because it is right. If a free society cannot help the many who are poor, it cannot save the few who are rich."

The result is to burden each elected, appointed, and career public official with responsibility for deciding which standard applies and when. The scope for disagreement was evident during congressional hearings on the Iran-Contra affair, which was in many respects a nationally televised argument over fundamental ethical premises. A principal figure in the intrigue, Lieutenant Colonel Oliver L. North, was deputy director of the political-military affairs bureau at the National Security Council (NSC) from 1981 until November 1986, when President Reagan dismissed him. While the questions asked during his testimony were often phrased in terms of underlying duties, such as to tell the truth, North appealed to the opposing, results-based standard in his answers.

John W. Nields, Jr., the House committee's chief counsel, asserted the ethical principle of truth telling by asking, "Did you ever say, 'You can't do that, it's not true and you cannot commit the President of the United States to a lie'?" North replied, "I don't believe that I ever said that to anyone, no." Nields pressed on, "So none of these people, director of central intelligence, two national security advisers, attorney general, none of them ever made the argument, 'It's not true, you can't say it'?" Again, North replied, "No."

While Nields used the principle of truth, North responded in terms of results. North argued that Congress should be investigated for a "fickle, vacillating, unpredictable" policy toward the Nicaraguan Contras. He, on the other hand, did what was necessary to accomplish the administration's policy goals, irrespective of underlying ethical boundaries (or law). That Nields and North did not agree is hardly surprising; different ethical standards lead to different views of acceptable behavior.

The two ways of thinking induce different responses to problems and offer competing premises upon which to make decisions. This is why changing decision-making premises (meaning the philosophical framework) is so useful in thinking through ethical dilemmas. A series of questions triggers the open-mindedness that incorporates both impartiality and responsibility.

1. What philosophical tradition underlies your proposal or posture?
2. What other moral principles could guide action and alter the proposal or decision?

3. What considerations emerge from alternative philosophical positions?
4. Why would a public manager try to design a proposal that reconciles different philosophical perspectives?
5. Should anything else be thought about?
6. In your view, is the proposal personally acceptable and ethically persuasive?

(Try applying these questions to the cases that conclude subsequent chapters in this book.) In the end, the individual decision maker is left with the judgment and the responsibility for exercising it.

Views on Public Service

Examining different ideas enriches our thinking by providing nuance and depth. At the same time, these ideas complicate matters by offering different views of public service and behavior befitting different roles. Ideologically, contemporary public service follows the Platonic tradition that stresses public interest as distinguishable from self-interest. According to Bruce Jennings (1989a, p. 175), this is precisely what judgment entails in the political arena within which public service operates. "Political judgment, in the classical sense of the term, is the capacity to tell the difference between public and private ends. It is also the ability to spot a private interest masquerading as a public good." Machiavelli's very name has come to signify the opposite: rational, self-interested decision making conducted in the long and short term. (In contrast to the classical Platonic tradition of abandoning personal interests, the rational self-interest theory underlies arguments for pay parity with private-sector counterparts.)

Contrasting notions of organizational and professional roles complicate matters further. Again, American democratic and bureaucratic practice combines both main ideas, the trustee and the delegate, associated with philosophers such as Locke, Bentham, and Mill. The trustee, an interpreter, acts statesmanlike in the community's best interest as the decision maker sees it. The U.S. Supreme Court, the U.S. Senate, political executives, and senior administrative generalists fit this category, as do claims of electoral mandate. A famous speech by English philosopher Edmund Burke coincided with the American Revolution: "Your representative owes you, not his industry only, but his judgment." The delegate, on the other hand, is more like a conduit who purposefully brings the constituency's views to bear and faithfully reflects them. This stance is typified by public opinion polls and some elements of populist and representative bureaucracy.

In sum, we have an ethics stew simmering on the back burner for every public manager. Ethical choices bubble up from ideas about morality, about public service, and about organizational and professional roles derived from classical philosophy and political thought. The sheer number of options drawn from philosophical traditions indicates that philosophy will not make our choices for us. Instead, it clarifies the reasoning behind those choices. The burden of multiple sets of ethical standards is all the heavier because the public manager uses public authority and enormous government power to back up decisions. As a result, the obligation for *informed* ethical reasoning—thinking through a dilemma and making a morally reasonable decision—falls on the shoulders of the individual public manager.

Purity Versus Receptivity

The purpose behind mastering the conceptual tools of ethical analysis here is to make moral judgments about one's own actions and decisions, not to evolve into a judgmental, self-righteous arbiter of other people's behavior (see the section on vigilante ethics, page 98). Imputing intent and motivation is dangerous business. While that is a traditional element in judging legal culpability in the courtroom, a jury is used, along with confronting accusers, advocacy representation, and other safeguards.

Because true motives may be camouflaged from the decision maker—never mind an observer—accurately tracing back from action to intent is tricky at best. A survey on the Iran-Contra affair asked respondents whether wrongdoing "was primarily due to poor judgment and misplaced zeal by people of good character, or was primarily due to blatant disregard of law and ethics by people of poor character" (Roper Organization, 1989). Responses were split, with 44 percent choosing good character and 40 percent selecting poor character (15 percent didn't know).

If we allow for human error, faulty reasoning, or incorrect facts, then what we observe may not be what was intended. There are observational snags, too. Perhaps what we witness as an isolated action is part of a series, and therefore we misinterpret the single data point. Every so often, an excuse is substituted for a requested explanation and people end up talking past each other. An excuse states why one should be considered innocent or blameless *despite* an action, while an explanation cites the reason for *choosing* that action.

Because it is so difficult to confidently distinguish surface from substance at a distance, judging others' behavior easily degenerates into charges of selective enforcement or casual labeling: Unethical! Hypocrite! There are many reasons for apparent inconsistencies and contradictions in ethical reasoning and behavior.

> *Courage.* The problem may be more a matter of following through on what one knows to be right when it is unpleasant or costly or demands sacrifice.
>
> *Multiple Roles.* We may adjust our behavior and reasoning to conform to different roles with different associated standards, and when incompatible claims (such as public interest and family loyalty) clash, the choice of an appropriate primary role may lead to behavior otherwise unacceptable.

Camouflage. Motivation is a tough call, and the underlying reason may not be clear even to the decision maker.

Rhetoric. An appeal to noncontroversial, vague values (such as justice or honesty) is quite different from an explanation of ethical reasoning. For example, what values are tapped by arguing that "the most important thing about government is democratic process"? Moreover, this statement obscures the mode of reasoning.

Confusion. Public interest has been defined as the majority (sum of individual interests) and the aggregate (shared, overarching interest). Representation can mean being a delegate or a trustee. Conceptual ambiguity may lead to misunderstanding and mixed signals.

Excuse, Not Explanation. Offering an excuse (reason one should be held blameless) instead of an explanation (reason for a choice) is a common source of confusion.

Consensus. Agreement is intuitively satisfying, and there is a temptation to claim all ethical ground in order to satisfy everyone. This may communicate unsound reasoning or political expediency.

Hard But Different Choices. Not all ethical problems are the same. If the dilemma is real and values or standards do conflict, then choices may reflect different assessments of, for example, the stakes or values involved. Immediate life-and-death issues are often treated differently, or at least more carefully, than others.

Error. Reasoning may be faulty or partial. Intention may be undermined by factual error or omission.

Selectivity. If every decision warranted and received thorough analysis, we would be immobilized. Pressures on time and attention mean that many decisions and actions are prompted by common sense or conscience rather than reflection or deliberation; sometimes we choose to downplay the wrong issue and fail to see a choice's serious ethical implications.

These ten reasons for seeming inconsistencies and contradictions induce a wise manager to *reserve most moral judgments for self-application* and to leave some matters to psychologists or clergy. Emphasizing a strong moral commitment, President Bush nonetheless took a forbearing stand in his 1989 inaugural address when he said, "A president is neither prince nor pope, and I don't seek a window on men's souls. In fact, I yearn for a greater tolerance, an easygoingness about each other's attitudes and way of life."

Appeal to Consensus. When it comes to giving explanations, consensus is intuitively satisfying, perhaps because public service is concerned with appearance and widespread public support. There is a temptation to claim all ethical ground in order to satisfy everyone, including oneself. Stuart Gilman (1989, p. 21) concurs: "Most people . . . will move across ethical systems and use more than one approach to grapple with an ethical dilemma. We feel more ethically certain when we derive a common answer using two or more different ways of moral reasoning."

In a historic specimen of ethical explanation (excerpted in Exhibit 5.2), President Gerald Ford explained his decision to pardon Richard Nixon in 1974 on grounds of secular duties and religious rules, pragmatic effects and political results, and an intuitive appeal to conscience. He asserted a commitment to ethical integrity by seeking "to be true to my own convictions and my own conscience." Conforming to the ethical reasoning model laid out in the next chapter, he explicitly accepted responsibility on the basis of his public role as president rather than on friendship. He noted his fact-finding efforts, referred to advice, and cited preeminent values of substantive justice (which Ford defined as equal treatment) and procedural justice (due process). He spoke of moderating justice with compassion and exhibited empathy for the affected party.

The subsequent drop in President Ford's standing in opinion polls suggests that even a beautifully crafted ethical explanation may not work. People may still think you are wrong, or worse. A universal claim to being right may backfire by undermining credibility and conveying unsound reasoning, self-interest, or expediency. Ethical explanation may smack of a public relations campaign. Justifying decisions on ethical grounds is no guarantee of professional or politial success or approval. But that is not the point: if success governs ethical choices, then standards and principles (and codes of conduct) apply only if they produce tactical advantages. This Machiavellian argument would have public managers strong like a lion, wily like a fox, and devoted exclusively to results.

Over the Long Haul. Long-term purity—indelible, unmixed, and unchanging adherence to a single way of thinking—is unlikely if public managers are like other people, whose capacity for thinking abstractly and applying general principles varies over time. Despite methodological and epistemological criticisms (Gilligan, 1982; Hirschmann, 1989), research by psychologist Lawrence Kohlberg and his colleagues has deeply influenced contemporary thinking about cognitive development.

Kohlberg identifies six general, universal patterns that are sequenced in invariable stages of cognitive development based on the individual's use of generalizable abstractions (1981). These six orientations or "total ways of thinking" he terms "stages of moral development" (1980, p. 31). The stages progress from the preconventional level (stages 1 and 2) concerned with physical and hedonistic consequences, to the conventional level of conformity and loyalty (stages 3 and 4), and finally to the postconventional level of autonomous, principled reasoning (stages 5 and 6). According to Kohlberg (1980, pp. 91–93), the stages are these:

Stage 1. Punishment and obedience orientation
Stage 2. Instrumental relativist orientation (market relations)
Stage 3. Interpersonal orientation (intention, pleasing others)
Stage 4. Law and order orientation (authority, duty, order)

Exhibit 5.2 Presidential Explanation.

The following excerpts are from President Gerald R. Ford's remarks on signing proclamation 4311, granting a pardon to Richard M. Nixon on September 8, 1974.

I have come to a decision which I felt I should tell you and all of my fellow American citizens, as soon as I was certain in my own mind and in my own conscience that it is the right thing to do. . . .

My customary policy is to try and get all the facts and to consider the opinions of my countrymen and to take counsel with my most valued friends. But these seldom agree, and in the end, the decision is mine. To procrastinate, to agonize, and to wait for a more favorable turn of events that may never come or more compelling external pressures that may as well be wrong as right, is itself a decision of sorts and a weak and potentially dangerous course for a President to follow.

I have promised to uphold the Constitution, to do what is right as God gives me to see the right, and to do the very best that I can for America.

I have asked your help and your prayers, not only when I became President but many times since. The Constitution is the supreme law of our land and it governs our actions as citizens. Only the laws of God, which govern our consciences, are superior to it. . . .

Theirs [Richard Nixon and his family] is an American tragedy in which we all have played a part. It could go on and on and on, or someone must write an end to it. I have concluded that only I can do that, and if I can, I must. . . .

I deeply believe in equal justice for all Americans, whatever their station or former station. The law, whether human or divine, is no respecter of persons, but the law is a respecter of reality.

The facts, as I see them, are that a former President of the United States, instead of enjoying equal treatment with any other citizen accused of violating the law, would be cruelly and excessively penalized either in preserving the presumption of his innocence or in obtaining a speedy determination of his guilt in order to repay a legal debt to society.

During this long period of delay and potential litigation, ugly passions would again be aroused. And our people would again be polarized in their opinions. And the credibility of our free institutions of government would again be challenged at home and abroad. . . .

In this, I dare not depend upon my personal sympathy as a long-time friend of the former President, nor my professional judgment as a lawyer, and I do not.

As President, my primary concern must always be the greatest good of all the people of the United States whose servant I am. As a man, my first consideration is to be true to my own convictions and my own conscience. . . .

I do believe that the buck stops here, that I cannot rely upon public opinion polls to tell me what is right. . . .

I do believe, with all my heart and mind and spirit, that I, not as President but as a humble servant of God, will receive justice without mercy if I fail to show mercy.

Finally, I feel that Richard Nixon and his loved ones have suffered enough and will continue to suffer, no matter what I do, no matter what we, as a great and good nation, can do together to make his goal of peace come true.

Stage 5. Social contract legalistic orientation (utilitarian overtones, procedural rules)

Stage 6. Universal ethical principle orientation (logical comprehensiveness, universality, consistency of abstract ethical principles)

Interestingly, Kohlberg (1980, p. 92) identifies stage 5 as the "official morality" of the U.S. government and Constitution.

In looking over this list, it is useful to bear in mind the following: "It is not the invoking of 'high principles' that credits a subject with high-stage thinking, but rather the way that a subject sets up the problem and deals with the claims of all participants in a dilemma" (Rest, 1980, p. 121). This formulation stimulates objections and disagreements over moral content (Wilson, 1980), over invariable evolution, over the relative weight assigned to the use of abstract principles in lieu of humanistic concerns, and over the theory's usefulness for predicting or understanding behavior. (Each stage is identified via expressed reasoning rather than actual behavior.)

More important to understanding ethical reasoning is the fact that "people at different developmental stages perceive moral dilemmas differently" and empirical tests confirm that a person's orientation is not permanent (Rest, 1980, pp. 109, 113). "Instead of existing as fixed traits, moral character occurs in a series of developmental stages" (Sprinthall and Sprinthall, 1988, p. 17). Furthermore, stages are *orientations*, meaning that, at any one time, an individual mixes the current, preceding, and next stages. Whether one agrees with Kohlberg or not, it is useful for understanding ourselves and working with others to allow that we are all engaged in an ongoing process of moral development.

Impartial and Open-Minded

Purity in ethical judgment is hard to come by. Motives and reasoning usually are mixed and are bound to change over circumstance or time. *In public service, the search is for compatibility and balance, reconciliation and accommodation.*

Moral absolutism rejects alternatives; moral relativism fails to distinguish among them. Public service rejects both by combining empathy, responsibility, and receptivity. The moorings for action are secured in moral character, and thinking is anchored in moral principles, including obligations to implement and comply with the law and to promote the public interest.

Our passionate, messy world of public service violates purity and precision at every turn. The way Debra Stewart (1984, p. 20) sees it, "Most managers are neither pure deontologists, nor pure utilitarians, but rather operate according to a kind of ethical pluralism . . . [a] synthesis of moral systems." The recommendation is not for fickle or expedient reasoning but rather that alternative perspectives be used so managers can see their behavior as others do. This "double focus" would have each of us "strain to experience one's act, not only as subject and agent, but as recipient, sometimes victim" (Bok, 1978, p. 30). (See Chapter Seven on stakeholder analysis.)

Many managers' judgments change with circumstances. A flexible manager, responsive to human distress, may not see all ethical problems as identical and amenable to a single, invariable verdict. He or she may prefer to blend consistency and flexibility, along the lines of mitigating factors in courtroom sentencing. Different values and stakes may alter the calculus as when, for example, an immediate threat to life outweighs the otherwise cherished value of telling the truth.

An unyielding, adamant position represents moral absolutism, which always applies timeless principles to every situation. Seductively simple, this view by and large negates individual judgment (not to mention compassion, mercy, and other unexceptional values).

By contrast, many managers pursue accommodation or reconciliation. They distinguish between "the principle of compromise and the compromise of principle," and understand that "willingness to compromise in order to reach an agreeable, ethical solution is very different from a willingness to jettison ethics altogether in a compromise of principle" (Guy, 1990, p. 19). According to Tom Peters (1987a, p. 241), coauthor of management books that have topped the bestseller lists, "The reality—whether you are in the executive branch of government or the legislative branch or the private sector—is that there has never been an effective leader yet who has not devoted 90 percent of his time to consensus building. All effective managers spend most of their life building consensus around the key issues where they want to make a difference." Peters' *Thriving on Chaos* (1987b) prescribes that one "demand total integrity."

Managers put it all together by selecting pragmatically from a number of right choices as they shift from abstraction to practical problem solving. What is needed to overcome an ethical impasse or resolve an ethical dilemma is *impartial open-mindedness*. This is individual ethical pluralism that tolerates moral ambiguity (Denhardt, 1989). It recognizes the acceptability as well as the probability of varying standards, principles, and rankings of what is right and important in different ethical choices. (See Chapter Six's decision-making model and Chapter Ten's agency process.)

Receptivity is distinct from promiscuity, the ethical relativism that rejects the validity of ethical judgment in the belief that right and wrong are only culturally defined or simply idiosyncratic personal opinions. Relativism leads to indiscriminate decision making. In its highly reduced version, relativism tumbles into the wanton, amoral "do your own thing."

Nor does sincere open-mindedness mean plugging in theories until one finds the perfect rationalization. This is the charade of sifting through ethical arguments until an appropriate justification is found for a decision already made (the "linear reasoning" in French, 1983).

Ethical locus remains an unsettled issue in American society. In an opinion poll conducted by Kane, Parsons and Associates (1989), 48 percent of the respondents said that there are absolute standards of right and wrong, whereas 44 percent said that right and wrong are related to the specific society a person lives in.

Open-mindedness allows "that there might be diverse traditions, beliefs and opinions about morality within a society but that this does not preclude widely shared agreement on the morality of certain basic practices" (American Society for Public Administration, 1989, p. 102). In that spirit, this author suggests altering decision premises and circumstances to double-check ethical judgments or reconcile different philosophical perspectives to imaginatively resolve a thorny problem.

What does this open-mindedness do to personal integrity? Being true to oneself does not mean shutting others out in order to sleep at night; it means managers seeing themselves the way managers actually live, related to other people and ideas. *Impartial open-mindedness is the first-order test of genuine empathy in public service.* The decision calculus calls for bending over backward to compensate for bias. Astute managers take care not to see *only* what they are told; empathy is balanced with analysis. Public service mandates thinking inclusively, listening closely (which begins with fact-finding), and striking a balance among competing ethical perspectives (and values).

The impartial public manager is ethically driven, not ethically empty. Unfortunately, a habit of empathy and concern for facts and legal obligations may be condemned as alleged "bureaucratic caution." The manager in public service is often on the receiving end of ethical judgments. A decision maker bent on moderation, inclusiveness, and reasonableness may appear hypocritical, indecisive, or self-serving for those very reasons. Tolerance, breadth, and delay, byproducts of the search for balance, may be interpreted as lack of conviction as well as lack of resolve. It may be small consolation to remember that a temperate inclination is not temporizing, that looking around is not at all the same as looking over one's shoulder.

An inclusive perspective aims not at stopping action but at making action *and* integrity possible. It is part of the definition of integrity, of being whole, of what it means "to serve with honor" (the title of the 1989 report of the President's Commission on Federal Ethics Law Reform).

Vigilante Ethics

A danger here is that we will abuse ethical judgment by being too hard on ourselves or on others, by using ethics to intimidate instead of inspire. Using ethics like a vigilante's rope in an old film version of the American West, we can wield ethical judgment to bludgeon public service into submission by demanding perfection or lifelong uniformity. Lord Acton's observation a century ago that "power tends to corrupt and absolute power corrupts absolutely" emphasizes the danger of militant claims to moral superiority. Excess is all too real a threat in relations with employees, with dependent service recipients, and even with the boss.

The American tradition of public service sees both rule and result philosophical postures as dangerous when they are exaggerated and alienated from each other. From a stand usually rejected in American administration, ideologues justify wiping away all concern for the opposing ethical standard. This runs contrary to consensual accommodation, the customary composite of American politics. The dogmatist is a true believer for whom ethical rules are untempered by pragmatism and who sacrifices policy objectives to first principles and rules of conduct at whatever cost. Zealots, by contrast, sacrifice principles to policy, and their appetite for results cancels out all rules of acceptable behavior. (The key, of course, is having the power to choose the particular purposes that justify neglecting all principles.) Reduced to simple extremes, both lead to fanaticism.

In American public service, uncompromising visionaries, whatever their vision, are restrained by law, limited and shared power, and *moderating virtues.* Humility and charity are unfashionable but not outdated virtues for public managers plying public power for public purpose. Years ago, Stephen K. Bailey (1964, p. 235) specified three "essential mental attitudes" in public service, including recognition of "the moral ambiguity of all men and of all public policies"; "the contextual forces which condition moral priorities in the public service"; and "the paradoxes of procedure." By adopting (or resigning ourselves to) impartiality and open-mindedness, we can draw upon the philosophical traditions to inform ethical judgment but not replace it. Ambiguity is the price of flexibility, and responsibility is the price of reason.

Case: A Matter of Convenience

Here is the problem. Both you, a senior manager, and your newly hired assistant, a newcomer to the county, commute separately every day from a suburb not too far from the airport, past which the major highway runs. This evening you will be detained unexpectedly at an important meeting called by your boss, the commissioner. As luck would have it, you have promised to pick up your spouse at the airport tonight. The arrival was scheduled deliberately to coincide with the office's regular closing time. Do you ask your assistant to pick up your spouse?

This case highlights incongruent obligations, conflicting loyalties, clashing values—the stuff of ethical dilemmas. But it is purposefully small stuff, with personal convenience an underlying issue. Practicing on low stakes, the decision maker echoes the daily choices that sum to a habit of ethical behavior.

Many ethical dilemmas are part of daily routine. "As one midlevel manager in a large construction firm says, 'I'm not worried about bid-rigging, antitrust, the Boesky affair, or the Chicago Board of Trade. These are not the kinds of issues I see. I need tools to help me identify potential ethical problems that can be hidden in situations I face every day'" (Rice and Dreilinger, 1990, p. 104).

Do You Ask Your Assistant To Pick Up Your Spouse?

Check responses with which you agree.
No, because
_____ 1.   it is coercive to request personal favors from subordinates.
_____ 2.   the employee may expect a job-related favor in return.
_____ 3.   the assistant is not a friend, so a personal favor is out of order.
_____ 4.   your prior promise to your spouse means you cannot attend the meeting.
Yes, because
_____ 1.   the assistant is passing right by the airport, it is no big deal, and you would do it for someone else.
_____ 2.   you made clear that it is voluntary and purely personal.
_____ 3.   the problem is job related.
_____ 4.   you are in a jam and it is not your fault.

     The familiar context in this case shows how different modes of ethical reasoning lead to different resolutions.
Examine the *no* reponses.
   1 = apply rule derived from role
   2 = result is critical factor
   3 = apply rule derived from role
   4 = rule applies (prior promise), not role
Examine the *yes* responses.
   1 = nonreflective, commonsense response
   2 = mix rule and result
   3 = irresponsible—abdicates to organization
   4 = irresponsible—substitutes excuse for explanation
Would your obligations and/or preferred responses change if
   The assistant volunteers to help?
   A routine obligation like day care is substituted?
   A houseguest is substituted for your spouse?
   The assistant is a friend?
Why? What is the reasoning guiding your response?

Chapter 6

Strategies and Tactics for Managerial Decision Making

Using a decision-making model open to contending viewpoints and values, managers tool up here for fact-finding, accommodation, and selective trade-offs that lead to informed, principled choices. With thinking anchored in moral principle, the manager now is asked to take three broad steps: (1) take a harm-averse stand, (2) admit that collective action is bound to hurt someone in some way, and (3) reconcile steps 1 and 2. Using tools for deciding *what* counts, the manager reconciles the responsibility to avoid doing harm with collective action and selective action. Central guidelines developed throughout the book are synthesized in this chapter for ready reference. Using a checklist, an application melds models and tools together to resolve a case on friendship and impartiality. The chapter concludes with a device for taking personal soundings on ethical responsibility and a case for exercising ethical reasoning.

Ethics must not be reserved for experts or philosophers. If practitioners do not practice it and if decision makers ignore it, then public service and the public are in real trouble. Stuart C. Gilman, Director of Education, U.S. Office of Government Ethics, told the author (July 1990), "For managers, ethics is only ethics when we're doing it." Public managers must be equipped to do what they cannot afford to eliminate and cannot legitimately delegate.

Question: What does a public manager do when a weighty problem refuses to disappear and routine solutions do not work satisfactorily? Answer: Mull it over, seek advice and information, apply specialized knowledge and analytic techniques, and reason it out. The same is true for ethical problems. *Ethical reasoning is a form of specialized problem solving.* Its methods provide tools for making choices, and equipment is standard on all models. The package includes public service values, a systematic perspective, fact-finding, screening tools, and feedback devices and assessment tools. Of course, like all crafts, public service depends on the qualities of the craftsperson wielding the tools; fine equipment works best in the hands of someone with personal virtue, professional courage, and a decisive turn of mind.

Decision-Making Models

The three models discussed in this chapter expose managers to different ways of thinking through ethical problems. Helping to clarify a manager's cognitive reasoning process, they are useful for reconstructing and then polishing one's own rational model. They also offer the manager some elbow room—individual choice.

The best problem-solving method is the one the decision maker uses. Ethical analysis is not menu driven, like computer software: if this, then that, and hit the key. There is no mechanical procedure, no automatic scheme, no standardized bubble sheet of correct responses to ethical dilemmas.

Instead, choices, nuances, and fine-tuning favor individual tailoring. A manager might initially select among the analytic frameworks discussed here on grounds of practicality, theoretical appeal, or situational fit. Some managers may wish to try several models if the problem is truly momentous. The choice among models turns on the manager's assessment of suitability and affinity. Is it appropriate? Satisfying? Does it square with time, resources, inclination, and circumstance?

The author's preference for merging the three models is shown in the application below. A compound method has it all—that is its strength and weakness. Some managers may reject testing decisions against several standards because, having selected a preferred ethical stance, they object to a combination (recall the discussion in Chapter Five about appealing to consensus). On the other hand, the genuine flexibility and built-in expansiveness may attract other decision makers not put off by complexity, factual and intellectual demands, or the time required. A composite perhaps is best reserved for the truly exceptional dilemma.

An analytic framework lets the decision maker break down a problem into manageable parts in order to examine them, then resynthesize them, and make better decisions. Sorting out and selecting among ethical claims—for what, to whom, and why—are central tasks in ethical analysis. The ethical values and principles at risk and the decision's consequences are figured in. Some decision-making models (including Nash's, below) explicitly wed duties and outcomes. Various models diverge over an accent on results (Cooper, below) or impacts on affected parties (Rion, below). Other models, not shown here, emphasize personal morality (Denhardt, 1988).

Calling on Integrity and Imagination. Terry Cooper (1990) tells us that the ethical process means examining and ranking what is important (values) and general rules for guiding action (principles) in a given decision. Accepting the emotional component of people's decision making, Cooper sets two goals for the ethical manager. The first is to maintain a sense of integrity and avoid an "ethical hangover" when a decision incongruent with our self-image begets anguish (p. 24). The implication is that most of us would like to look in the mirror and see someone we can respect. (Oscar Wilde's *The Picture of Dorian Gray* depicts progression in the opposite direction.)

Cooper's second goal is stretching "the moral imagination" (p. 22). A series of steps generates alternative solutions through serial reasoning from a results-based perspective.

1. Specify all conceivable alternatives.
2. Match probable positive and negative consequences with each alternative.
3. Identify principles related to each alternative.
4. Rank principles or values at stake and justify priorities as if to someone else or publicly.

With choices generated, the task now is to select among them. Working on the assumption that public service role obligations are accepted, the decision-making method can be summarized in four steps (Cooper, 1990).

1. Review the facts and get what you need to know.
2. Understand roles and values, both your own inclinations and imposed obligations.
3. Consider all possible options and possible results.
4. Anticipate how you would feel about and explain your decision.

The fourth step in part parallels the publicity tests suggested at the conclusion of Chapter Three. According to Cooper (p. 24) "Resolution is reached when we discover an alternative that satisfies our need to have sound reasons for our conduct and our need to feel satisfied with the decision."

Accommodating Duties and Results. Laura Nash proposes twelve questions that are grounded in the two broad philosophical traditions discussed in Chapter Five but that are expressed concretely and designed for practical business decisions. Substitute *agency* for *corporation* in the fourth question and add *legislative body* to the tenth, and public-sector applications become apparent.

Have you defined the problem accurately?
How would you define the problem if you stood on the other side of the fence?
How did this situation occur in the first place?
To whom and to what do you give your loyalty as a person and as a member of the corporation?

What is your intention in making this decision?

How does this intention compare with the probable results?

Whom could your decision or action injure?

Can you discuss the problem with the affected parties before you make your decision?

Are you confident that your position will be as valid over a long period of time as it seems now?

Could you disclose without qualm your decision or action to your boss, your CEO, the board of directors, your family, society as a whole?

What is the symbolic potential of your action if understood? If misunderstood?

Under what conditions would you allow exceptions to your stand?*

Nash's method combines major (simplified) traditions in formal moral reasoning to explore the ethical content of workaday decisions in organizational settings and in language meaningful to a manager. Loyalty conflict (question 4) "is a workable way of smoking out the ethics of a situation and of discovering the absolute values inherent in it" (1981, p. 84); and disclosure or scrutiny (question 10) "is a way of sounding those submarine depths of conscience and of searching out loyalties" (p. 86). Nash sees the symbolic message as aimed at domestic consumption within the organization and for external communication with the public. Questions 9, 10, and 12 test decisions against change. As in several cases in this book, changing selected circumstances clarifies reasoning and reveals critical factors in making moral judgments. These three questions are especially suggestive from the standpoint of the public interest and public service.

On the job, when demands prohibit delay, a mental checklist is a useful device for filtering and organizing information quickly. A checklist modeled on Nash's framework is given in Exhibit 6.1, with an abbreviated version designed for easy recall. Together they represent a useful and inclusive method for making ethical decisions. The elementary standard—know the law—from Chapter Four is the starting point.

Decisions are made with the heart and the mind but sometimes rejected by the pit of the stomach. The visceral test—"Can I live with this?"—serves as a final check, a precaution with the force of feelings behind it. The question taps into anticipated consequences and the likelihood of follow-through. Then it remains to monitor and evaluate the decision as it is implemented.

Six Good Questions. The abbreviated version of the decision-making model shown in Exhibit 6.1 combines the inclusiveness of Nash's model with pointed questions from Michael Rion's *The Responsible Manager* (1990). Rion builds a

---

Exhibit 6.1. Decision-Making Checklist.

☐ 1. Facts (including law)

☐ 2. Empathy and inclusion

☐ 3. Underlying causes and precedents

☐ 4. Stakeholders and responsibilities

☐ 5. Motives and objectives

☐ 6. Possible results and rationality

☐ 7. Potential harm (stakeholders)

☐ 8. Participation

☐ 9. Long-term time frame and anticipated change

☐ 10. Disclosure and publicity

☐ 11. Appearance and communication

☐ 12. Universality and consistency

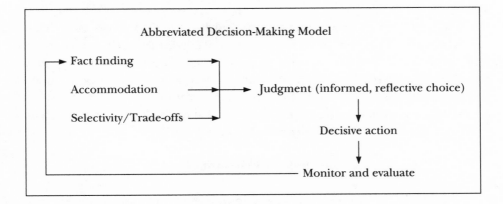

framework for practical decisions by business managers under severe time pressures. His construct poses six questions (pp. 13–14, original emphasis deleted).

1. Why is this bothering me? Is it really an issue? Am I genuinely perplexed, or am I afraid to do what I know is right?
2. Who else matters? Who are the stakeholders [affected interests, individuals, or groups] who may be affected by my decisions?
3. Is it my problem? Have I caused the problem or has someone else? How far shoud I go in resolving the issue?
4. What is the ethical concern—legal obligation, fairness, promise keeping, honesty, doing good, avoiding harm?
5. What do others think? Can I learn from those who disagree with my judgment?
6. Am I being true to myself? What kind of person or company [or agency] would do what I am contemplating? Could I share my decision "in good conscience" with my family? with colleagues? with public officials?*

The first question highlights the difference between a real ethical dilemma and the courage to follow through on ethical obligations. It is especially handy for short-circuiting evasive waffling used to postpone unpleasant or costly action. In Rion's approach, ethics is not just a rational process, although it is a deliberative one. Having to live with the outcomes, managers should be comfortable with them.

The third question needs to be distinguished from the excuse that "it's not my job" or the argument that no one is responsible for collective decisions in a public agency. This question adds an element of reasonable selectivity to the proposition in Chapter Four, "We cannot hide behind our supervisor or our desk to escape responsibility." A public manager wantonly doing "good works" would soon burn out or exceed legal authority and the budget. The question now is *how* to opt reasonably and selectively for responsibility.

Opting for Responsibility

Recall the old story about a government employee who complains to the teacher that someone at school is stealing his child's pencils. The father explains that it is the *principle* that bothers him, not the pencils—he gets all the pencils he needs at the office! Of course, behavior is not always this transparent, but it does seem easier to pin down, without qualification or queasiness, someone else's responsibility than one's own. When it comes to tough calls, it may also be easier to get bogged down in nuances and definitions as a way of bypassing decision making. At any rate, responsibility is not as difficult to define as to exercise.

An earlier discussion organized ethical claims according to roles from which they originate and depicted for simplicity's sake as five separate clusters (see Exhibit 1.2). By extending that image, responsibilities can be visualized in three dimensions, along a vector that runs from the informal, personal, and self-imposed responsibility to the formal, public, and externally imposed obligation. In actuality, roles are interrelated, interact, overlap, and sometimes conflict, blotting out or magnifying segments of other multifaceted clusters. The result is a profusion of do's and don'ts, not all of which can be acted on simultaneously.

Daily events activate multiple responsibilities; they create dilemmas and spark the need for selectivity when a manager cannot meet all responsibilities at the same time. John F. (Jack) Azzaretto's example (unpublished cases provided to author, May 1990) embroils the manager in harassment, the law, agency pressures, values such as fairness, and trust. "An employee comes to you to reveal that she feels her supervisor's actions may constitute sexual harassment. She is reluctant to press further for fear of reprisal and the indignation of co-workers toward her because this supervisor is well liked. When you ask her what she would like you to do, she replies, 'Don't get involved—I'll handle it myself.' Do you ignore this situation?" (The Equal Employment Opportunity Commission's guidelines under Title VII of the Civil Rights Act of 1964 define harassment as discrimination. Section 1604[d] of the guidelines states, "With respect to conduct between fellow employees an employer is responsible for acts of sexual harassment in the workplace where the employer [its agency or supervisory employees] knows or should have known of the conduct unless it can show that it took immediate and appropriate corrective actions.")

The decision-making model we adopt affects the responsibilities we accept and how we choose among them when choice is necessary. Decision makers use some sort of framework to sort and accept ethical claims. The framework is a decision-making model; our adopted model cues and sorts claims (legitimate? compelling?) and keys our choices among them. Figure 6.1 illustrates this idea in one clean thrust.

Avoid Doing Harm. In many models, the number one concern is how people are affected (leading to stakeholder analysis, discussed in Chapter Seven). A typical starting point is accepting the minimum prescription to avoid harming others. "Customarily, ethics in public administration means the obligation to avoid injury" (Stewart, 1984, p. 19). To avoid doing harm or inflicting injury is crucial for Rion, Nash, and others. It tops unobjectionable lists of commonsense moral values and rules (Goodpaster, 1984, p. 4) and, rendered as *caring*, is among the values around which there is general consensus (Guy, 1990, p. 14). It is a stringent standard under ordinary circumstances and even more so when regulatory and redistributive impacts guarantee that people are helped and hurt differentially.

The harm-averse stand is so important in public service that it is added

Figure 6.1. Decision Makers Use a Framework to Sort and Accept Ethical Claims.

Doonesbury   BY GARRY TRUDEAU

DOONESBURY copyright 1988 G. B. Trudeau. Reprinted with permission of Universal Press Syndicate. All rights reserved.

to the ranks of basic guides to action. Exhibit 6.2 shows these essentials of ethical performance in public service. They serve as general guides by which to order competing ethical claims.

Although the dictum of doing no harm deeply influences ethical reasoning and action, an ethical and pragmatic regard for competing claims forces us to moderate it through selectivity and trade-offs. Selectivity calls for ranking ethical claims on the manager as a way of establishing priorities.

Ranking Roles (Tool 1). In some instances, a manager may prefer to set priorities according to the source of the claim and the operative roles (see Exhibit 1.2). To do this, the decision maker selects one ruling cluster and sidesteps or downplays others. (This is behind the argument about citizen versus official dissent in Chapter Two.) While this works well for fundamental obligations in public service, other applications may produce crude oversimplifications that lead to Morozov-like deformations (see Chapter One).

The potential damage to important values and ethical claims can be minimized by several checks. Anticipate follow-through by inquiring, "Can I live with this?" Apply the acid test of prospective publicity and ask what kind of person would do this and whether you want to be and be known as that kind of person (see Chapter Three).

Ranking Responsibilites (Tool 2). When avoiding harm is at issue, a useful approach to setting priorities draws upon type of ethical claim and taking responsibility for one's actions. Ranked in order of diminishing strictness, ethical claims include:

1.   The most stringent, the negative obligation—avoid harm.
2.   Remedy or relief—for problems we provoke.

Exhibit 6.2. Doing Public Service.

PRINCIPLES
1.   Obey and implement the law (Chapter Two).
2.   Serve the public interest (Chapter Three).
3.   Avoid doing harm (Chapter Six).

ACTION GUIDES
1.   Take individual responsibility for decisions and behavior (Chapter Four).
     No escaping responsibility by
       hiding behind the boss or desk,
       hiding behind subordinates,
       hiding behind ignorance.
2.   Take responsibility for what is done and how it is done (Chapter Four).
3.   Treat incompetence as abuse of office (Chapter Four).

---

3.   Affirmative aid—for problems others cause.
4.   The least stringent, doing good works—voluntary charity.

Public service's posture of avoiding harm begets an obligation to correct direct or indirect problems we create. This distinction is not an academic nicety or analytic luxury. By way of illustration, federal regulations (40 CFR 1508.8) divide environmental impacts into two categories: direct, "caused by the action and occur at the same time and place"; and indirect, "caused by the action and are later in time or farther removed in distance, but are reasonably foreseeable."

In thinking about the effects of actions or decisions, the ethical manager applies the rule of reason. For example, the evaluation of "reasonably foreseeable significant adverse effects" required for implementing the National Environmental Policy Act (by regulations issued in 1987 by the Council on Environmental Quality, in the Executive Office of the President) requires disclosure of incomplete or unavailable information. "Reasonably foreseeable" is defined as including "impacts which have catastrophic consequences, even if their probability of occurrence is low, provided that the analysis of the impacts is supported by credible scientific evidence, is not based on pure conjecture, and is within the rule of reason" (40 CFR 1502.22[b]).

A third and less rigorous claim moves the decision maker from the realm of obligation to responsibility (see Exhibit 1.2). It is a positive responsibility: to help. This line of reasoning is by no means unique to American public administration; many religions teach, first, not to do evil and, second, to cultivate good.

Charity, the fourth ethical claim, is the least stringent. It is voluntary, self-generated, and dictated by time, energy, and personal inclination. Although doing good deeds is commendable, it is not necessarily ethical to do them at public expense or through public office (as the case at the end of Chapter Two illustrates).

Threshold Test (Tool 3). What about a problem a manager did *not* cause? Apply a threshold test adapted from Rion and others in which the more that each of the following four factors applies, the more punch behind the obligation (Rion, 1990, pp. 64–65; Stewart, 1984, p. 21):

1. Vulnerability: a need or problem clearly exists, presents potential harm.
2. Proximity: the manager knows or should know that a need or problem exists.
3. Capability: the means exist to help without excessive risk (danger, liability).
4. Dependency: last resort, no one else is apt to help.

These factors elaborate the commonsense yardsticks of proximity, saliency, and gravity that are used in Chapter Four to discriminate among top management's responsibilities. The multifaceted notion of proximity can be broken down further by distinguishing among physical access, reporting lines, and cognizance.

While the *threshold test* is most useful when immediate physical danger is threatened, it easily extends to injury of any sort, from material loss to severe violation of basic ethical values or principles. It is especially relevant to sorting out self-generated ethical claims. Although not everyone would agree that "[t]hese conditions provide a warrant to inject personal judgments" (Dobel, 1990, p. 360), they do promote vulnerability and dependency as critical factors in assessing ethical responsibility. At minimum, they should trigger earnest reflection.

Ranking responsibilities and the *threshold test* reveal the dilemmas in the case at the end of this chapter. They also explain this book's emphasis on a *future generations* test. With neither voice nor vote to participate or to protest irreparable harm, future generations are the most dependent stakeholders of all, and public officials are their only institutional trustee.

Realistically, because the point of this all is ethical action, time constraints and urgency are part of a manager's calculation of priorities, even—or especially—ethical ones. Still, some managers may prefer more specificity in a form geared to public service. Regulations governing environmental impact statements (40 CFR 1501.8[a]) supply suggestive (and results-based) criteria for calculating priorities. The eight criteria include: potential for harm; scope or size of proposal; analytic limitations undermining certainty; public need, including the effect of delay; number of affected people and agencies; information uncertain or unknown (time needed); level of controversy over action; and legally imposed time limits.

Of course, managers can fine-tune any assessment technique by refining or adding criteria by which responsibilities are selected and ranked. Some possibilities are mandated mission and legislative intent, cost, reversibility, and future effects and beneficiaries.

Application

With the help of the foregoing tools, we can use an amalgam of the three approaches (from Cooper, Nash, and Rion) to resolve a perplexing case. Picture the scene: as personnel director, you learn at a top-level staff meeting that the municipality's retrenchment plan calls for reorganization and cuts in managerial staff. The tentative blueprint has the city's Department of Community Services absorbing the small elderly services unit, whose program director, a close friend of your family, is slated for termination. The city manager, whose judgment you respect, mentions the program director's poor performance and as the meeting adjourns reminds everyone that the discussion is confidential as usual. As you leave, you remember that your friend is about to make a substantial down payment on a new home. *How would you handle this?*

Reviewing the decision-making checklist shown in Exhibit 6.1 is a good beginning. By putting ourselves in the personnel director's role, we can use the checklist to elicit acute considerations.

1. *Facts.* Does the city manager know about the imminent down payment?—No. Is the city manager aware of the friendship?—Yes. Is your friend aware of prospective termination?—No. Are you sure your friend depends upon her municipal salary to finance housing?—Yes.

Is information confidential just because the city manager says so? Is a strictly legalistic view right or an excuse? You strike a middle ground by asking yourself, "Is this privileged information, known to me through my job but not known generally?"—Yes. A draft model ordinance (designed to aid municipal attorneys in drafting municipal ethics codes) defines confidential information as "all information, whether transmitted orally or in writing, which is of such a nature that it is not, at that time, a matter of public record or public knowledge" (National Institute of Municipal Law Officers, 1990, p. 3).

Does your jurisdiction prohibit using public office for *anyone's* personal gain and divulging confidential information?—perhaps. But either way, you know confidentiality is a widely accepted administrative value because federal standards (see Exhibit 6.3) and state law in more than half of all states forbid the use of confidential government information.

2. *Empathy.* How would you feel if financial ruin threatened you? Can you put yourself in the city manager's shoes? How important is confidentiality in *your* job? How are other people in the community affected by your helping or not helping your friend?

3. *Causes.* Thinking about causes helps you define the problem and solutions. Your friend brought on her termination herself through poor performance but not the retrenchment's coinciding with the new house. Therefore, the problem is not keeping the job but avoiding financial disaster.

4. *Stakeholders.* Friendship does make ethical claims on you, but the difficult part of public service is that personal friendship is rejected as a legitimate basis of action—it is nontransferrable from the personal to the public realm. You must weigh reponsibilities and obligations to *all* affected parties, including the city manager, who unknowingly put you in a difficult position; your family friend; yourself, spouse, and family; the municipal organization; and residents and taxpayers.

5. *Objectives.* The city manager's motives are not clear, but because he

Exhibit 6.3. Judge Nebeker's Memorandum.

The following information is excerpted from a September 12, 1988, memorandum from the director of the U.S. Office of Government Ethics on the independent counsel's 1988 report concerning the activities of Attorney General Edwin Meese, III. Reference is to Section 201(c) and Section 205 of Executive Order 11222, still in force in 1988.

> Assisting a friend is not in and of itself prohibited by the Executive Order. But, assisting a friend in a manner which misuses official position for the friend's private benefit, which gives that friend preferential treatment not properly afforded, which causes a Government decision to be made outside official channels, which affects the public's confidence in the integrity of its Government, or which leads an informed and reasonable person to believe that any of these things have occurred, is what this section was in part intended to prohibit. . . .
>
> Section 205 states "[a]n employee shall not directly or indirectly make use of, or permit others to make use of, for the purpose of furthering a private interest, official information not made available to the general public."
>
> This provision of the standards of conduct is directed not only to information which is by statute confidential or classified, but also to the large amount of information which is neither, yet clearly not information generally available to the public . . . [which may mean preferential treatment or its appearance].

did not know about the down payment, because confidentiality is standard procedure at these staff meetings, and because you trust his judgment, you assume he intends to act for the best. You even may feel that he knowingly put you on the spot and ought to do something about it. The obligation to prevent injury emerges from checklist items 2 and 3, above, but what about *your* objective? Are you acting to protect a friend through special treatment?

12. *Universality and Consistency.* At this point you skip to checklist item 12 because you realize that you happen to have specific information that warrants consideration on behalf of *anyone* in a precarious situation, not only your friend. Your intention is *not* to use privileged information from public office solely to protect a friend.

6. *Possible results.* What happens if your friend loses her job and cannot make the mortgage payments? How can you face her accusation of betrayal? What happens if she learns about the retrenchment plan from you, does not buy the house, but then does not lose her job? If you were to betray a trust for friendship's sake and your friend knows you have other friends too, can she ever trust you again? Can you be effective in your job without the city manager's trust? What if everyone disclosed confidential information at whim? Can government function if public trust takes second place to employee needs? To personal friendship?

7. *Potential harm.* Your friend faces financial harm. The city manager's trust is at issue. You also realize that the organization is at risk—do you want to work in an organization that would allow something like this to happen to an employee, even one being fired? Does the city deserve an administration like this? You decide something should be done to prevent injury.

8. *Participation and 11. Appearance.* Because of the friendship, you conclude it would be best for communication to come from someone else. Given the fact-finding in checklist item 1, above, you begin to think about bringing the city manager into the picture.

9. *Change and 10. Disclosure.* You do not see these items as directly applicable to the problem you face.

Next, you turn to assess the options stimulated by your thinking:

1. Do nothing: say nothing.
2. Tell your spouse, who is not bound by confidentiality.
3. Tell your friend immediately and directly.
4. Inform the city manager of your friend's impending down payment.
5. Say nothing but be prepared to help your friend financially.
6. Casually hint to your friend about impending shake-ups.
7. Leak the retrenchment plan to the media.
8. Tell your friend and other municipal employees that budget cuts mean that a shake-up is imminent and suggest that they avoid new commitments at this time.
9. Say nothing, and help your friend get another job when the time comes.

Can you stand by and do nothing? Is this your problem? The obligation to keep confidentiality (involving legal compliance, loyalty, and trust) clashes with another top-ranking obligation, to refrain from doing harm. Although you are not directly causing the problem, inaction or silence could result in serious injury. Therefore, your obligation is reduced but still compelling. You may remember the story about George Washington refusing to help a job-seeking friend: "As George Washington, I would do anything in my power for you. As President, I can do nothing" (Bailey, 1964, p. 241). You feel that *his* obligation of affirmative help was lighter than the one you face, the obligation to avoid doing harm.

Pragmatism affects your choice among alternatives. Given your municipal salary, the remedy or relief of supporting your friend's new home is not realistic; financing your own mortgage is hard enough each month and soon both families would be insolvent. Helping in the job hunt does not mean omitting the friendship or poor performance appraisal from a reference, but you know of many publicly advertised openings and your expertise can really help a friend here.

You can think of no way to sidestep the conflict. Embroiling your spouse unties no ethical knots and is itself unethical. Even a hint or two to your friend ("cutbacks in towns across the region counsel postponing life choices") abides by the letter more than the spirit of the obligation. Even worse, ignoring other employees possibly in comparable positions results in favored treatment for a friend. Leaking the story as an unidentified source means breaking confidence on a grand scale plus trying to escape personal responsibility. A general tip-off to employees personally or through the media still breaks confidence, stimulates gossip, and would cause anxiety and distress. Inflicting minor injury on many, including the innocent (those with good job performances), to protect a friend from more serious harm makes you uncomfortable.

Using the threshold test, you determine that there is a need or problem, you do know something, you are capable of helping but at either some professional or some personal cost. However, you are *not* the last resort, and this realization along with considerations of participation and appearance lead you to speak with the city manager. You request that he inform your friend and the others targeted in the retrenchment plan.

Now comes the hard part. Assume that the city manager, whose judgment you respect, declines to make the retrenchment plan public, citing potential employee demoralization and not giving advance notice for affected agencies to undercut the plan by soliciting citizen opposition. He explains that the decision is still tentative, and he does not feel that widespread employee stress is a reasonable price for your friend's financial security. He also refuses to give *your* friend special treatment. Empathically, you reconsider obligations and options from the city manager's perspective.

If you still believe that his response fails to meet the ethical claims that are emerging from your analysis and you genuinely believe that anyone should be told, not just your friend, then you decide to go farther. You try to persuade the city manager and explain your ethical posture. Your task is to convince him that the information should be disclosed to those at severe risk; the city has a responsibility to employees, too. You point out that your professional code (that of the IPMA) bids you "to insure that full and early consideration is given to the human aspects of management plans and decisions." You argue that information deeply affecting people ought to be made public or at least available to directly affected parties, especially when withholding it causes serious harm.

If that fails, you acknowledge that the city manager's ethical preference or lapse does not absolve you of the reponsibility that you already determined is yours. You then reassess capability in terms of *excessive* risk to yourself (job, integrity, family, friendship, professional identity) and the values and principles associated with all participants, including your good friend, the municipal organization, city residents, the profession, and others.

Presuming an authentic assumption of ethical responsibility in this case, you decide that legal compliance and avoiding the conflict of interest represented by respecting privileged information are preeminent obligations in public service. IPMA's code reinforces your commitment to "treat as privileged, information accepted in trust." You decide to say nothing, to help your friend in her job search, and to initiate an outplacement program for all municipal employees. (This last idea illustrates inventive resolution—Cooper's "moral imagination"— at work.)

You conclude by asking, "Can I live with this?" You test the emotional components of your decision and assess the likelihood that you will follow through. To find out, you decide to let the decision sit for a time, but you feel pushed by the pace of events. Your personal anguish is sincere, and you ask yourself, "Am I right?" Insofar as you attempted to use reasoned, unbiased judgment in an informed, systematic way, yes. Does everyone agree with your resolution? No; that is why this is a dilemma that recurs with different faces and different choices at all levels of public service.

Accepting Responsibility (Self-Testing)

Given the principle of individual ethical claims, accepting and selecting responsibilities are critical to a public service built on accountability. Moving from the abstract idea to the concrete heightens the noncognitive aspects of decision making. Can you live with this? Take responsibility for it? And the consequences? This applies the visceral test and makes tangible an abstract or general decision.

The symbolic template shown in Exhibit 6.4 can be laid over decisions as a self-testing device. This author is *not* recommending that it be adopted as a public communication or official routine by an agency or office. Rather, public managers can scan the ethical soundness of their decisions against their willingness to sign—*as if* for the public record—the ethics responsibility statement.

A state manager captured the point of the exercise by quoting Nobel laureate Gabriela Mistral: "El perfecto valor consiste el nacer sin testigos todo lo que seriamos capazes de hacer ante el mundo entero." Translation: "A perfect value consists in doing without witness all that we could have done in front of the entire world."

Exhibit 6.4. Ethics Responsibility Statement.

(Not intended for agency adoption)

I take personal responsibility for making this recommendation or decision in the public interest, with consideration given to future generations.

_____	_____
(signed)	(date)

I am prepared to explain this recommendation or decision publicly, to the press, and to my agency, service recipients, and (if a public-private partnership or an interjurisdictional project) collaborators.

_____	_____
(signed)	(date)

I take personal responsibility for making this recommendation or decision in an ethical manner.

_____	_____
(signed)	(date)

No Closure

Is this all there is? Of course not. But this book is for public managers, who are not and do not want to be philosophers or theologians. Managers prefer other pursuits, which are easy to respect. Just turn on a faucet, cross a bridge, or catch a plane.

Why not a few authoritative rules, and settle the problems once and for all? Simplistic rules are no solution in our complicated world, and not the point; judgment and action are. Not everything can or should be reduced to a snappy slogan on a bumper sticker or a twenty-second sound bite. The polar extreme of hairsplitting and quibbling over exquisite niceties does not help managers either. Remember Lewis Carroll's *Through the Looking Glass*? Tweedledee says, "Contrariwise . . . if it was, it might be; and if it were so, it would be: but as it isn't, it ain't. That's logic."

After thousands of years of discussion and tons of paper, closure is improbable (and impossibly arrogant). Then, too, anyone promising the *last* word on the subject rejects the challenging future anticipated for public service.

Case: Gloomy Prognosis

The text of this case is from Kenneth J. Garcia, "Prognosis Gloomy for Trauma Network," *Los Angeles Times*, Apr. 10, 1990, pp. B1, B8. Copyright, 1990, *Los Angeles Times*. Reprinted by permission.

> **Health care:** Some say the strapped system can be saved by sending most gun and knife injuries to county facilities.
>
> The deterioration of the county's emergency health-care system may mean a return to what paramedics call the "Wild West days" before the trauma system existed, and that means many more people would die, according to trauma surgeons, other physicians and hospital officials. . . .
>
> Already, 25,000 people injured across the nation die each year after they reach hospitals. Last year, Los Angeles County trauma centers treated more than 14,000 patients—a number that continues to rise while the number of trauma units declines.
>
> The trauma system has crumbled primarily because of the large financial losses incurred by the hospitals, some of which used to be designated as trauma centers, believing that it would bring in millions of dollars and much-valued prestige. Instead, they lost millions, in part because of new government and health insurance cost controls, but mostly because of the large numbers of indigent patients that entered their doors. Some of those patients ended up staying at the hospitals for months recovering from their injuries, running up sky-high medical bills.

Since the county's trauma network opened seven years ago, 11 of the original 23 member hospitals have pulled out of the system and others have threatened to do so unless the operation is revamped.

The rapidly failing health of the trauma network is so troubling to emergency service officials that they are considering sweeping changes to salvage what is left of the system, thought to be the nation's finest when it opened in 1983.

Unless they make those changes, the officials say, the gaping holes in the trauma net will foster a return to the pretrauma times when emergency surgeons had little status and there was little organization over how and where critically injured patients should be transported.

Topping the list of proposed changes is a radical, two-tier system in which nearly all "penetrating" trauma victims—most of them gang members suffering from bullet wounds—would be taken to county trauma centers, and nearly all "blunt" trauma victims would be treated at private hospitals. The gaping wounds caused by knives and bullets, and usually associated with gang warfare, make up the vast majority of the penetrating trauma cases, while the blunt injuries are usually caused by falls and car accidents.

The idea recognizes the fact that gang members almost never carry medical insurance and don't pay for their medical care. And doctors at private hospitals . . . have said they pulled out in part because of the "criminal element" that injured gang victims brought to their community.

The new system, if approved, would allow most of the private hospitals to treat trauma patients who carry medical insurance while the county hospitals would be left with the brunt of the non-paying gang victims.

The proposal has been criticized by physicians and hospital administrators who believe that it would further segregate indigent patients and create a privileged trauma-care system for those with medical insurance.

In addition, they say, it would eventually force city and county paramedics to use more helicopter transport for critically injured patients, an expensive and logistically difficult endeavor on the crowded streets of Los Angeles.

The proposal "would be my last choice, because frankly I don't think it would be safe, but it may be the only choice left to save the trauma network," said Virginia Price-Hastings, head of the county trauma program. "We're going to have to look at ways of changing the system or somehow create a whole new system that will work in this county. But I have difficulty favoring any idea that would change the system for social, and not medical, reasons."

However, supporters of the idea say that to keep the status would be akin to placing the critical-care network on life support. . . .

"I think separating blunt and penetrating trauma cases is an interesting, even creative possibility for salvaging the trauma system," said David Langness, vice president of the Hospital Council of Southern California. "Yes, it might ghettoize knife and gun club victims, and that's unfortunate. But our county hospitals are the best at treating those type of combat-type injuries, so why not give them a chance to save them all?"

"In the end, the purpose is to save the trauma system, so the risk of creating a two-tiered system might be worth it if it saves the system itself." . . .

[According to Dr. Allen W. Mathies, president and chief executive office at the private hospital whose withdrawal precipitated the crisis,] "In the beginning, there was a general lack of recognition for what the costs would be, the need for long-term care for many of the patients and the potential liability of the physicians."

"But it's like in those Gallup polls where when the question is asked, 90% of the people believe that access to health care is a basic right. But when asked whether they would raise their own taxes to pay for it, 80% of them say no. Without that basic commitment to a trauma system, it becomes very difficult."

How do technical criteria affect the service delivery decision and obscure its ethical dimensions?

What public service values are protected or threatened by the policy proposal?

What type of ethical reasoning dominates thinking here?
- How would the proposal change if reasoning changed?
- Would you recommend using alternative decision-making models as a control, or is this phony? Too time consuming?

We may use different standards or ways of thinking in different settings. In this public policy dilemma, is your thinking affected by different factors?
- Service users' dependency on public services?
- Potential for severe injury (vulnerability)?

Many believe that public service ethics is built on the obligation to avoid injuring others and that decision makers are obligated to offset or reduce the harmful effects—intentional but unavoidable, direct and indirect—of their decisions or actions.
- What does this principle suggest in this case?
- Do you agree with this principle?

- What different principles could be used for distributing public services (for example, age instead of class)?

Questions about ethical implications can be asked at three levels: according to the decision maker or individuals affected, the organization or policy, and the system or society.

- Is any set of concerns omitted in this case?
- With what results (for example, reducing indirect harm)?

Do you agree that "the purpose is to save the trauma system"? Sometimes, immediate individual interests vie with long-term institutional or social interests.

- How could county officials think about reconciling public service values and severe consequences for individuals, for the hospital, and for the trauma network?
- How is reasoning affected by ranking responsibilities and using the threshold test?

Are options clarified by separating ethical from practical matters, or is that just an academic exercise?

- Should ethical concerns outweigh pragmatic matters?

Chapter 7

Understanding Who and What Matters: Stakeholder Analysis

In this chapter, stakeholder analysis operationalizes open-minded reasoning. A diagnostic tool helps answer the question of *who* counts and *what* counts. Significant players in ethical dilemmas, ethical managers count as well. Principled discrimination in responding to ethical offenses equips managers to discount trivialities and survive professionally with their integrity intact. A case calling for stakeholder analysis concludes the chapter.

Ethical analysis is all about ambiguity and confusion—that is what the word *dilemma* implies. Stakeholder analysis is a method of viewing a scenario from the potential victim's perspective, for taking the empathic leap to public interest without sacrificing too much or too many.

Stakeholder analysis has a duty-based core, although at first glance it may appear wholly and solely focused on results. The underlying reasoning draws on both of the philosophical perspectives discussed in Chapter Five, but results do play a leading role in the analysis. A manager, acting on the principles of reciprocity in human relations and respect for the other person, searches for some way to bring practice in line with principle. The task, then, is to specify who and what is threatened by adverse repercussions in order to lighten or relieve them. (Admittedly, it may be used self-servingly to predict likely response or possible opposition; this conjures up the suspicion about mixing pragmatic and ethical rationales.)

Who Matters

Many factors, many actors, and many impacts thicken the plot. Stakeholder analysis is a tool for identifying and sorting them out. Likely as not, the stakes are numerous, complicated, and important.

Ethical managers exercise reasonable selectivity among responsibilities and choose their battles in a principled way. The principle proposed in Chapter Six of abstaining from doing harm is moderated by the need for collective action that actually may inflict some injury. The task of ethical analysis now shifts to pinning down the potential injury and victim. While more is involved than a simple calculation of net good over harm, public service requires one to act in the public interest, and general harm bars action. However, decisions rarely reduce neatly into no-harm/go choices. Instead, particular groups, regions, sectors, individuals, interests, or values are vulnerable to someone's good idea, as the case at the end of this chapter illustrates.

Self-interested resistance is the crux of the not-in-my-backyard (NIMBY) attitude toward, for example, a prison site; it rejects solutions that sacrifice one locale or group to a common good more broadly enjoyed. It is the moral of the poll cited in the case that concludes Chapter Six. NIMBY and like problems are compelling reasons for examining basic assumptions (What would happen were there no backyard?) and innovatively redesigning alternatives.

Because collective action in an interdependent world is bound to hurt someone's pocketbook, sensitivities, surroundings, values, or principles, collective problem solving is possible only if we allow for the possibility of someone getting hurt in some fashion and to some degree. Collective or government action is possible only through a combination of sacrifice (often involuntary), relief or compensation, and trade-off. That trade-off allows for acting in the public interest and distributing costs and benefits differently to different segments of the public.

Stakeholder analysis is a method of specifying who and what is affected. It is *not* a search for interest groups couched in the rhetoric of ethics. It asks, "Who else matters?" (Rion, 1990, p. 46). Three categories provide an answer (Dreiford Group, 1988, pp. 26-28; Rion, 1990, pp. 43-55). The point is to be as inclusive as possible and consider the long and short terms. Affected stakeholders include the following:

1. *Internal:* the organization or agency, including mission, superiors, employees, and the decision maker
2. *External and direct:* clients and suppliers, lawmakers, taxpayers, and community residents and businesses
3. *External and indirect:* those keyed to general interests, spillovers, and the long term, including citizens and society, other jurisdictions, the private sector, and future generations

Analysts will surely disagree about particular classifications, but that is not as important as including all affected parties. Bear in mind the three levels of ethical impacts: the decision maker or individuals affected, the organization or policy, and the system or society. By changing the level of abstraction, stakeholder categories can account for all three levels.

Ranking Obligations to Stakeholders. Once affected parties and potential adverse impacts (who is being hurt and how much) are identified, the next step is to rank the weight of obligation to each. A simple but unworkable method is to choose one of the three categories and base priorities on it. That makes a sham out of the exercise, leaves out too many stakeholders, and treats all stakes the same.

A more useful alternative is to rank the stakes, the values associated with interests, and to come up with a composite measure of adverse impact. Using a measure along the lines of the stakeholder diagnostic presented in Exhibit 7.1—a practical tool for aiding deliberation, not a quick fix for ending it—the decision maker can assign scores to selected factors.

Although the stakeholder diagnostic shown in Exhibit 7.1 uses six *equally weighted* factors in the index, the decision maker can adapt it to different ethical concerns by varying the weight of different factors or adding new ones. The manager selects the factors and assigns the values. For example, a high score on "negligible policy impact" in the sample diagnostic suggests injury for trivial results and explicitly factors in utility gauged by aggregated impacts. While duty-oriented purists may drop it from the calculation, some analysts would consider tolerating any harm at all for only material, nontrivial reasons.

Repeating the scoring for each of the stakeholders allows comparisons among them. The higher the score, the less acceptable the decision for that stakeholder. Adding the scores together furnishes an aggregate measure of the overall

Exhibit 7.1. Stakeholder Diagnostic.

Category (check one)   *Description of Stake*

☐   Internal   _____

☐   External and direct   _____

☐   External and indirect   _____

Factors	Score	High (3)	Medium (2)	Low (1)	None (0)
Dependency on government (in accessible alternative services)					____
Vulnerability of stakeholders (potential injury)					____
Gravity (versus triviality) of stake or threat					____
Improbable relief or remedy					____
Risk to fundamental value					____
Negligible policy impact					====
Add column for total score					____

Score triggers manager's considering obligatory action or relief   ☐ Yes   ☐ No

Manager recommends obligatory action or relief   ☐ Yes   ☐ No potential harm. A decision that causes severe permanent harm or injury to the dependent (service recipients) or vulnerable (ill, poor) and damage to crucial values receives a high score. An aggregate score of 18 across the board should prompt managers to reject the proposal outright. The intention here is to provoke rethinking and some reflection on the meaning of public interest.

A score of 18 for individual stakeholders in the sample diagnostic could trigger thinking about modification, mitigation, remedy, or relief. While this is surely a burden, the effort could restrain action at deviant points on the continua shown in Chapter One. By way of precedent, there are monetary compensation, job retraining, outplacement programs, affirmative action, and programs for reducing health and safety risks to employees.

Individual responsibility, truth telling, and publicity combine into an obligation to accept willingly the responsibility for one's actions. Add to this the obligation to modify behavior if the results are harmful. Thus feedback is important to building in the capacity to monitor and modify. The willingness to listen is a component of ethical decision making.

Appetite Curbs. Two problems cause indigestion if stakeholder analysis is swallowed whole in a single gulp. One is a matter of concepts and principles of justice, such as distribution, redistribution, compensation, and others (Beauchamp and Pinkard, 1983, pp. 128–169). The notion of compensation is too often reduced to financial payoffs. We should know better; even the ancient idea of *lex salica* (a sixty-century penal code also including some civil law acts) allows for payment *or* atonement (Pollock-Byrne, 1989, p. 47). The ethical (and political) ramifications of buying off the injured party or buying citizen cooperation are all too obvious. Is it too harsh to wonder whether what is being bought off sometimes is the decision maker's guilty conscience? Duty-based reasoning argues that some things or people should not be bought; the price is never *right*.

For those with an eye on results, reducing harm via compensation raises the specter of discriminatory, class-based problem solving rationalized on ethical grounds. Because the price of a rich injured party is higher than a poor one's, economical implementation of ethically justified solutions targets the poor. If public service sincerely values social equity, why should poor neighborhoods, or poor countries for that matter, get the solutions to society's problems (prisons, nuclear waste dumps, and so on)? Because they are poor? Weak? What level of economic distress transforms compensation into coercion? An opposing sentiment clarifies this line of argument. If the value of efficiency prevails in tax policy and assuming the diminishing marginal utility of money, do we really have an *ethical* rationale for taxing the rich?

The second problem is a problem only if one objects to a results-based, somewhat utilitarian view that condones, although under constrained circumstances, the involuntary sacrifice of individuals, their interests, or values to some "greater" good. This is, of course, a problem with all collective action that parcels out costs and benefits to different members and in different degree. A primitive duty-based critique may protest that the trade-off means "using" another person, and any price for human dignity is ethically intolerable. This kind of moral absolutism freezes government and public agencies into immobility.

Amplifying Standard Analysis

Stakeholder analysis is a powerful analytic tool. With appropriate research and inclusive participation, authentic empathy replaces patronizing paternalism or self-interested projection. It can be an effective counterbalance to elitist planning and arrogant policy-making that imperiously assign pros and cons and define the public interest expertly but autonomously. Duty-based reasoning can use stakeholder analysis as a net to capture the affected principles and values. Results-based thinking can use it to tally and trade off the effects of decision (or indecision).

   Stakeholder analysis is also a powerful decision-making tool. Thomas C. Schelling (1981, p. 37) explains (although not speaking of stakeholder analysis itself) how hard decision making is. "I have often been glad that I wasn't in charge. It is easy enough to see plainly that there is too much inequality (or illiteracy, or ill health, or injustice) and to help to reduce it, knowing that despite all efforts too much will remain. But if it were up to me to decide *how much* inequality is not much, or how much injustice, or how much disregard for the elderly or for future generations, I'd need more than a sense of direction." The tool even has been incorporated into the Cummins Engine Company's corporate training program (Nelson, 1990).

Cost-Benefit Analysis. Probing devices such as stakeholder analysis correct for some analytic distortions and omissions in cost-benefit analysis and other techniques by adding ethical dimensions of action, inaction, and delay. (The case at the end of this chapter demonstrates the potential for doing so.) Originally applied to public works by the U.S. Army Corps of Engineers in the pioneering days of American public administration, cost-benefit analysis now is relatively refined but still ethically lopsided. The technique garnered new clout in the deregulatory push of the 1980s. In 1981, President Reagan issued Executive Order 12291 (46 CFR 13,193), according to which major rules proposed by executive agencies are required to undergo cost-benefit scrutiny.

   Public policy analysis and regulatory review routinely use cost-benefit analysis to examine decisions in which lives, health, safety, and quality of life are expressed in dollars. One issue is the "elastic nature" of the value put on human life that ranges among different federal agencies from $1 to $3.5 million (Scanlan, 1990, p. A7). Analytic limitations are exposed in regulations governing environmental impact statements (40 CFR 1502.23), which dictate that "when a cost-benefit analysis is prepared, discuss the relationship between that analysis and any analyses of unquantified environmental impacts, values, and amenities. For purposes of complying with the [National Environmental Policy] Act, the weighing of the merits and drawbacks of the various alternatives need not be displayed in a monetary cost-benefit analysis and should not be when there are important qualitative considerations. . . . [A]n environmental impact statement should at least indicate those considerations, including factors not related to environmental quality, which are likely to be relevant and important to a decision."

Environmental Stakes. Stakeholder analysis can also assist decision makers in working through controversial problems such as hazardous waste cleanup. In testimony before a Senate committee, an administrator in the Environmental Protection Agency said, "The [Superfund] program can pursue either complete cleanup at some sites or incremental cleanup at many sites. It cannot fully accommodate both goals simultaneously" (Congressional Budget Office, 1990, p. xxviii). The two critical issues Congress faces are developing comparative assessments "so as to provide the greatest benefit to the public welfare" (Congressional Budget Office, 1990, p. 49) and establishing environmental priorities on contamination. A study by the Congressional Budget Office (1990, p. 50) concludes, "The complexity and controversy of these risks to human health and the environment increase the need for a better system to evaluate potential costs and benefits of federal hazardous waste programs." This is a tall order, but stakeholder analysis and ethical analysis in general promise some help.

The tie between environmental concerns and ethics is in admitting future generations into the calculus as external, indirect stakeholders. Where environmental degradation is concerned, future generations are both highly dependent and highly vulnerable. Corroborating that tie, the vice chairman of Corning Incorporated said at a conference on business ethics, "I think that in this day and age, every responsible person in business or elsewhere had better be or become something of an ethicist or an environmentalist" (Campbell, 1989, p. 20). The case at the end of this chapter inspects that tie.

The Personal Stake

Public managers do not need stakeholder analysis to tell them that *they* are affected parties, too. Integrity, reputation, financial security, and career prospects dictate a genuine and legitimate concern for oneself. In his influential *Inside Bureaucracy*, Anthony Downs (1967, p. 53) argues that "every official acts at least partly in his own self-interest, and some officials are motivated solely by their own self-interest." While personal cares are not permitted to usurp public interest or disable impartiality, ignoring them altogether may undermine analytic integrity and ultimately impede follow-through. Unless altruism is the standard in all things and all cases, a manager can better identify and separate out personal stakes by considering them than by ignoring them. Stakeholder analysis permits a manager to own up to self-interest and personal costs. It clarifies general issues, undercuts hypocrisy and self-deceit, and avoids later paralysis or regrets.

Personal Qualms. Sometimes an ethical manager is the object of unethical behavior, sometimes a witness to it, or occasionally even an active party (however unwilling or accidental) in it. The manager then is in the uncomfortable position of either tolerating unethical conduct by himself or herself or by others or doing something about it. Here we revisit the pragmatic themes raised at the beginning of this book: What counts? What is at stake? How can managers ensure both professional success and ethical survival?

Here, again, the individual and the setting interact. Innumerable examples of heroism and steadfast resistance to injustice remind us that even passive acceptance or inaction is a choice, although not necessarily an ethically neutral one. Of course, they remind us as well of the personal risk and potential cost. Assuming that we work without blinders on, the choice is among eight generic options:

Denial	Notifying supervisor
Hypocrisy	Working for change
Sabotage	Whistle-blowing
Disqualification	Resignation

The fact is, none of the options is fully satisfactory for figuring out which way to turn.

Filtering Offenses. Denial, probably used as often as any other single option, is self-deceit. It works nicely for petty conveniences and immaterial human error— we forget that he put that pen in his pocket. The idea that ethical offense is a matter of degree, of gradations, is the point of the exercise given in Exhibit 7.2. Managers routinely sort misdeeds by discounting for imputed motive, intent, impact, and widespread agreement (in the agency or community) about wrongdoing and other factors. *Selectivity*— choosing your battles in a principled way— *does not change the ethics of the violation but does affect the response* (reaction, remedy, penalty).

Where do you draw the line? Judith N. Shklar (1984, p. 8) observes, "Most of us may intuitively agree about right and wrong, but we also, and far more significantly, differ enormously in the ways in which we rank the virtues and the vices." What is the difference between pocketing a pen and taking home a PC? The dollar value? Only in part; the smaller infractions have a huge aggregate impact. Similarly, is the *number* of pages duplicated on the office machine the issue, or is the principle of personal use of public property the issue? Are impacts measured as one-shot, cumulative, or aggregate, and does the result affect a manager's response?

Reasonable selectivity runs the risk of appearing to be arbitrary enforcement of standards or biased treatment of individuals. Problems arise precisely because it is so hard to specify decision-making criteria in advance. Yet, these criteria are important precisely when the manager is picking and choosing.

To think that everyone makes mistakes or has a price does not entail

Exhibit 7.2. Choosing Your Battles.

Here is a list of seventeen practices. What do *you* believe?

1 = very unethical   2 = basically unethical
3 = somewhat unethical   4 = not particularly unethical
                    5 = not at all unethical

How unethical do you consider these . . . practices?	Rating
1. Using agency services for personal use.	_____
2. Padding an expense account up to 10 percent.	_____
3. Giving gifts/favors in exchange for preferential treatment.	_____
4. Taking longer than necessary to do a job.	_____
5. Divulging confidential information.	_____
6. Doing personal business on work time.	_____
7. Concealing one's errors.	_____
8. Passing blame for errors to an innocent co-worker.	_____
9. Claiming credit for someone else's work.	_____
10. Falsifying time/quality/quantity reports.	_____
11. Padding an expense account more than 10 percent.	_____
12. Calling in sick to take a day off.	_____
13. Authorizing a subordinate to violate agency rule.	_____
14. Pilfering agency materials and supplies.	_____
15. Accepting gifts/favors in exchange for preferential treatment.	_____
16. Taking extra personal time, late arrivals, longer lunch hours and breaks, early departures.	_____
17. Not reporting others' violations of policies/rules.	_____

Observations

From studies of business managers: "If you rated every item the same, you are truly unusual. . . . Managers perceive degrees of ethicality . . . seeing some things as *more* or *less* unethical than others."
–Do public managers also see practices as a matter of degree?
"Don't ask what the *correct* responses are." No practice is accepted or rejected universally by the business managers. Yet, there are norms: items 8, 5, 10, 9, 11, and 14 were rated most unethical (in descending order).
–Do you agree with this assessment?
–What practices would you, your boss, and your subordinates add to this list?
–Delete from this list?
Item 8 is rated most unethical by business managers.
–In your opinion, would most public managers agree with this choice? Why?
–What ethical action guides does this practice disable?
–Use Chapter Six's tools to analyze item 8.

Now repeat the exercise, asking several questions.

What do your peers believe?
What do you think top agency management believes?
What about agency clients? Would they agree?
How frequently do you think your fellow managers follow this or that practice? How frequently do you?

A serious mismatch between your views and those you attribute to your boss, peers, and clients serves as an early warning sign of troubles to come.

equating all offenses. A working proposition is that *the more* un*ethical we judge a behavior, the less likely we are to practice it or tolerate others' doing it.* For example, many people would agree that endangering a child's life is far more offensive than lining one's pocket. The problem is that seeing ethical offense as a matter of degree may carry a high emotional price tag when trivialities descend into transgressions.

One risk is that by looking the other way too much and too long, we end up teetering precariously on that infamous slippery slope, the gradual numbing of ethical discrimination. Watergate figure Jeb Stuart Magruder described his slide down that slope, along which ethical judgment about right and wrong is lost. In his words, "It's a question of slippage. I sort of slipped right into it. Each act you take leads you to the next act, and eventually you end up with a Watergate" (quoted in Terkel, 1973, p. 15).

Magruder was not the only one to have lost a sense of right and wrong. At hearings in 1973, Senator Herman Talmadge asked John Ehrlichman, a senior White House aide, "If the president could authorize a covert break-in, you don't know exactly where that power would be limited. You don't think it could include murder or other crimes beyond covert break-ins, do you?" Ehrlichman replied, "I don't know where the line is, Senator" (quoted in Moyers, 1988, p. 94).

"No man ever became extremely wicked all at once," wrote Juvenal in the second century. Thomas Paine, the Revolutionary War pamphleteer, observed, "A long habit of not thinking a thing wrong gives it the superficial appearance of being right." At some indeterminate point unknowable in advance, we can lose altogether the capacity to make moral judgments. Or act upon them.

Bending the Rules. When managerial discretion, selectively choosing one's battles, and maintaining ethical integrity interact, bending the rules may seem like a good idea. A district chief with the Internal Revenue Service (IRS) contends that most managers have no systematic technique. In an IRS publication, Edward J. Roberts (1990) says,

> Every time I interview an individual for a managerial position, I ask the question, "Do you bend the rules?" My intent is to determine if the applicant realizes that he/she will have to interpret regulations, evaluate situations and make decisions regarding complex issues; that there is no answer book for the ongoing "tests" and challenges that managers face everyday. Most applicants understand and articulate this principle. Some individuals realize that the issue of integrity defines the difference between bending and breaking the rules while others simply contend that they recognize a "bend the rules" situation when "they see it." When I probe further, I find that most managers and would-be managers have no pre-established criteria or "game plan" to test whether bending the rules is appro-

priate. Instead, a vague generic concept of what is good is used to decide if and how the rules are to be bent.

Roberts goes on to note, "Bending the rules, in and of itself, is not good. We walk the line when we bend rules. We must be sure-footed in our approach and balanced in our views. We must also be disciplined, testing each situation and each proposed decision."

Using implicit stakeholder analysis, ethical integrity, and the principle of public scrutiny, Roberts proposes questions about what a manager wants to do. Is it good for the agency, taxpayers, and agency employees? Does it support integrity? Does it stand up to publicity? "If I owned this agency, would I do this?" For Roberts, *yes* answers mean following Admiral Farragut's order: "Damn the Torpedoes, Full Speed Ahead." A *no* answer elicits reassessment.

Some public managers may retort that Roberts's last question misses the point of public service. Some may object that discretion in enforcing the tax code opens the door to favoritism or political harassment—not entirely unknown in the agency's history (Burnham, 1990). Because the agency's power and employees' discretion are indisputable realities and given the agency's reach into personal pockets and across the entire economy, ethical judgment and action in the IRS warrant special care. Recall Chief Justice John Marshall's point in *McCulloch* v. *Maryland* (1819): "The power to tax is the power to destroy."

Deception. Michael Walzer argues on behalf of accepting necessary lapses for public purposes as part of the job. "Here is the moral politician: it is by his dirty hands that we know him. If he were a moral man and nothing else, his hands would not be dirty; if he were a politician and nothing else, he would pretend they were clean" (1973, p. 168). Walzer's words apply to politicians, but his reasoning extends to public managers. (For counterviews on deception, see Sissela Bok's *Lying*, 1978.) This kind of reasoning is used to justify sting and covert operations as authorized forms of lying and deception.

A second option, hypocrisy, is denial on a public level. It is designed to deceive. It has been degraded lately into a slur against opponents. Pretense, often justified by loyalty to clients or colleagues, induces cover-ups as, for example, in Watergate or the "blue code of silence" in some police departments. By definition, hypocrisy is terminal for ethical integrity. In the seventeenth century, La Rochefoucauld said, "Hypocrisy is the tribute which vice pays to virtue."

Sabotage is also a public lie but one often undertaken in the name of ethical principle. It is contrary, however, to ethical values such as truth telling and loyalty and to administrative principles such as legal compliance and accountability. The contradictions are so intense that behind sabotage there often is a disgruntled employee indulging in personal retaliation.

Going Through Channels. Disqualification (or recusal, in formal terminology) lets a biased decision maker off the hook by keeping the job *and* the interest that presents a conflict. Blind trusts and negotiated agreements are other forms of excusing oneself, but from the other end of the conflict. Requiring procedures for recognition, disclosure, and substitution, disqualification is essential—unless public service recruits automatons unconnected to family or community.

From experience as an elected official in a small town, this author knows that in small, stable communities or company towns, where everyone is acquainted or connected to an interest, sidestepping conflict through strict disqualification criteria means that nothing could ever get done and government decision making would be crippled. Interwoven relationships may also arise in large jurisdictions. In the spring of 1990, New York City Mayor David Dinkins and the city council's president were barred from voting on franchise renewals for cable television because their relatives own stock in companies affiliated in other ventures with the media conglomerate that owns interest in the cable companies. When the network of ties, friendship, institutional and individual contribution, stock ownership, and relatives threatened to stymie the appointment of a conflict-free substitute, a newspaper headline read, "When Life Itself Is a Conflict of Interest" (Purdum, 1990, p. E8).

From the outside, it is hard to differentiate the option of working for change within the organization from self-serving compromise. It also may be hard from the inside. Jeb Stuart Magruder pointed out that the hired hand or aide tends to go along. "It's very difficult to set your own standard and continue in the power structure. I always felt I could do more by staying in the system. Maybe that's just the way of satisfying my conscience" (quoted in Terkel, 1973, p. 15). This may be just the time to hold up a mirror and review Chapter Five's reasons why ethical arguments are so difficult to assess accurately.

It also may be the time to think of the story of General Harold K. Johnson, the Vietnam-era army chief of staff. As a Japanese prisoner and survivor of the Bataan Death March in World War II and a commander during the Korean War, General Johnson's physical courage could hardly be disputed. Colonel Harry G. Summers, Jr. (1989, p. xviii), tells how, during the Vietnam War, Johnson went to tell the president that "the United States had no strategy worth the name in Vietnam, that all the principles of war were being violated, and that American soldiers were being killed needlessly. On the way there, however, he thought better of it and convinced himself that he could do more by staying on than he could by resigning. 'And now,' he said, 'I will go to my death with that lapse in moral courage.'" Formerly holding a chair in military research at the Army War College, retired colonel and journalist Summers (p. xvii) concludes, "Everyone knows that taking a moral and ethical stand may have disastrous consequences for one's career ambitions. But General Johnson's comments are testimony that the consequences of not taking such a stand may be far worse."

Going to one's supervisor, another option, also presents problems. Although it is true that federal and many state and local standards obligate disclosure of fraud, waste, or abuse, it is also true that these rules run counter to our indoctrination as team players, starting with Little League, 4-H, and scouting.

Sometimes disclosure is even called *ratting*, a term no more complimentary than *snitch*. A humane and human manager, making allowances for trifles and petty errors, lapses into denial on occasion. Nonetheless and despite personal discomfort, a public administrator has a responsibility to the agency and the public that preempts individual loyalty.

Blowing the Whistle. Blowing the whistle means going outside routine channels; it means making an end-run play by using special reporting channels (for example, ombudsman, hotline, inspector general) or even going to the media. James Bowman (1980, p. 18) uses Alan Campbell's definition: "a popular shorthand label for any disclosure of legal violations, mismanagement, a gross waste of funds, an abuse of authority, or a danger to public health and safety, whether the disclosure is made within or without the chain of command."

Whistle-blowing is *not* a casual choice. It is imperative that everyone—the organization and the individual—see whistle-blowing as a last resort. As the ranger's experience in the case that opens this book suggests, there is simply too much evidence of personal pain and retribution by peers or superiors in public agencies and corporate life for any other view of whistle-blowing. It is "one of the most threatening forms of organizational dissent" (Jos, Tompkins, and Hays, 1989, p. 552), and managers who elect this option are advised to prepare for criticism, ridicule, and ostracism.

Nevertheless, whistle-blowing is done. Inspectors general offices in the Department of the Interior and the Environmental Protection Agency report that most allegations of conflict-of-interest violations are received via agency hotlines (General Accounting Office, 1987, p. 7). Of course, there are formal protections in many jurisdictions; federal employees theoretically are protected against reprisals for making complaints to inspectors general offices. Many state and local employees are similarly protected. The other side of the coin is protecting the alleged wrongdoer against the unscrupulous or mistaken, who would damage a reputation and career anonymously and at low cost (and in contrast to civil disobedience).

Sometimes the protections work. Yet personal costs, factual disputes, impugned motives, and ruined careers are permanent fixtures. They are evident in a whistle-blowing case over Alaskan land claims from the Taft administration of eighty years ago, as recounted in an early casebook in public administration (Stein, 1952). Despite today's formal protections, recounted repercussions belie an automatic victory for truth and justice. To this add the anguish over self-image and identity when a loyal team player with strong institutional ties breaks ranks—with no guarantee of effectiveness.

Because of the risk potential for the organization and individual on many levels, the whistle-blowing option demands rigorous procedural protections for complainant *and* accused. Otherwise, whistle-blowing is subject to abuse in personal vendetta, partisan conflict, or policy dispute and looms as an administrative scourge.

All in all, whistle-blowing is suitable only after verification of facts, soul-searching, and administrative channels are exhausted. Before reaching for the whistle, managers are advised to answer these six questions:

1. Is the violation serious enough to warrant the risk to the manager and the organization?
2. Are you prepared for this action to become known, for heroism to mutate into betrayal?
3. Are you sure of your facts? Are you sure you are right?
4. Are you sure that superiors are not trying to correct the situation?
5. Is your motive purely in the public interest?
6. Are you ready to accept the consequences if you are wrong?

Six affirmative answers, and ethical managers do the right thing.

On the other hand, are you ready to accept the consequences if you are right but fail to act? The adage "The only thing necessary for the triumph of evil is for good men [and women] to do nothing" synopsizes the results of everyone's silence. Taking action means taking responsibility and showing courage.

Resignation. When personal integrity is, in fact, compromised—and each manager must make this decision personally—the resignation option separates public service from forced servitude. Highly publicized resignations in the Department of Justice under Attorney General Edwin Meese verify its use. But before making a rash decision, later regretted, a manager can secure time for deliberation by submitting privately to a self-audit. Redraw the maps in Figure 1.2 and verify the mismatch between acceptable and actual diamond shapes. If the distortion is intolerable and/or unalterable from your office, do what you have to do. An *ethical career professional* puts the emphasis on the first and third words. There is a quiet heroism in that.

Case: The Highway Project

The following case is reprinted by permission of The Dreiford Group, copyright 1989. It was presented at Ethics in Government: An Intricate Web, conference sponsored by the American Society for Public Administration, Washington, D.C., Nov. 12–15, 1989.

> As director of his state's Department of Transportation, Alan Sykes was accustomed to making difficult and often controversial decisions. However, the situation in which he was currently involved seemed to him to be more troublesome than most.
>
> A proposal had been advanced to develop a major highway system through a currently "underdeveloped" area of the state. The governor was fully behind this proposal, and had stated his belief

that undertaking the highway project at this time would be advantageous for a number of reasons.

Alan remembered a recent staff meeting at which the governor had explained his position on the highway proposal. "Everyone knows that business and industry are on the verge of expanding into the Clark County area," the governor had pointed out. "That means that eventually we're going to have to build this road system anyhow. We can do it more cheaply if we do it now, and can also, in some measure, control the direction of development."

One staff member had questioned the governor's assumptions. "Really, sir, expansion into the Clark County area is only speculation at this point. There are other areas of the state which are equally likely, perhaps even more likely targets for development."

"Well, expansion into Clark is going to be that much more attractive if this project is begun," the governor had answered. "And while I'm certainly concerned with the interests of all parts of this state, I'm sure that you're all aware that I have always had a special commitment to the welfare of the Clark area."

Since the governor had begun his political career many years previously as a state representative from Clark County, Alan was well acquainted with his "special commitment" to that area. On the other hand, Alan also knew that the governor was an eminently fair man. Despite his love for Clark County, the governor would never support any project there that either was unneeded or would divert resources that could better be used elsewhere.

Alan's department immediately contracted for a cost-benefit study on the proposed road system. That study was part of what was currently troubling him. The problem was not that the study clearly failed to support the governor's position; it was that the conclusions that could be reached from the study were much more ambiguous than Alan had hoped.

If certain figures were used to project the growth of the Clark County area, then it seemed highly likely that the highway project would be beneficial. On the other hand, if other, possibly equally valid, figures were used, the highway project would be shown to be unnecessary and probably damaging to the state's economy. Selecting which set of figures to use meant choosing a prediction of the future—a shaky task at best.

One vision of the future suggested that because of tax advantages, an available labor pool, and the attraction of a rural area that was relatively near the state's population centers, Clark County would be likely to grow greatly during the next decade. Other visions of the future showed that there were two other areas of the state that had all the attractions that Clark did, as well as additional advantages—nearness to a source of hydroelectric power in one case; a larger labor pool and a marginally better location in the other. What seemed most likely to Alan was that building the highway in Clark County might be the catalyst to its development. However, Alan wasn't totally convinced that development in other areas of the state might not benefit more people than would development in Clark.

Alan also remembered the first day his wife had heard about the project. "Why, how clever of you, Alan," she teased. "You did this all to be able to wash your hands of my brother Bill, didn't you?"

Alan hadn't even thought of Brother Bill until that point, but he realized that Bill, the owner of a faltering construction company near Clark County, could not help but profit if the highway proposal were accepted. Whether Bill won a contract to help construct the road itself, or whether he worked on the construction that would be part of the area's business development, Bill would at last be out of Alan's pocket. He might, although it seemed unlikely, even pay back some of those "small loans" from Alan that had kept him afloat over the past years.

On the other hand, Alan was aware that he would have to be careful to ensure that he did nothing that would even appear to be unfairly advantageous to his brother-in-law.

There was yet another aspect of the situation that troubled Alan. Environmental groups who had learned of the road proposal were strongly opposed to it. Much of Clark County was forested, and the environmentalists were concerned about the fate of those forests if the highway project went through. Also, two of the most pristine rivers in the state ran through the area, and the environmentalists believed that not even the most stringent of industrial controls could preserve the rivers' condition if development occurred.

Alan himself had a strong environmentalist bent, and he personally felt that keeping Clark County green as long as possible was an admirable goal. Moreover, he had been in contact with many people from Clark County who had moved there, or whose families had lived there for generations, precisely because of the county's unspoiled nature. These people, as well as many of the farmers in the area, were adamantly opposed to the road project.

On the other hand, Clark County was a generally low-income area, and there were at least as many people whose primary concern was feeding their families as there were those who were dedicated to preserving the ambiance of their surroundings.

Alan's dilemma, then, was how to structure the report he was to present on the highway project. His personal inclination was to make use of those figures favoring other areas over Clark for expansion. But, as an appointee of the governor, Alan felt strongly that he should support the governor's positions whenever possible. Quite conceivably, not to do so could affect Alan's personal future. And it was not really that difficult for Alan to make a case, both to himself and to others, that would demonstrate that Clark County should get this highway system.

What are some of the ethical issues that Alan faces in this situation?

If you were Alan, what would you do to resolve this situation?

Alan is a political appointee. Would the way in which you chose to resolve this issue differ if Alan were a career civil servant?

Assume Alan's position. What resolution do you recommend? Try using the stakeholder diagnostic (Exhibit 7.1) and decision-making checklist (Exhibit 6.1) to clarify the ethical dimensions of the problem(s). How do they aid resolution?

What are the hidden analytic premises with ethical implications in Alan's cost-benefit study?
- Is objective information neutral?

Does Alan have a conflict of interest, or is this a red herring?
- Is it too early in the process for this to matter?
- Is the link or effect too tenuous?

What internal and external stakeholders are involved? What ethical values?

Can state statutes and regulatory protections adequately address the environmental stake?

What ethical issues arise when economically developing regions in the state want to preserve Clark County's natural amenities? In some developing countries, some business interests and farmers object to preserving the rain forest or animal reserves.
- Is compensation or relief obligatory?
- If so, by whom? To whom?

Is government ethically obligated to protect the environment? Consider the public interest, extended time frame in decision making, future generations, and whether irreparable, severe injury with no possible relief (using current technology, not conjecture) should trigger obligatory action.

Should ethics be a part of government and business working together to address environmental issues? Explain.

Part Three

Ethics and
the Agency

Chapter 8

Designing and Implementing Codes

Part Three moves from the individual to the workaday organizational level and examines ethics in the agency. This chapter compares governmental codes and model statutes by type, function, and provisions; it provides a benchmark for current practices, a forecast of likely developments, and adaptable innovations. Highlighted provisions run from the typical to the exceptional and include conflict of interest, financial disclosure, appearance of impropriety, post-employment curbs, and blanket coverage. After recommending guidelines for developing a viable code and then managing it effectively, the chapter ends with a case study on the guidance offered by standards of conduct.

Since Hammurabi, Moses, and Hippocrates, we have operated on the theory that it is easier to do the right thing when we know what that is. As a result, codified standards of conduct have become a popular vehicle for clarifying minimum expectations about acceptable behavior. Codes are now being adopted, refined, or strengthened in jurisdictions all over the country.

All the dialogue over the years has produced prototypical arguments for and against codes. Implemented codes are coercive and spawn more red tape; they reduce managers' maneuverability and restrict practical options. An unenforced code's symbolism is a weak message, just a piece of paper scribbled over with platitudes. Codes alter the course from aspiration to asphyxiation, from ethics to obedience, and substitute rules for reasoning. But must we rely on mysteries, guiding behavior by unspoken, axiomatic norms?

The controversy spawns three generic choices. We can adopt intricate rules with interpretations, advisory opinions, and complex enforcement mechanisms and protections. Alternatively, we can elect blanket prohibitions that are simple to understand and apply but inflexible and difficult to live with. Or we can select no explicit rules, no categorical prohibitions, no articulated standards. Increasingly choosing the first option, many governments today seem to respond to the questions, "If not cure-alls, then what good are codes? What can they do" with a simple answer. Ethics codes do *less* than everything and *more* than nothing.

Proposing the first codification of federal conflict-of-interest statutes, President Kennedy outlined the pros and cons of ethics codes in his message to Congress on April 27, 1961.

> The ultimate answer to ethical problems in government is honest people in a good ethical environment. No web of statute or regulation, however intricately conceived, can hope to deal with the myriad possible challenges to a man's integrity or his devotion to the public interest.
>
> Nevertheless formal regulation is required—regulation which can lay down clear guidelines of policy, punish venality and double-dealing, and set a general ethical tone for the conduct of public business. . . .
>
> Criminal statutes and presidential orders, no matter how carefully conceived or meticulously drafted, cannot hope to deal effectively with every problem of ethical behavior or conflict of interest. Problems arise in infinite variation. They often involve subtle and difficult judgements. . . . And even the best of statutes or regulations will fail of their purpose if they are not vigorously and wisely administered.

Experience in federal, state, and local governments has proven him correct on every count.

A few current samples illustrate the potential, complexity, loopholes, and even perverse outcomes from writing and implementing standards of conduct. They also illustrate the variability in standards among the more than 80,000 government units in the United States. *Formal standards, legal sanctions, public expectations, and acceptable administrative behavior vary significantly across the country.*

- Although an investigation into advance knowledge was inconclusive, a police chief in Buffalo, New York, was found in violation of ethics standards when he purchased a house in an urban renewal district two days after the renewal plan was announced. His daughter had worked on the city's renewal plan (Potamianos, 1990).
- Private interest in official action reared its head in Ohio in 1989. A bill was introduced into Ohio's state legislature to provide that "the relationship of a public official or employee, or of his family members, to a church or other religious organization solely as a member, participant, worshiper, or volunteer shall not be considered as manifesting a substantial and improper influence on him with respect to his duties or as otherwise constituting a conflict of interest." This bill was a response to an ethics commission's opinion

advising four city officials including the mayor that the ethics law prohibited them from participating in decisions about property held by a church of which they were members (Judd, 1989, pp. 25–26).

- California's Fair Political Practices Commission's summary of enforcement decisions and its bulletin (FPPC) cites individuals by name, affiliation, violation, and sanction. Some other commissions summarize and sanitize reports of rendered opinions.

- Chicago's Board of Ethics (City of Chicago, 1988, pp. 60, 99) limited spousal interest by taking the view that "[a] city employee who negotiates an agreement for the city with a corporation represented by the law firm where the employee's wife is a lawyer [but not directly participating] does not by virtue of his wife's employment have an economic or financial interest in the negotiations." Another finding: sisters-in-law are not covered by the nepotism restrictions in the ethics ordinance.

- A 1986 letter to a federal employee from the U.S. Office of Government Ethics (1990b, pp. 643–646) advises, "To avoid adverse appearances, we think you should consider imposing limitations on the use of the (agency's) gift acceptance authority. Under [statutory] gift acceptance authority, the agency, rather than the employee, accepts the payment. As a result, the adverse appearances . . . are not necessarily present. . . . Even so, we generally suggest that agencies avoid accepting reimbursements from organizations that do business with or are regulated by the agency." The letter goes on to distinguish appearance by nonprofit versus for-profit status of the gift-giving entity. For nonprofits, "the appearance problem is not substantial since the entity is not in a position to profit as a result."

Given the variability, why bother with what is going on in other jurisdictions and professions, when keeping up-to-date locally is hard enough? One reason is that practices elsewhere provide a benchmark against which to compare current local practices—a way to take a sounding and gauge future direction. Learning from others' mistakes is more efficient than repeating them. Permutations among states and localities represent adaptable innovations in a domestic version of technology transfer.

One of the first steps in writing codes is scanning other jurisdictions for ideas about standards and procedures. In 1990, Alaska did it, and the year before, Los Angeles did it. The Council on Governmental Ethics Laws compiles a state-by-state catalogue annually. National public interest organizations are proposing model statutes, while professional associations, research institutes, and national consulting groups contribute to the interjurisdictional give-and-take.

Before moving inside government codes and processes, public managers may wish to glimpse them from *the other side*. What is serving on a commission like? University professor Sarah P. Morehouse recounts her experiences as chairperson of an ethics commission in a New England town (Lewis, 1986, p. 45): "Being on the commission means having to rack your brain for solutions to problems very, very real to the participants and the answers aren't easy . . . and both sides think they are so right. Here we are, sitting in judgment and the answers are painful to come by. This is an area of conflict and questions where everybody wins because of the nature of the questions raised and publicity surrounding them.

"Also, I think this is some the gutsiest stuff you can do."

Not everyone demonstrates this sensitivity. Figure 8.1 offers a different perspective that raises the specter of abusing ethics through, for example, militantly claiming moral superiority (see also the section on vigilante ethics in Chapter Five).

Code Objectives and Types

The eventual success or failure of a code and related enforcement processes depends on what one hopes to accomplish by adopting them. West Virginia's Governmental Ethics Act of 1989, Chapter 6B-1-2(b), is a model of restraint:

> It is the purpose of this chapter [new ethics law] to maintain confidence in the integrity and impartiality of the governmental process in the state of West Virginia and its political subdivisions and to aid public officials and public employees in the exercise of their official duties and employment; to define and establish minimum ethical standard for elected and appointed public officials and public employees; to eliminate actual conflicts of interest; to provide a means to define ethical standards; to provide a means of investigating and resolving ethical violations; and to provide administrative and criminal penalties for specific ethical violations herein found to be unlawful.

Figure 8.1. Formal Rules and Procedures Raise the Specter of Abuse.

By permission of Johnny Hart and Creators Syndicate, Inc.

Codes are best associated with three general but realistic objectives: to encourage high standards of behavior, to increase public confidence, and to assist decision making (Zimmerman, 1976). Different objectives lead to different models. Legislated codes provide legal penalties and protections as necessary and effective constraints on official power, public authority, and the potential for abuse of administrative discretion. Administrative standards and procedures assist decision making and managers by providing an operational framework tied to workaday realities. "Managers need to know what is regarded as acceptable and what is not. . . . Can an organization afford to have its members trying to guess what its standards are?" (Bowman, 1981, p. 61).

A *credo*—for example, the Athenian oath, the federal Code of Ethics for Government Service, or ASPA's so-called code—is aspirational and inspirational, more a positive statement and pledge of commitment, more a list of do's than don'ts. A combined approach encompasses sanctioned aspirations (should), minimum standards (shall), and prohibitions (shall not). The American Bar Association's Model Code of Professional Responsibility is a composite, with three parts: canons, stating the norms or general standards; ethical considerations, stating aspirational principles; and disciplinary rules, which are mandatory minimum rules of conduct.

A productive starting point is realistic managerial objectives: *the internal, direct clients are the ethical managers and employees; the purpose is to assist them* in ethical behavior and decision making. This is West Virginia's message, quoted above. Codes do *not* improve the moral climate in the true meaning of the phrase, despite sincere wishes and wrongly placed bets. One state-local report states that the code, disclosure, commission, and penalties "will improve the moral climate and contribute to the prevention of corruption in government in the future" (quoted in Common Cause, 1989b, p. 6). This is unfortunate because it is unrealistic, and reality is bound to come up short. Agency codes may alter behavior via coercion, by outlawing a range of behaviors, but they target only enforceable, minimal taboos. Ethics codes do *not* prevent conflicts of interest—these are inherent in public service. If duly enforced, codes give guidance on avoiding some transgressions, working out some problems, and detecting violators.

No code will turn willful crooks into law-abiding public servants. There is no empirical evidence to support an ethics deterrence theory; down that road lies futility. In regard to overhauling the Senate's code, Senator Adlai Stevenson of Illinois remarked, "If there are culprits in our midst, they are unlikely to be deterred by ethics codes" (U.S. Senate, 1980, p. 137). In its report, *To Serve with Honor*, a presidential commission studying ethics law reform more recently observed, "Laws and rules can never be fully descriptive of what an ethical person should do. They can simply establish minimal standards of conduct. Possible variations in conduct are infinite, virtually impossible to describe and proscribe by statute. Compulsion by law is the most expensive way to make people behave" (President's Commission on Federal Ethics Law Reform, 1989, p. 1). At the local level, S. Stanley Kruetzer (who drafted a code for New York City and was chief counsel of a New York State legislative ethics commission) "recounts how, when he wrote to 100 mayors about ethics codes, they responded along the lines of 'we know in our hearts what right and wrong is and no code will prevent someone from the wrong'" (Lewis, 1986, p. 14).

A managerial and manageable code builds on five critical elements: a reasonable objective; affirmative values that guide action; a coherent set of understandable standards, including do's and don'ts; a set of enforceable, meaningful sanctions; and procedural safeguards. Although particulars vary from jurisdiction to jurisdiction, a code's effectiveness turns on four general processes, listed here with sample mechanisms.

> Enforcement procedures: disclosure, impartial commission
> Protections for all concerned: grievance and appeal procedures, whistle-blower aids
> Meaningful sanctions and penalties: recusal, administrative intervention, noncriminal actions
> Implementation mechanisms in the agency: orientation, training, evaluation and outside dissemination, self-governance

Workable codes comply with three guidelines. First, they reduce rules and procedures to as few as necessary and as simple as possible to do the job. Second, they tailor operations to particular administrative realities. Third, they recall that the direct, internal clients of agency intervention are the ethical managers and employees. Commonly, components cover some or all of seven major categories:

1. Fundamental, understandable prohibitions (conflict of interest, abuse of office)
2. Financial disclosure
3. Appearance-of-impropriety standard
4. Impartial commission (with investigatory and advisory authority)
5. Supplementary restrictions (outside income, post-employment)
6. Criminal sanctions and administrative penalties
7. Procedural protections for complainant and employee

Codes are best written in the spirit of Alexander Hamilton's comment about the newly proposed Constitution: "I never expected a perfect document from imperfect men." At best, a code is a mechanism for communicating and enforcing minimal standards (at least conflict of interest) and headlining commitment to them. To convey standards, codes should be "simple and straightforward, and should focus on the affirmative values that must guide public servants in the exercise of their responsibilities" (Volcker Commission, 1989, p. 14).

Even the best code will not substitute for good government or good people. Sissela Bok (1978, p. 250) cautions that "codes must be but the starting point for a broad inquiry into the ethical quandaries at work."

Current Practices in the States

Most states now bar the use of public position for personal gain (see Exhibit 8.1) and have antibribery statutes on the books (Common Cause, 1989b, p. 16). However, only about a dozen states have "something comprehensive enough to be called a state code of ethics" (Weimer, 1990, p. 2).

Exhibit 8.1. Majority Practices in the States.

The information presented here comes from data in the Council on Governmental Ethics Laws 1990 report. Because of reporting failures, the figures represent *minimum counts*. Ethics, elections, campaign finance, and lobbying oversight authorities are included.

	Minimum No. of States
Designated board, commission, or office with legal authority in the area of ethics	36
Jurisdiction over appointed officials *and* state employees	30
Own investigatory authority	33
At least one ethics body authorized to issue advisory opinions or interpretations	36
Opinions rendered are always public	33
Some type of financial disclosure by senior state appointees*	29
Restrained Activities as of January 1, 1990 (by state constitution, case law, statute, executive order, administrative action, or union contract):	
Using public position for personal benefit	35
Providing benefits to influence official actions	34
Using confidential government information	28
Receiving gifts by officials or employees	33
Representing private clients before public bodies	27
Competitive bidding†	25
Receiving fees or honoraria	28
Outside employment or business activities	27
Post-employment restrictions	23

*Only thirteen states require personal disclosure from all state employees earning over a specified income, and twenty-two states require personal disclosure from volunteer members of state boards and commissions. When elected officials are included, thirty-six states require financial disclosure.

†This is included among majority practices because of the likelihood that the count is higher. Note that the 1986–1987 report (with more extensive reporting) showed competitive bidding as a restrained activity in thirty-six states.

Diversity best describes the overall pattern of state ethics laws and practices. (Variability and experimentation in public service ethics are good examples of the results of federalism.) Competence, jurisdiction, organization, and specific prohibitions vary from state to state.

Data from the Council on Governmental Ethics Laws' *Blue Books* (1990) and a study from Alaska's legislative staff (Weimer, 1990) reveal only a few standard practices. A majority of states (thirty-six) do have a designated board, commission, or office with legal authority in the area of ethics. (Common Cause, 1989b, p. 18, identified thirty-two independent state ethics commissions in 1989.) Of these, thirty have jurisdiction over appointed officials *and* state employees. Although the Council on Governmental Ethics Laws (COGEL), the National Municipal League, and Common Cause call for a commission's jurisdiction to extend to elected or appointed officials *and* employees in *all* government branches, actual practices vary among the states. Practices associated with a majority of the states are shown in Exhibit 8.1.

The scandal trigger is apparent from initiation dates. While only four state codes predate 1973, nineteen states adopted codes in response to Watergate between 1973 and 1979, and five between 1980 and 1988. That the pace of activity picked up more recently is hardly surprising given headlines across the country. According to a study by R. Roth Judd, the executive director of Wisconsin's ethics board, in 1989 alone codes went on the books in Arkansas, New York, and West Virginia; were proposed in Idaho and Vermont; and died in Georgia's senate judiciary committee. All told, there were more than five dozen legislative and judicial actions involving thirty-one states in 1989 (compiled from Judd, 1989, p. 36).

At least thirty-three of the thirty-six state ethics commissions are empowered to conduct investigations on their own volition (see Exhibit 8.1). States differ markedly in enforcement mechanisms and procedural protections, however. West Virginia's 1989 act, a comprehensive statewide ethics law, is the first state statute to provide for a special prosecutor.

In thirty-six states at least one ethics body is authorized to issue advisory opinions, declaratory rulings, or interpretive statements. This function allows for variability and adaptability and is vital if either code or administrative structure is complicated. A proactive protection for the ethical manager, before-the-fact advice helps the individual find a path through what can be a confusing labyrinth.

In practice, advice directly supports the code's core, the conflict-of-interest rules. Most requests to Connecticut's commission for advisory opinions between 1978 and 1983 involved possible conflict of interest by state employees (Lewis, 1986, p. 26). Similarly, much of the federal advisory assistance—7,000 telephone calls for advice—involves interpreting and applying conflict-of-interest statutes (U.S. Office of Government Ethics, 1990a, p. 7). During the ethics commission's first decade of operation in Massachusetts, the number of formal opinions issued declined substantially, to be replaced by informal staff letters and reviews of town counsels' opinions. The commission's report (Commonwealth of Massachusetts, 1988, p. 1) explains, "This shift reflects the fact that as precedents set by the formal opinions established more of the law's general guidelines, the ability to address individual situations through informal correspondence, often restating opinions previously addressed by the commission, increased."

Conflict of Interest. Designed to assure that the pubic interest is pursued by creating barriers to personal interest, the standard pertaining to conflict of interest is logically fundamental to codes at every level of government. Beyond this, little uniformity appears across jurisdictions (see Exhibit 8.1).

COGEL and the National Municipal League restrict conflict to the financial or economic. The league explains in the introduction to its 1979 model state law that "conflict of interest laws are concerned with financial conflicts which set apart an individual officeholder from most of the general public." California's 1974 Political Reform Act similarly narrows conflict to financial matters (Cowan Commission, 1989a, p. 147). "A public official has a conflict of interest when all of the following occur":

1. the official makes, participates in, or uses his or her official position to influence a governmental decision;
2. it is foreseeable that the decision will affect the official's economic interest;
3. the effect of the decision on the official's economic interest will be material;
4. the effect of the decision on the official's economic interest will be distinguishable from its effect on the public generally.

More expansive formulations extend conflict to "financial, social, and political relationships and transactions which may compromise or give the appearance of compromising their [public servants'] objectivity, independence or honesty" (Josephson Institute, 1990, p. vii).

Financial Disclosure. A conventional way of encouraging compliance with conflict-of-interest prohibitions is financial disclosure, "the 'linchpin' of government ethics laws" (Weimer, 1990, p. 2). Disclosure serves three purposes: (1) encouraging employees' attention to conflict prohibitions and potential, (2) using public scrutiny mechanisms for prevention and enforcement, and (3) letting action be taken and violations corrected. One state ethics commission's executive director noted, "filers are reminded of what their financial interests are and of the need to avoid affecting them by their official acts" (Lewis, 1986, p. 17).

While disclosure does symbolize a commitment to fundamental standards, its utility as an enforcement mechanism indicates that someone has to read, verify, investigate, and act on the reports. Common Cause (1989b, p. 40) argues that filing alone is "not enough. To be effective, financial disclosure must be public." Common Cause's position (p. 8) is clear-cut: "In short, public disclosure forces the law to be taken seriously."

With thirty-six states requiring some type of financial disclosure and federal service featuring two types, the many variations on the specifics come as no surprise. Laws in nineteen states require certain local officials to file, but executive orders issued on ethics in at least eighteen states over the years sometimes included a disclosure directive (Common Cause, 1989b, pp. 16–17). Sample forms, usually available from local and neighboring ethics agencies, provide provocative reading and are sometimes eye-openers for transition teams and new recruits.

Different administrative positions may have different disclosure requirements, keyed to salary and/or discretionary authority. For example, federal public disclosure is much more detailed than confidential reporting. In Pennsylvania, state, county, and local elected and appointed officials and public employees must file a disclosure with the state, while senior appointees in Philadelphia must file an additional disclosure to comply with a mayoral executive order. The Massachusetts State Ethics Commission reports that it reviewed approximately 45,000 disclosures between 1979 and 1988 and can boast of a 95 percent compliance rate. "What began as one of the commission's major activities has become a routine matter within the agency, and a basically accepted requirement of public life for those officials and employees who must file (Commonwealth of Massachusetts, 1988, p. 2). New York State's Ethics in Government Act of 1987 requires employees who earn less than about $53,000 or hold "non-policy-making" positions to submit a limited disclosure form.

Information subject to disclosure varies from specific dollar amounts to narrow or broad categories (Common Cause's recommendation). Coverage may extend to assets, income, financial transactions, liabilities such as personal and bank loans, gifts from nonfamily sources, and reimbursements for travel and other activities. Disclosure is usually limited to immediate family and dependents, and no state requires reporting beyond this traditional circle of personal relationships (Weimer, 1990, p. 10). Some jurisdictions such as Philadelphia allow nonreporting even for immediate family members. Definitions in model statutes from the National Municipal League, Common Cause, and COGEL are broader, to some extent allowing for mixed, blended, and unorthodox domestic arrangements.

There seems to be no strong empirical evidence that the prospect of financial disclosure has led people to avoid or resign from public service, but the allegation has been part of the discussion for some time (Neely, 1984). Careful crafting is needed to balance privacy and disclosure, burden and benefit. "Virtually all state courts have upheld the constitutionality of financial disclosure" (Weimer, 1990, p. 15).

Appearance of Impropriety. The standard regarding the appearance of impropriety is central to federal standards. The media often apply it irrespective of a jurisdiction's formal standards. Appearance is *not* a universally adopted and legally enforceable standard. COGEL's draft model statute adopts it, as do many professional codes, including the American Bar Association's well-known Canon 9. Common Cause's and the National Institute of Municipal Law Officers' codes do not. Among the cities in the municipal study described later in this chapter, Philadelphia, Chicago, and Buffalo expressly require avoiding the appearance of impropriety. Definitional lapses make a legally enforceable appearance standard problematic at best. Given the variations in legal provisions and state practices, the most definitive conclusion is that the jury is still out on appearance as an *enforceable* standard suitable for public service codes.

Revolving Door. The number of states with post-employment restrictions climbed to twenty-three by 1990 (Council of State Governments, 1990, pp. 144–145). What may soon become another standard practice among the states usually prohibits the lobbying of former agencies on matters in which the official or employee was personally and substantially involved. "Such restrictions must be defined narrowly so as not to discourage highly qualified professionals from entering government service, infringe on the constitutional rights of present state officials, or prevent the flow of communication and understanding between the public and private sector" (Weimer, 1990, p. 2). Other common provisions place permanent bans on disclosing privileged information.

Coming Attractions. In the evolutionary, adaptive system described above, today's innovation gives us a glimpse of tomorrow's standard practice. The ethics business is booming, and training adds a new element. With education pinpointed as "a key element to an effective ethics code," most states require commissions to publish reports or handbooks (Weimer, 1990, p. 6). Ethics education is mandatory for selected federal employees as of 1989, in California and in Los Angeles as of 1990, and proposed for Alaska in 1990. The 1989 report of the code-drafting commission for Los Angeles posited that "the central function of an ethics code is to prevent—rather than punish—unethical conduct. To achieve that goal, the commission believes an educational and training program must accompany the new code" and recommended mandatory training and ongoing education (Cowan Commission, 1989b, pp. 11–12).

A second development is the use of forward, multiyear, or protected funding in several jurisdictions to insulate the ethics commission from political pressure, executive or legislative retaliation, and budgetary vagaries. A third emerging practice is seeking and sometimes getting direct subpoena powers for ethics commissions. Yet a fourth area to watch in state code provisions is inclusive coverage of all jurisdictions and all branches of government statewide. Fifth, post-employment restrictions and treatment of part-time, contractual, and volunteer government officials and employees are volatile issues in which developments only hint at an emerging consensus.

There are whispers of other things to come. Consider the wisdom of shaping financial disclosure to contemporary life-styles and responsibilities associated with dual-career couples, blended families, adult guardianships, adult children living in a household, and life partners. The increase in number, status, and influence of legislative staff members in state governments suggests that extending or adopting code provisions may mark a future phase. In states such as Connecticut and Minnesota, the state code is a term and condition of employment by virtue of its incorporation into union contracts.

State agendas consistently overlook the way in which individual privacy conflicts with the public's right to know. In principle, this is a concern even if only the flawless or fearless participate. Examples of intrusion and confidentiality issues still in their embryonic stage include polygraph and integrity tests and medical and insurance records. If the goal is to recruit the best (not the perfect) people into public service, then working with the media, professional associations, public interest groups, and statutory safeguards could help protect administrators' privacy in some carefully selected realms such as medical records, health insurance claims, intimate family relations, and other matters traditionally private and functionally irrelevant to job performance.

Model statutes are visions of the future to the extent that they are influential. Common Cause was recently a key player in California, West Virginia, and Massachusetts. Core elements in its model statute for state government include prohibitions on abuse of office for personal gain and on conflicts of interest; standards of conduct to prevent and avoid abuse; personal financial disclosure for candidates and high-level officials; and a strong, independent commission with investigatory and civil enforcement powers. Its *A Model Ethics Law for State Government* (1989a) covers detailed disclosure, prohibitions against conflicts and procedures to avoid and prevent them, post-employment restrictions, a strong ethics commission, and investigatory procedures that assure due process.

Federal Offices and Standards

Conflict-of-interest prohibitions are central to federal standards of conduct. Ranging from affirmative ideals to unequivocal restrictions and on to the criminal code, these standards include the more positive, prescriptive Code of Ethics for Government Service (P.L. 96-303) enacted in 1980; detailed proscriptions administratively adopted by executive orders; plus regulations from the U.S. Office of Government Ethics and individual agencies; and criminal conflict-of-interest statutes in 18 U.S.C. 201-209.

Federal conflict-of-interest statutes date from the Civil War, but the principle can be traced formally to 1789 when an Act to Establish the Treasury Department (1 Stat. 12, 1789) created the very first domestic federal agency and prohibited conflict of interest (and promised a financial reward for whistle-blowers). Section 8 of the act states that "no person appointed to any office instituted by this act shall directly or indirectly be concerned or interested in carrying on the business of trade or commerce." The many federal statutes were first codified in 1962 and, except for post-employment provisions, have not been amended "substantially" since then (U.S. Office of Government Ethics, 1990b, p. 814). The general conflict-of-interest law is found in 18 U.S.C. Section 208. The Ethics Reform Act of November 30, 1989, revised this section by adding civil prosecution and injunctions to criminal prosecution.

Broader and more stringent standards have been adopted administratively. There are the executive orders (E.O.), including Lyndon Johnson's 11222 (1965) and George Bush's 12674 (1989) and 12731 (1990), with the latter adding limits on outside earned income. The U.S. Office of Government Ethics (OGE) promulgates implementing regulations. Jointly with the OGE, agencies issue supplementary rules and procedures. These reckon with agency particulars, including organic act limitations, statutory gift acceptance authority, and procurement, human subject research, or other functional specialities. E.O. 12731, Section 301(a), directs agency heads to augment the OGE regulations with "regulations of special applicability to the particular functions and activities of that agency."

According to a memorandum from the U.S. Office of Government Ethics (1990b, p. 814), "There is a significant difference in the range of conduct covered by these two sets of standards. Conduct covered by the criminal statutes is what Congress has determined is punitively inappropriate in public service. The regulatory standards of conduct for executive branch officials, which cover a larger range of conduct, reflect a presidential determination. . . . Such conduct does not rise to a level requiring use of criminal process."

U.S. Office of Government Ethics. The OGE was initially created in the federal Office of Personnel Management by the Ethics in Government Act of 1978, then given separate agency status when the act was amended a decade later. The 1988 reauthorization act defines the OGE's mission as "overall direction of executive branch policies relating to preventing conflicts of interest on the part of officers and employees of any executive agency." A small agency with a budget to match, the OGE is vulnerable as one of the relatively few discretionary components in the federal budget.

Since 1989, the executive order in force has required the OGE to promulgate regulations establishing a "single, comprehensive and clear set of executive branch standards of conduct." (E.O. 12674 specifies they be "objective, reasonable, and enforceable.") The seriousness of this charge is shown in the OGE's swift response; it published interim regulations in the *Federal Register* (January 18, 1990) to standardize rules and correct deficiencies in agency ethics programs. Although the OGE's tasks extend beyond regulatory authority to include financial disclosure, education and training, guidance and interpretation, enforcement, and evaluation of conflict-of-interest laws, its regulatory reach touches every executive employee in federal service and every agency.

Compliance and the Ethics Industry. Although compliance may appear to be a growth industry in the nation's capital, the evidence is contradictory. Agency budgets belie the growth prediction, but that may change. While only one agency in the OGE's survey had a separate line item for ethics in 1989 (U.S. Office of Government Ethics, 1990a, p. 2), E.O. 12674 states that agencies should have separate budget line items when "practical," and the 1990 order repeats the directive.

Staffing is another indicator that is sending out mixed signals. In ninety-nine agencies that account for almost five million employees, there were only 125 full-time equivalent employees working in ethics in 1989, but thousands are involved part-time (U.S. Office of Government Ethics, 1990a, p. 22). In April 1990, the U.S. Department of Housing and Urban Development (previously rocked by one of the biggest scandals to hit a federal line agency, as discussed earlier) advertised the position of ethics officer at HUD headquarters in the ethics office of the assistant secretary for administration. The notice for vacancy no. 00-MSD-90-0057 reads as follows: "The incumbent, serving as Director of the Office of Ethics and the Deputy Agency Ethics Officer, is responsible for directing a staff charged with developing, coordinating, and managing the department's programs regarding ethics and standards of conduct. The incumbent will develop policies and procedures, assure proper review of disclosure reports, provide advice and assistance to HUD executives on ethics-related issues, and assure that remedies are effected to correct violations or potential violations of HUD standards of conduct."

Whether in a growth phase or holding pattern, compliance already ranks as big business in the executive branch. With administrative and criminal standards and numerous agencies and offices involved in oversight, reporting, investigation, prosecution, and other activities, the overlap and complexity is impressive even for Washington. The roster includes the OGE itself, the Merit System Protections Board, U.S. attorney offices, the special counsel's office, inspectors general offices, general counsel, agency heads, designated agency ethics officers, and units in the Departments of Justice and Treasury inaptly called public integrity units. To the list add special units, committees, and procedures in different agencies such as the Department of Defense. Then, too, there are presidential commissions and the President's Council on Integrity and Efficiency, and congressional hearings and investigations.

The compliance clamor is at a predictably high decibel level. Consider the designated agency ethics officer (DAEO) described in HUD's position notice. A DAEO "serves as a technical resource to the IG [Inspector General], but the DAEO's primary duties are to provide training and counseling to agency employees on conflict of interest matters and to review financial disclosure statements" (General Accounting Office, 1987, p. 7). In 1989, 76 percent of all DAEOs were in legal offices and only 4 percent in personnel offices (U.S. Office of Government Ethics, 1990a, p. 22). If that is not convincing enough, note the title of a 1986 OGE publication, *How to Keep Out of Trouble*.

Enforcement. The many investigatory authorities make the ethics aspect of life in federal service a little confusing. In a study of the Department of the Interior and the Environmental Protection Agency, the General Accounting Office (1987) described the following three general routes to "ethics enforcement," meaning investigation of alleged violations of conflict-of-interest standards.

> *Agency enforcement.* "The investigation . . . is primarily the responsibility of the Inspectors General. . . . Also, allegations the DAEOs receive . . . are to be forwarded to the IG. The IG investigations may result in the case being referred to the Department of Justice for further investigation and possible prosecution or forwarded to others within the agency for possible administrative action (e.g., a reprimand or dismissal in cases involving current employees)" (General Accounting Office, 1987, p. 7). No uniform, formal referral process has developed in federal agencies (U.S. Office of Government Ethics, 1990a, pp. 23–24), and cases may be referred to one of the ninety-four U.S. attorneys' offices (General Accounting Office, 1987, pp. 8–9).
>
> *Prosecutorial enforcement.* "The process by which the Public Integrity Section [of the Justice Department] and the U.S. Attorney's Office investigate and prosecute a conflict of interest case is . . . the same as any other criminal investigation or prosecution. . . . Cases that are prosecuted . . . are sometimes resolved by a finding or admission of guilt under other criminal statutes, such as those prohibiting false or fraudulent claims (18 U.S.C. 287), false or fraudulent statements (18 U.S.C. 1001), and perjury (18 U.S.C. 1621–1623). . . . [T]he final test of prosecutive merit in a conflict of interest case is the likelihood of obtaining a felony conviction" (General Accounting Office, 1987, pp. 10–11).
>
> *Agency administrative actions.* Disciplinary actions for violations of non-criminal standards include termination, suspension, restitution, reassignment, reprimand, admonishment, recusal, and divestiture. Taking administrative action does not preclude criminal sanctions and the IGs review the action. "The IGs said they commonly refer cases that are declined by Justice to the employee's bureau-level supervisor for administrative action" (General Accounting Office, 1987, p. 12). In 1989, about one-quarter of the over 2,000 adverse actions on standards violations dealt with misuse of government vehicles and other property, while less than 2 percent related to conflicting financial interest and less than 3 percent to conflicting outside action (U.S. Office of Government Ethics, 1990a, p. 27).

Financial Disclosure. The Monitoring and Compliance Division of the OGE collects and reviews the public Executive Personnel Financial Disclosure Report, the SF 278. The thousand or so Senate-confirmed presidential appointees (excluding federal judicial officers) file disclosures annually and upon terminating federal service. This drives an impressive transition-period workload for the unit, which reviewed and certified 474 disclosures to the Senate in one fourteen-month period (U.S. Office of Government Ethics, 1990a, p. 11).

Annual filers of public disclosures include the president and vice president, and officers and employees at senior grades 16 and above on the federal General Schedule, which categorizes jobs according to eighteen grades and a progression of pay rates. This means that high-level managerial, supervisory, and policy positions and the entire career Senior Executive Service (SES, established by the Carter administration's 1978 Civil Service Reform Act) file disclosures that are available for public review. Others are military ranks at pay grade 0–7 or above, administrative law judges, employees determined by the OGE, selected senior postal service officers and employees, the OGE's director, and agency DAEOs.

In 1989, incumbents filed more than 14,000 annual public reports, and the career SES achieved a 99 percent compliance rate (required: filed ratio, calculated from the U.S. Office of Government Ethics, 1990a, p. 27). In the entire executive branch in 1989, only one case of filing a false public disclosure was referred to the Department of Justice, and there were no referrals for failing to file (1990a, p. 24). Adding reports from more than 2,700 new entrants and 1,700 from terminations gives some sense of the magnitude of the public disclosure enterprise. In 1989, 591 reports were publicly released in response to requests, almost one-half of which came from the news media (1990a, p. 29).

Initiated by executive order in 1965, confidential disclosure is required from more than 200,000 employees each year (compared to the cumulative 45,000 during a decade of operation in Massachusetts). The overall compliance rate reached almost 93 percent in 1989 for civilian and military filers. Dollar amounts are not required, and nonbusiness ventures are excluded. The directive for reporting household interests reflects a traditional (or perhaps delusional) view of the American household even when it was adopted.

The confidential reports led to some 2,300 actions, amounting to only a little over 1 percent of the total number of reports actually filed (U.S. Office of Government Ethics, 1990a, pp. 28–29). Actions such as divestiture, disqualification, reassignment, letters, waivers, or warnings taken on the basis of public disclosure reports totaled fewer than 1,500 or just shy of 11 percent of all SF 278s filed. (The career SES accounted for fewer than 700 of all actions.)

The President's Commission on Federal Ethics Law Reform concluded that financial disclosure is valuable and allows review and employee counseling but warned against excessive detail. "[T]he use of unduly narrow categories for specifying asset value and income seems to the commission to result in a needless burden on filers without providing particularly useful information to the public and also increases the risk that filers will make inadvertent mistakes" (1989, p. 81).

Municipal Highlights

Standardization is no more characteristic of local than of state practices. A 1990 study by Paul Potamianos of fifteen large municipalities uncovered few common features. The authority behind codes and standards varies: two municipalities rely on state-promulgated municipal codes; one combines state statute and municipal provisions; another has no ethics legislation from state or municipal government; one uses a general council policy only; and four, the largest jurisdictions in the survey, have detailed, extensive municipal codes.

Each city in the study has a population of over 300,000 (six have over a million). All together, they account for more than twenty-one million residents. Every region of the country and both mayor-council and city manager forms of government are represented on the list: Los Angeles, San Diego, Jacksonville, Miami, Atlanta, Chicago, Minneapolis, Buffalo, New York City, Oklahoma City, Philadelphia, Austin, Dallas, San Antonio, and Washington D.C.

Code provisions also vary, and a majority of the surveyed jurisdictions have relatively few standards in common. Only six of twenty-three identified conflict-of-interest provisions apply in a majority of the cities (Potamianos, 1990): direct and indirect interest in business dealing with the city is forbidden or restricted; representing private interests before the city is forbidden; disclosure and use of confidential information is prohibited; use of position for personal pecuniary gain is banned; limits on honoraria, travel, and gifts are imposed; and disclosure of interest is required. As a result, legalistic answers to the case at the end of this chapter would vary from city to city.

On conflict of interest, the draft code of the National Institute of Municipal Law Officers, a code intended to be used by municipal attorneys when they draft municipal codes, limits interests to "direct or indirect pecuniary or material benefit." However, it requires disclosure of financial or personal interest in proposed municipal legislation and forbids "special consideration, treatment or advantage to any citizen beyond that which is available to every other citizen" (National Institute of Municipal Law Officers, 1990, pp. 3, 5–6).

Only two of twenty-three financial disclosure provisions are majority practices among the fifteen cities. Financial and economic disclosure is generally required from city officials and employees, as is disclosure of real estate other than one's home. Three procedural majority practices are having a commission or board of ethics, giving it investigatory authority, and giving it authority to issue or request subpoenas. No majority practices were identified in the areas of procedural protections, abuse of office, or whistle-blowing.

Chicago's ethics code was issued by Mayor Harold Washington by executive order in 1986 and passed by the city council in 1987. The unanimous council vote of 49-0 conceals the earlier struggles. The first executive director of the City of Chicago's Board of Ethics, Harriet McCullough, furnishes cases on municipal compliance and integrity from the trenches, as it were, in Exhibit 8.2.

By referendum in June 1990, voters in Los Angeles approved a full-blown code largely developed by the drafting commission but accommodating some city council amendments. Under the leadership of Geoffrey Cowan (former chairman of California's Common Cause), the commission made itself independent of city government and city financing. It took a relatively strict approach to conflict

Exhibit 8.2. From the Trenches.

The following cases are reproduced courtesy of Harriet McCullough, consultant and former executive director of the Board of Ethics, City of Chicago.

Outside Employment. A city employee had duties which included assisting persons in their efforts to file for United States citizenship under the new federal law. The city provided these services free of charge. This employee has an opportunity to work part-time in the evenings for a private law firm. This part-time work would have involved providing services for compensation which are similar, if not identical, to the services he provided to the public, free of charge, as a city employee. Should he accept the job?

Family Involvement. A city department and a corporation were negotiating an agreement that would bring substantial economic benefit to the corporation through city action, such as tax abatement, capital grants, and street reconstruction. A law firm was retained to represent the corporation in negotiation with the city, and a deputy commissioner represented the department. The wife of the deputy commissioner was a lawyer employed by the firm representing the corporation. However, as an employee, she was not involved in the negotiations, nor did she assist the group of lawyers at her firm who were. Is there a conflict of interest? What, if any, actions should be taken?

Play Ball. One of the city's professional sports teams sent season passes to aldermen [elected council members] and selected city employees. At the time these passes were received, the City Council was reviewing various proposals submitted by this particular sports club which would involve major expenditures of city funds. Is it permissible for the aldermen to accept these season passes? What about the city employees?

Fly Away. Several city officials received promotional materials from a major airline which included free tickets to fly round-trip between Chicago and any of three midwestern cities. The city runs the airports. Should Department of Aviation officials respond differently from other officials? A year earlier, another airline had distributed coupons which could be exchanged for two round-trip tickets to a European city. Does the distance and desirability of the locale matter?

Deals. I received the following offer in a phone call from another department: "If you will arrange the installation of the new PCs by Christmas, I'll try to get your authorization for trucks through by then." Did the employee who made that offer do anything unethical? If so, what should I do about it?

---

issues by incorporating financial and noneconomic ties that potentially interfere with impartiality, induce bias or favoritism, or give that appearance. The commission's options report on resolving conflicts of interest summarized the state's 1974 act and then went further, noting that Los Angeles had imposed by virtue of its city charter a stricter test for recusal. The city attorney's office decided matters on the basis of "whether the public could reasonably conclude that there is an *appearance* of a conflict of interest" and used a not-in-the-public-interest standard (Cowan Commission, 1989a, pp. 147–148).

As a result of the June referendum, Los Angeles has the most comprehensive ethics package of any city in the country. A strong ethics commission can call for a special prosecutor if the city attorney has a conflict of interest. Revolving-door restrictions limit post-employment and government employees' involvement with former employers' contracts.

Statewide Uniformity? Although most states' ethics laws do not extend to localities, at least fourteen states blanket officials and employees in state, county, and municipal governments (See Exhibit 8.1, p. 145). The observations made earlier in this chapter about borrowing from other jurisdictions should not be mistaken for arguments in support of uniformity. (Chapter Ten proposes adapting rules to particular administrative realities rather than touting them as universal remedies.)

The trade-off is obvious: the logic and simplicity of statewide uniformity versus tailoring a local code to local needs and conventions. National professional associations have discovered that variable community standards can be a sticky issue. Differences in size and complexity add other dimensions, such as strong implicit or distinctive moral codes, the size of the talent pool, readily observable and widely known behavior, and family connections to local businesses receiving municipal contracts (sometimes complicated by local contracting requirements).

Duplication of effort, a longtime administrative taboo, warrants some thought. Harriet McCullough, whose experience in both Chicago and Los Angeles puts her in a unique position to know, says, "The passage of ethics legislation in large cities can be a huge task. It takes time, commitment, compromise, political posturing, citizen involvement, media attention, and lots and lots of debate" (McCullough, 1990, p. 1). A statewide approach avoids repeating the task, but the debate itself is useful.

Localities are treated differently in different states and in different model statutes. Common Cause endorsed uniform standards years ago, while the National Municipal League did not include local jurisdictions in its 1979 model statute. More than two decades ago, New York's state legislature defined conflicts of interest and required each jurisdiction from counties to school districts to adopt its own code. According to the New York State Commission on Government Integrity (1988, p. 2), the state's 1987 Ethics in Government Act "had little application to local government," and 95 percent of all municipalities in the state are "totally unaffected" by its provisions. Noting "a confusing patchwork of contradictory, inadequate and sometimes overly restrictive ethics codes, some of which are unenforceable and some of which are simply not enforced" (p. 1), the commission recommended a municipal ethics act.

In contrast, in California, selected state, county, and city officials as well as state and local employees designated in the conflict-of-interest code are required to file annual statements of economic interest. City officers include mayors, council members, city managers, chief administrative officers, planning commissioners, and city attorneys. On the other coast, the Massachusetts State Ethics Commission ("the primary *civil* enforcement agency") reports that the state's conflict-of-interest law "has regulated the conduct of public officials and employees in the Bay State since 1963. The law limits what public employees may do on the job, what they may do after hours or 'on the side,' and what they may do after they leave public service and return to the private sector. It also sets the standards of conduct required of all state, county, and municipal employees in Massachusetts, articulating the premise that public employees owe undivided loyalty to the government they serve, and must act in the public interest rather than for private gain" (Commonwealth of Massachusetts, 1989, p. 2). Municipal employees saw a perverse kind of progress over one decade. While the fifty complaints to the Massachusetts commission in 1979 involved no municipal employees, they were the subjects of about four-fifths of the more than 750 allegations in each of fiscal years 1988 and 1989.

Managing the Code

An effective code demands a developmental process. It starts with a conflict-of-interest prohibition, defines what else is imperative in the community, moves on to enforcement, and finally shifts to more subtle aspects of implementation, such as training and before-the-fact advice. From beginning to end, the process is more like doing individualized programming for a broad application than buying off-the-shelf software for a particular task. (Managers who have survived installation of a new computer system may appreciate the analogy.)

Ready-made standards and model provisions possibly suit more populous or complex jurisdictions. For smaller jurisdictions, some specific concerns are the need for and reasonableness of the appearance-of-impropriety prohibition, detailed public financial disclosure as a meaningful way of implementing conflict-of-interest prohibitions, nepotism and dual employment restrictions, and investment limitations. The list could go on. Taking size and diversity into account would contribute sensible and tenable standards and also acknowledge the variety that characterizes American public organizations and governmental structures.

A former senior federal official and now a professor, Robert C. Wood sums up the major points (quoted in Cox 1988, p. 10): "Codes of conduct should be crafted from a rich empirical base, understandable in the climate of the particular agency, making sense to those to whom they apply—down-to-earth, realistic. They should not appear as commandments from on high, generalized statements of good intentions, lofty aspirations incapable of specific human responses. They need to be fashioned out of the everyday work life, become integral parts of staff development activities; a support to effective performance, not a burden. The goal is to underscore that the standards of honesty go hand in hand with those of efficiency and competence."

Even with a code and a nonpartisan commission in place, most of the work remains: to integrate the code's standards into the agency's way of doing business, its culture, its style. Gary Edwards, executive director of the Ethics Resource Center, says that codes do make a difference but only if they are well managed

(Lewis, 1986, p. 17). In addition to executive example and leadership, serious implementation throughout the agency is vital. For a code to be *operative, fair, and meaningful,* it must be related to the organization's management and incentives. These concerns translate into five general guidelines for managing the agency's code.

1. Show hard evidence—top management's ongoing, serious commitment to standards and to implementation.
2. Show the flag—immediate superiors' and line managers' integration of ethical concerns into the routine work environment.
3. Link ethical concerns and behavior with career path and with the agency's reward structure.
4. Safeguard against arbitrary or selective enforcement, favoritism, or abuse.
5. Communicate standards and expectations publicly and repeatedly to employees, vendors, clients, the media, others.

Case: The New Position

The following case is reprinted by permission, from Frank Cassidy, "Survey on Responsible Administrative Behavior," University of Victoria, British Columbia, Canada, July 1987, with minor modifications to conform with U.S. usage.

> Jim McDonald, assistant engineer, was a dedicated municipal employee, a firm supporter of the merit system, and apolitical. The newly appointed city engineer, David Fedorak, was a former assistant deputy commissioner and a person who not only had strong political connections but also took pride in these connections.
>
> The city's economy was in a depressed state. The council was controlled by a group elected on a platform of lower taxation and reduced services. The engineering department was having a serious problem maintaining services.
>
> Shortly after his appointment as city engineer, David was approached by Carl Richter, deputy commissioner of transportation and a former colleague. Carl asked David whether he could find a position in the municipality for his wife Jennifer, since she was unable to find satisfactory work within state government because of Carl's position as deputy commissioner.
>
> *Was this ethical of Carl? . . .*
> Jennifer Richter has a B.S. degree with majors in psychology and English, completed 18 years ago.
>
> During budget discussions with his senior staff, David announced that he was proposing a new staff position, which would directly report to him, called a "program coordinator" with a $40,000 salary. He vaguely described the job description as provid-

ing a coordinating function with the other municipal departments. He also indicated that he had conducted an informal interview with a person who had the experience and qualifications perfectly suited to the position.

Was this ethical of David? . . .

He referred to Jennifer Richter by name and expressed the wish that she would be a part of the engineering team in the near future.

Was this ethical of David? . . .

One week prior to the presentation of the budget to the committee, David was admitted to a hospital with a bleeding gastric ulcer. David would not be returning to work for about two to three months and he was not to be contacted on matters relating to work. Jim, who now had to defend and justify the new budget to the council, had agreed with David on all matters except the new position. Jim went and saw the city manager to seek his advice.

Was this ethical of Jim? . . .

Jim told him that he thought it was a political appointment rather than a good organizational one. The city manager listened to Jim but said that this situation was the responsibility of the engineering department and that Jim would have to deal with it.

Was this ethical of the city manager? . . .

Jim then considered going to the mayor but, due to the lack of response of the city manager, did not do so.

Was this ethical of Jim? . . .

Jim decided that the best strategy was to present the budget and justify all items with equal enthusiasm, just as David would have.

Was this ethical of Jim? . . .

But when it was his turn to present the budget, Jim realized that he could not defend the introduction of this new position. His lack of enthusiasm was very obvious to the council.

Was this ethical of Jim? . . .

Is this simply a case of bad personnel management or personal expedience?

- What are the ethical dimensions, if any, at each step in the sequence of events in the case?
- Is there any real difference between personal expedience and managerial prudence?

A standard view is that impartiality and merit (versus pressure and patronage) in personnel selection are core values in professional public service. Are these *ethical* values? What is *your* view?

- What other values figure into this case? Are they all compatible? Important?

At each step in the sequence, who is affected and what is at stake? What is the offense?

What are the responsibilities of the different players in this case?

– How would you suggest the players juggle their multiple responsibilities in a principled way?

Does your jurisdiction have an ethics code or standards of conduct?

– If so, does the code offer guidance for the different players in this case?

Does your professional association have an ethics code?

– If so, does it offer guidance for Carl, David, the city manager, and Jim?

Many public managers are members of professions with codes of conduct. Several such codes are reprinted in Rena Gorlin's *Codes of Professional Responsibility* (1990). Do professional standards of conduct offer meaningful guidance for the different players in this case? See the following creed and codes.

The Engineer's Creed, adopted by the National Society of Professional Engineers in June 1954, states that "as a professional Engineer, I dedicate my professional knowledge and skill to the advancement and betterment of human welfare."

The Code of Ethics for Engineers, adopted by the National Society of Professional Engineers and as revised in January 1987, reads as follows:

I. FUNDAMENTAL CANONS. Engineers, in the fulfillment of their professional duties, shall

1. Hold paramount the safety, health and welfare of the public in the performance of their professional duties.

2. Perform services only in areas of their competence.

3. Issue public statements only in an objective and truthful manner.

4. Act in professional matters for each employer or client as faithful agents or trustees.

5. Avoid deceptive acts in the solicitation of professional employment.

II. RULES OF PRACTICE

3(a). Engineers shall be objective and truthful in professional reports, statements or testimony. They shall include all relevant and pertinent information in such reports or testimony.

4(a). Engineers shall disclose all known or potential conflicts of interest to their employers or clients by promptly informing them of any business association, interest, or other circumstances which could influence or appear to influence their judgement or the quality of their services.

(Reprinted by permission of the National Society of Professional Engineers.)

The American Society for Public Administration's code of ethics, adopted in 1984, prescribes that members "support, implement, and promote merit employment and programs of affirmative action to assure equal opportunity by our recruitment, selection, and advancement of qualified persons from all elements of society." And the International City Management Association's code of ethics, as revised in 1976 (with guidelines and rules of procedure added in 1987), enjoins members to "handle all matters of personnel on the basis of merit so that fairness and impartiality govern a member's decisions pertaining to appointments, pay adjustments, promotion, and discipline."

Chapter 9

Ethics and the Boss

Turning the spotlight on organizational interaction, this chapter focuses on the supervisory function, a central managerial responsibility. In a host of ways, including modeling, the manager shapes ethical conduct and the ethical agency. Supervising employee time is an ongoing stress point and demands special care. Work force diversity, alternate recruitment channels, mixed administrative settings, and collaborative relationships as illustrated by the procurement function figure prominently among today's challenges. A case on supervising working hours completes the chapter.

Public managers are doers and deciders; that is the crux of the job. As Bayard L. Catron, professor of public administration at the George Washington University, remarked to the author (June 1990), "ethics is first, foremost, and finally about conduct." The upshot is a passion for action in preference to personal introspection, and that means dealing with other people. *A public manager's primary ethical concern is behavior toward other people.*

Service recipients or clients are especially "meaningful others" lately, probably in response to the surge in social services, the injection of equity and compassion by the *new public administration,* and the responsiveness-as-marketing concerns associated with entrepreneurial public management. (Today's dictum of *customer* service neglects the dependency, vulnerability, and civics aspects of many public services.) Recognizing users' dependency on public services, a focus on clients as external, direct stakeholders is a beneficial development. In effect, it repudiates the petty tyrant exercising government authority, the small-minded bureaucrat so aptly described by Dostoyevsky (n.d., pp. 108–109) in nineteenth-century Russia. "I was a spiteful civil servant. I was rude and took pleasure in being rude. Mind you, I never accepted any bribes, so that I had at least to find something to compensate myself for that. . . . Whenever people used to come to my office on some business, I snarled at them and felt as pleased as Punch [English puppet] when I succeeded in making one of them really unhappy. I nearly always did succeed. They were mostly a timid lot: what else can you expect people who come to a government office to be? . . . All I did, as a matter of fact, was to indulge in a little innocent fun at the expense of . . . the people who came to my office on business, for actually I never could become a spiteful man." (Note how he divorces the office from the person and rationalizes his behavior.)

An emphasis on clients is all to the good, but not to the exclusion of all others. Dependency and vulnerability, factors that affect ethical responsibility, touch subordinates with a heavy hand. Because agency managers and employees are direct stakeholders in agency actions and operations, supervision's ethical aspects must be core concerns. Moreover, omitting ethics from the supervisory relationship implies endorsing market exchange as the sole basis of human relations in public agencies. Given the hours spent on the job and maintaining professional proficiency, few managers would be willing to make this argument—or live with the consequences.

The Boss as Ethical Model

By way of illustration, step into this manager's shoes (via an ethical dilemma from Oklahoma's ethics training program for state managers): "For the last two performance appraisal cycles you have tended to give mid-range ratings to all of your employees. In the strict sense you have had one or two employees performing above the *Meets Expectations* level. You have justified your ratings because of the subjective nature of performance appraisal and the fact that your own boss (as the reviewer) prefers that you give the mid-range scores—'it makes things less complicated.' Are *your* actions justified?" Are your supervisor's? Why? Thinking this through requires appraising two supervisors—yourself and your boss—as well as subordinates.

Proposals about the ethical aspects of the supervisory function touch upon managers' *and* subordinates' behavior and, for that very reason, breed wariness in some minds. Doubts induce special care for the ethical dimensions of hierarchical relationships. A manager's treatment of subordinates sets the tone for the organization and imparts appropriate behavior to subordinates.

Public managers generally understand and accept this responsibility. In a study of executive accountability, almost four-fifths of a group of senior managers rated "frequent informal personal contact" as a "very effective" method for holding accountable those who report to them. Only informal personal contact and "regularly scheduled one-to-one discussion on progress and problems" were deemed very effective by a majority of respondents (Rosen, 1989, p. 36). John A. Betti, formerly responsible for a $100 billion budget as under secretary of defense for acquisition, explained to a business audience, "Often, the informal rules of acceptable behavior of an organization's culture are more influential in governing behavior than the formal rules. . . . Ethics is an important element of an organization's culture. Therefore, ethics is the responsibility of management, and is a matter of leadership . . . the leadership of an organization must *be,* and must *be seen,* as personally and professionally committed to good ethics. . . . They [managers] must demonstrate through their actions that they will not tolerate unethical behavior by anyone with whom they do business" (Betti, 1990, pp. 1–2).

In this vein, Peter Drucker (1989, pp. 229–230) tells us, "Every enterprise requires commitment to common goals and shared values. Without such commitment there is no enterprise, there is only a mob. . . . Management's first job is to think through, set, and exemplify those objectives, values, and goals."

Most of us learned how to deal with complex pressures and ethical dilemmas from our bosses in a modern version of apprenticeship called *modeling* or, if conscious and direct, *mentoring.* Social learning theory tells us that learning is fostered through observation and by example of those who control rewards and deal out penalties. Ethical modeling is an ancient notion that is more cosmopolitan than American or even Western public administration. An example from Buddhism (Bukkyo Dendo Kyokai, 1987, pp. 468–469) strikes a familiar chord: "If an important minister of state neglects his duties, works for his own profit or accepts bribes, it will cause a rapid decay of public morals. . . . Under such circumstances, faithful ministers will retire from public service, wise men will keep silent from fear of complications, and only flatterers will hold government positions, and they will use their political power to enrich themselves with no thought for the sufferings of the people."

In light of the importance of the supervisor as ethical role model, responses to a survey of members of the American Society for Public Administration are somewhat disquieting. Responding members disagreed (57 percent) or strongly disagreed (18 percent) with the comment, "Top management has a stronger set of ethical standards than I do" (Bowman, 1989, p. 107).

The results are partially explained by the tendency of survey respondents to rate their own ethics higher than other people's, a pattern repeated in *City & State*'s (1989, p. 105) readership questionnaire (although a large majority expressed the belief that public service peers are ethical). But, again, this is only a partial explanation. A professional in local government in the Northwest commented, "examples should be set by senior level of management. Unfortunately, that is the *most* unethical level within my organization" (Bowman, 1989, p. 107).

Work Force Diversity

The apprentice's screening capacity should not be downplayed. When it comes to dealing with other people in the office, old, automatic responses may no longer be as reliable as they once were. Disabled workers, the foreign educated, single parents supporting a family, adult children caring for aging parents, workers with nontraditional life-styles all make the office a much more complicated place than it was when the boss-as-model learned on the job.

Today's catch phrase is *cultural diversity,* and well it should be. White males will decrease to 40 percent of the work force by the century's end, compared to about 50 percent when Richard Nixon was president. Because the work force is changing, employee relationships are changing. Some behaviors may need rethinking. Others may call for full-scale *re*modeling.

Sexual harassment comes to mind as a serious example. From 1976 to 1985 the number of women serving at the municipal level of government rose by 260 percent ("Women Take On City Governance," 1989, p. 12). Today, women comprise 11 percent of the people on active military duty, but a 1990 Pentagon study depicts sexual harassment as the norm (Schmitt, 1990, p. A22). The public spotlight was turned on when a female midshipman at the U.S. Naval Academy blew the whistle and went public in protest over a particularly degrading incident.

There are many other examples of changing relationships and behaviors (see Timmins, 1990). When ICMA's code was originally adopted in 1924, city management was much simpler: no assistants, county administrators, consultants, women, or minorities (Tranter, 1987). Today they are part of the team, along with private-sector collaborators and two-career couples with investment interests and personal life-styles that raise questions and entail commitments different from those of the profession's formative years. Fondly recalled, the "good old days" conjure up simplicity, not equity.

The new faces, new cultures, and new customs and norms are adding fresh dimensions to employee relations and novel ethical issues. "Even now, the average manager may think: 'To be fair, I should assume everyone is the same and treat them that way'" (Solomon, 1990, p. B1). That response begs the question. It is not bigotry or biased treatment—both are intolerable in public service—but more subtly demeaning behavior, stereotypical thinking and treatment, inadvertent slights, and misunderstandings.

Both personal idiosyncrasy and cultural variation in habits, mores, values, and even body language complicate the manager's job. What motivates the employee? How does the manager build trust in the office? Does eye contact signal trustworthiness or belligerence? Is an informal chat before the meeting gets down to business an inexcusable waste of time or a team-building tactic?

Loosely paraphrasing Lawrence D. (Larry) Fisher, director of Oklahoma's human relations development department (in letter to author, Aug. 20, 1990), an Oklahoma story evokes the ethical dimensions of work force diversity. "At an agency meeting, a junior manager overhears a racist remark told by a Kiowa colleague about a Comanche. Should the manager say something?" Before answering, it is useful to think through three additional questions.

1. Does speaking up or keeping silent define professional behavior? Ethical behavior?
2. As you respond, do you visualize the junior manager as Native American or Caucasian? Do you visualize the Kiowa as the manager's supervisor, peer, or subordinate?
3. Does a public manager's ethnic identity determine appropriate behavior?

Answers to the first question may be moderated by seniority, reporting lines, appropriate context, professional roles, and other considerations. There is a significant distance between *should* and *would;* they are separated by courage, prudence, responsibility, and other matters. Is only the *how* and *when* affected by these considerations, or is the obligation also? (Chapter Six's tools for assessing responsibility may be of help here.)

The second question raises the specter of bias or prejudice affecting the reasoning. Was it truly impartial? An emphatic no to the third question emphasizes professional commitment to impartiality, even or especially in the face of ethnic, age, sex, or other personal characteristics. The answers to the three questions may stimulate rethinking of the initial problem. Once again, *should* the manager say something?

New York State has responded to diversity with a "strategic work force planning initiative" which offers the following perspective (New York State Department of Civil Service, 1990, p. 4): "Diversity has grown from purely a social agenda of enlightened government to include pragmatic concerns related to business viability for all employers, private or public. The very productivity that the state will need could be threatened by counterproductive workplace tensions if workers are unprepared to deal with cultural differences. Clearly, managers and supervisors will need greater skills in working with a multicultural and increasingly diverse work force." Mistakenly, and apparently bowing to the ethical neutrality argument (see Chapter Four), the New York plan (p. 70) argues that "this is not a social or moral issue, but rather a pragmatic one."

No one can predict for sure where diversity is taking public service, except to say that the work force will be different and the workplace probably so. In preparation, we turn to the ethical dimensions of employee time as an everyday area of control, awkward bloopers, outright abuse, and chronic misunderstanding. This issue taps many ethical aspects of interpersonal relations in the office, including those that directly affect every manager.

Time Abuse

Misuse of working hours and workers is a commonplace and costly problem posing serious ethical issues. It may constitute the rather simple appropriation of public property for personal gain or unauthorized use, which can be seen variously as intangible theft or conflict of interest. When the misuse stems from an unscrupulous supervisor's directive, the problem is abuse of office. Then too, the problem may be linked to carelessness or incompetence on the part of the employee or supervisor. All told, these behaviors are contrary to ethical standards in public service.

Time abuse is distinct from lost time, which refers to all time paid but not worked for any reason, including legitimate reasons. In this regard, how many employees understand that vacation time may be devoted to personal purposes, but that the employee is still on the payroll and still a public servant? It is up to the manager to explain that the ethical obligations binding on public employees still operate, and that this is not the time for conflicting or unauthorized moonlighting. Authorized outside employment usually presents no problem as long as it does not interfere with job performance, generate conflicts of interest, or appear improper.

A quick calculation in any agency reveals the serious financial implication of time abuse. With 17.6 million employees in government alone, the aggregate and cumulative potential loss is striking. Time is money in government, too.

More broadly speaking, productive use of working hours for public purposes is hardly a paltry matter. Payroll and benefits account for 75 percent or more of spending in many jurisdictions or agencies. As a big-ticket item for the organization *and the worker,* employee time and its ethical dimensions are a good candidate for discriminating reasoning by supervisory staff.

The federal government takes the straightforward position that personal use of working hours and government workers—like other resources or assets—is contrary to standards of conduct. The 1990 executive order states, "Employees shall protect and conserve Federal property and shall not use it for other than authorized activities." Its 1965 predecessor, E.O. 11222, stipulated that the "employee shall not use Federal property of any kind for other than officially approved activities. He must protect and conserve all Federal property, including equipment and supplies, entrusted or issued to him."

Even so, abusive supervisors and greedy, ill-advised, or wrong-thinking employees, abetted by careless supervision, perpetuate time abuse. The President's Council on Integrity and Efficiency took a survey of inspectors general to identify trouble spots. The U.S. Department of Health and Human Services' ethics handbook (1989, p. 9) categorizes one of these spots as misuse of public office: "A manager was admonished following an investigation which showed that on two occasions he had employees help him with personal chores while they were on official time." In this vein, the General Accounting Office (1989, pp. 54–55) reports, "Integrity issues cover not only conflict of interest and management actions in administrative matters but also the use of sick leave by federal employees."

Many states similarly prohibit personal use of working hours by statute, personnel rule, or legal opinion. Under the auspices of the Council on Governmental Ethics Laws, a committee (chaired by John Larsen, executive director of the Board of Ethics, State of Illinois) undertook to craft model ethics legislation for states and localities. Its 1990 draft version states, "A public official or employee shall not use public funds, *time, personnel,* facilities, or equipment for the official or employee's private gain or that of another unless the use is authorized by law" (Feigenbaum, Larsen, and Reynolds, 1990, Sec. 210; emphasis added). The last phrase is designed to allow for economic development ventures and the like that join state resources to private activities.

More knotty supervisor-subordinate interactions on both agency and personal time cause ethical problems in any office. Federal standards extend to superiors' requests to work *after hours,* as the U.S. Office of Government Ethics (1990a, pp. 833–834) spells out. "While one normally thinks of Federal property as being things, it also includes the time of federal employees while on government duty. Therefore, one employee cannot ask another employee to provide services in furtherance of purely personal projects while on official duty. And, if a supervisor asks someone he supervises to provide free personal services to the supervisor on non-official duty, the supervisor is requesting a gift from that employee which is prohibited by statute."

Less regulated environments tend to confine the ban to working hours (as implied in the case "A Matter of Convenience" at the end of Chapter Five). With respect to working hours only, the Josephson Institute takes a different tack and shifts responsibility so that it is the subordinate's responsibility to say no. This posture allows that, while the superior is obligated to the subordinate, obligations flow in the other direction, too. According to the Josephson Institute (1990, p. 8) guidelines, "Public employees should refuse to perform improper personal tasks on government time."

This advice strikes head-on against *team player* loyalties and an employee's economic dependence on the organization and is plumbed in Exhibit 9.1. These are matters of courage. Civil rights activist and author (*I Know Why the Caged Bird Sings*) Maya Angelou says, "Courage is the most important virtue . . . because without courage you can't have other virtues" (Fuchs, 1989, p. 13). Ethics is about doing the right thing; it is not always easy. Fiduciary responsibility to the public and the ethical principle that calls for taking personal responsibility support the Josephson Institute's posture.

Crossbreeding

A new recruit (like Mark in the case at the end of this chapter) may not even be aware of the ethical—never mind the managerial or legal—aspects of a directive or of norms different from those of other work environments. Cross-recruiting can be a positive, constructive, even creative step, but it also builds in some trouble spots. From the dollar-a-year or on-loan executive to the transplanted military officer, volunteer, or part-time worker, the potential is there for confusion, casual misunderstanding, or undiscerned conflicts of interest. Potential problems bid selectivity, followed by precautionary exposure to public service obligations and agency expectations.

A manager's task is to clarify agency work norms when the new employee crosses over from, for example, a military to a civilian post. Lieutenant Colonel Oliver North's comments at the 1987 congressional hearings exemplify the challenge. Describing his view of his role in the National Security Council for six years, he said, "I was simply a staff member with a demonstrated ability to get the job done. . . . My authority to act always flowed, I believed, from my superiors. My military training inculcated . . . in me a strong belief in the chain of command." Projecting can-do competence and a military allure, North testified

Exhibit 9.1. Just Say No.

A technician employed by the city (population 100,000) in the data-processing office complained to the city manager, to the corporation counsel, and later that same day, to a local television station that her supervisor had ordered her several times to do private jobs on city time and with city equipment. Once she was asked to install city equipment at a private site on her own time and felt she had to cooperate or "face the music."

After the investigators sifted through work orders, purchase orders, time cards, invoices, and the records of several local vendors, it looked as if charges soon would be brought against the supervisor and several other employees. The sergeant who led the police inquiry reported no information implicating high officials outside the data-processing office.

What are the ethical issues as distinct from legal or practical ones in this case?
–For the employee?
–For the supervisor?
Is the employee hiding behind her supervisor in order to escape responsibility? (See Chapter Four.)
Is the obligation to protect public time and property a license for suspicion? Is it a subordinate's *ethical* obligation to second-guess the boss? Does this disrupt the office?
Do you agree with Josephson Institute's standard?
–For all governments?
–For all public service agencies?
–For all public employees, no matter what position they hold in the hierarchy?
Should the technician, who admits to illegal activity, be rewarded for blowing the whistle?
–Does the technician appear to have answered the questions on p. 132? With what results?
Loyalty often is identified as an ethical value. What does loyalty mean in this case? To whom and for what?
–Is loyalty simply an appeal to personal bonds and sentiment, or does it rightfully exert an ethical claim in public service?
–How does loyalty affect accountability?
How does this case compare with "A Matter of Convenience" (Chapter Five)?
–What different issues affect your reasoning?

to a mind-set in which obedience and performance overrule legality and telling the truth. "I haven't in the 23 years that I have been in the uniformed services of the United States of America ever violated an order, not one," North stated. "In combat, my goal was always to understand the objective, follow orders, accomplish the mission, and to keep alive the men who served under me."

Some evidence suggests potential problems in recruiting from the private sector. One survey posed a general question about an excellent employee (in a spot similar to the employee in the case that begins on page 176). With no remaining vacation but unused sick days left, she calls in sick to attend her child's school play (Kane, Parsons, and Associates, 1989). While 38 percent of the respondents judged the employee's behavior "definitely wrong and unacceptable," 41 percent identified it as "in principle unethical but justified under the circumstances," and 19 percent saw it as acceptable (the others were not sure). What 41 percent of the respondents were actually saying was, "it is wrong but I would do it anyway"; in other words, rationalizing unethical conduct.

Values such as telling the truth and avoiding conflicting claims such as personal responsibilities versus occupational obligations obviously are not all that different in the world of private business. Although the pressures may be similar, in public service, where company time is public property, the moral compass points to the *unacceptability* of appropriating public property for personal use.

The business compass may point in a different direction. Loyalty, stamina, grit, and ability won the day over honesty and obeying the law in a poll of general public opinion taken during North's testimony. The poll asked, "If *you* ran a business, would you want to hire Oliver North as an executive?" A majority (56 percent) said they would, while about one-third (35 percent) said they would not and 9 percent were not sure (*Wall Street Journal*/NBC News, 1987). Some differences turn on the degree of private ownership. For example, while nepotism is contrary to public service standards, a parent hiring a child to work in a family-owned business is accepted, even expected.

The split opinion over calling in sick mirrors the competition among values and interests that crop up in current debates over family leave, flex time, job sharing, rehiring retirees, and other recent innovations. Of course, dogmatic insistence upon working hours to the exclusion of hours worked, productivity, or competing demands in an employee's life may induce reactive rigidity such as clock-watching, lackadaisical performance, and anxiety. It certainly tends to sacrifice compassion as an ethical value and stresses the organization as the preeminent if not exclusive stakeholder.

Team Ethic. Despite innovation and experimentation, many organizations that tend toward the private on the continuum depicted in Figure I.1 (page 4) play down the team spirit that characterizes so much of public service. The team ethic is the opening salvo on behalf of ethical behavior in the federal training film *Public Service, Public Trust.* The term *team* evokes close association, a network of affiliation, kinship of goals, and mutual supports, dependency, and dependability. It is only when a we/they line is drawn around the agency and public employees forget that the *we* extends to the public that the team ethic undercuts public service ethics.

Public service may be a team, but it is not an exclusive club. In response to cross-recruiting, managers can smooth the transition and build an effective, ethical team. For starters, managers can preach reality. "Those who make a successful transition from private sector to public sector learn to view our government not as a corporation, but as a political institution, driven by democratic principles. They learn how to build consensus and negotiate with those opposing them. They let go of the role of master and cherish the role of civil servant" (Kouses, 1987, Sec. 3, p. 3). The challenge is to help new members join and then succeed by letting them in on the house rules.

Managers are called upon to proselytize and inspire, advocate and model, hearten and reward; training, supervision, controls, and incentives are marshaled.

This is the time for straight talk, repeated talk, backed up by right action. Cross-recruiting is also a prime time for introducing the fusion route described in the introduction.

Nonprofits and Volunteers. Crossbreeding is a setup for special managerial challenges in nonprofit organizations, which are a nongovernmental part of public service. As the public service work force is diversifying, so is the type of agency and mode of organization. Defined by their IRS designation, nonprofit organizations are particularly important to public service.

The scope and functions of the *independent* or *third* sector have grown remarkably over the past two decades and are today both broad and pioneering. A partial catalogue includes health, educational, and professional organizations; charitable, benefit, and athletic associations; public advocacy, research, and consulting groups; legal aid and mutual societies; savings banks and credit unions; and a host of nongovernmental community services, both secular and religious. One example, the American Arbitration Association, dates to 1926, but the growth in dispute resolution has boosted its statistics to more than 55,000 arbitrators and mediators with a caseload that surpasses 50,000 annually (American Arbitration Association, 1989, pp. 3, 10).

The nonprofit umbrella covers many different career paths and opportunities in diverse fields. Nonprofits vary by size, revenues and financing modes, and mission. Some are local, some are national, and many speak for budgets and staffs that dwarf local governments. Some operate with a board of directors and function like a business, but without shareholders or owners.

Many nonprofits rely heavily on volunteers, often treated as unpaid staff. Almost 1.5 million volunteers (excluding blood donors) work for the Red Cross alone, and the total in all nonprofits is estimated at more than thirty million (Drucker, 1988, p. 30). Many of them, retirees and others, are new to the public service environment, its demands, and its ethical standards. Misguided compassion, however well meaning, can bring an agency to its knees and a community service to a standstill.

With one foot in the business camp and the other in public service, a nonprofit manager needs both eyes focused straight ahead. This means moving ethical modeling and public service expectations to the top of the manager's agenda. The reactive alternative risks letting scandal force a response.

No Boss, Multiple Masters

Given different work norms, relationships and interactions get even stickier when we venture outside the pyramidal agency and into the indirect, sometimes convoluted ways we have of doing the public's business. Not everyone involved in decision making or service delivery nowadays fits neatly in a superior-subordinate relationship with a defined role in a hierarchical office. This is a source of many ethical problems that face public servants and more-or-less-public agencies of all sorts.

Complicating matters are network relationships and matrix-type organizations marked by flat or variable authority structures and/or collegial relationships. Intersectoral, international, intergovernmental, and interjurisdictional arrangements complicate matters further. Parties to proxy, third-party, or indirect administration use loans, grants, and contracts and, like associates in public-private partnerships, share no common chief in the weblike administrative environment.

Collaborative relationships by definition share no single command structure, organizational culture, or compulsory or even habitual ethical standards. "Integration of collective efforts depends on a loosely coupled process of negotiation, bargaining, and collaboration between autonomous organizations. Multiple sets of decision and procedural rules are in effect" (Goodsell, 1985, p. 69). When public opinion and participation are added, we clearly see the "new" administration Woodrow Wilson ([1887] 1987, p. 12) described more than a century ago: "There is scarcely a single duty of government which was once simple which is not now complex; government once had but a few masters; it now has scores of masters."

"One basic issue cuts across most of the problems: how to allow maximum possible independence while assuring adequate accountability" (Rosen, 1989, p. 52). In a collaborative setting, where misunderstandings and foul-ups are predictable, it is helpful to put ethical standards and expectations up front and on the table. What do we expect from special government employees such as temporary advisers, expert consultants, or corporate, academic, church, or other members of blue ribbon commissions? Do they know the prevailing ethical norms? Legal requirements? Is a briefing prudent or patronizing? Is financial disclosure advisable?

Does it matter whether decision makers are unpaid volunteers or part-time rather than full-time employees? Evidence for the seriousness of the question lies in their large number and important functions. Many state and local commissions—including land-use, ethics, and other commissions—rely on volunteer appointees. More than 3.3 million state and local government employees are employed on a part-time basis (U.S. Bureau of the Census, 1989, p. v).

Different jurisdictions respond to the issues differently. New York City's code (originally enacted in 1959, with the most recent amendments effective as of 1990) is more restrictive for full-time paid employees. "Since regular employees gain their primary income from the city, stricter rules apply to them than to those classes of publics servants—part-time and unpaid—who are expected to have outside jobs and interests" (Valletta, 1990, p. 3). Volunteers on state boards and commissions are requested to file personal disclosures in at least twenty-two states and volunteers on local boards are similarly bound in at least ten states (Council of State Governments, 1990, pp. 129–131). In the federal government, the almost 8,000 special government employees who serve as advisory committee members or as experts and consultants are required to file confidential financial disclosure reports, although this mandate is weakly enforced (U.S. Office of Government Ethics, 1990b, pp. 29–30).

The profession is responding with new jargon that speaks to the increased likelihood of joint ventures. This is the era of "creative downsizing," alternative service strategies such as "privatization" and public-private "partnerships," and other innovative avenues to productivity.

Buying In. In the present climate, contact and communication with contractors and suppliers are especially sensitive. Much of the effort in this arena is confined to legal compliance rather than the integrity aspect of administrative ethics. (The case on pages 42–45 illustrates what can happen when there is a deep misunderstanding of public service obligations imposed by a contractual relationship with government.) With the object of avoiding any conflict of interest, regulations governing environmental impact statements declare, "Contractors shall execute a disclosure statement . . . specifying that they have no financial or other interest in the outcome of the project (40 CFR 1506.5[c]).

Contracting and procurement pose special problems and temptations inside government and out. The team's composition shifts, its objectives are shared only partially, and its coherence is marginal at best. Relationships are fluid and temporary; alliances and allegiances may change. In this atmosphere, tough and open talk, mutual responsibilities agreed to in advance, laid out ethical expectations, and leveraged ethics programs are among the best ways to reduce risk and sponsor ethical behavior. This method gets all participants to buy in.

Propelled by scandal and public concern, the U.S. Department of Defense (DOD) has taken the lead in the procurement function. This is logical considering the fact that its civilian acquisition work force totaled more than 550,000 in 1988 (Cheney, 1989, p. A-2). A commission appointed by President Reagan in 1985 reported that relying on government regulations alone is ineffectual and "suggested that effective self-governance by contractors might help insure the utmost propriety in the defense industry" (Defense Industry Initiative on Business Ethics and Conduct, 1990, p. 1).

The industry responded with the Defense Industry Initiative on Business Ethics and Conduct. Accounting for about one-half of all Defense Department contract funds, its signatory companies are obligated by DII principles "to self-govern by monitoring compliance with federal procurement laws and adopting procedures for voluntary disclosure of violations . . . and corrective actions taken" (Defense Industry Initiative on Business Ethics and Conduct, 1990, p. 35). In a 1989 report to the president, Secretary of Defense Dick Cheney (1989, p. 22) declared: "Within the context of vigorous law enforcement, contractor self-governance remains the most promising additional mechanism to foster compliance with the high standards expected of DOD's suppliers. The conduct revealed by recent DOD-DOJ [Departments of Defense and Justice] investigations, including Operation Ill Wind, is not representative."

That same ill wind has been blowing for 200 years; procurement fraud has been with us since the beginning of the republic. The very first congressional investigation, a 1792 inquiry into an Indian victory over troops serving under Major General Arthur St. Clair, was an eighteenth-century version of a defense procurement scandal. "Blame for the disaster was placed on the War Department, particularly the quartermaster and supply contractors, who were accused of mismanagement, neglect and delay" (Congressional Quarterly, 1974, p. 15). Historically, scandals often provoke a statutory response. In 1863, Civil War scandals led to passage of the "forerunner of the principal conflict of interest law in the federal government—18 U.S.C. Section 208" (Maskell, 1989, p. 1). Nonetheless, some behavior seems to resist change, perhaps because the "market price" is so persuasive.

New and usually more stringent procurement rules are very productive if the gauge is amount of legislation. Over and above objections to more bureaucratic paperwork, arguments against tightened standards of conduct are strong: unfair constraints on using professional expertise (several top officials did resign in the face of the new curbs); dissuading experts from temporary career moves; and unwise, hermetically sealed boundaries between the public and private sectors. On the other hand, practical experience counters with a strong case on behalf of unique procurement taboos. According to the U.S. General Accounting Office (1989, pp. 48–49), "On the basis of a questionnaire to contractor employees who had formerly worked for DOD, we reported that of 5,100 former personnel who had left DOD during fiscal years 1983 and 1984 and obtained work with a defense contractor, 32 percent, or 1,632 (1) had DOD responsibilities that could have affected their subsequent employer, (2) worked on the same project that they had worked on while at DOD, or (3) had responsibilities for DOD contracts that supported their subsequent work. We also found that 82 percent of former DOD personnel maintained business communications with DOD officials while working for a contractor; 45 percent of these communicated with former colleagues."

As risks multiply, so do administrative costs associated with reducing them. In a collaborative arena, relationships tend to be temporary, fluid, and wholly and solely dedicated to efficiently delivering a single good or service. Under these conditions, production-oriented managers may resist putting time and energy into *ethics*, of all things, when the relationship is designed single-mindedly on a market basis: get the job done. Unless a manager is willing to do the public's business on a buyer beware basis, this rejection leaves us with armies of contract compliance officers and lawyers pouring over detailed contract specifications in a suspicion-charged atmosphere.

Supplementary Tactic. As a supplementary tactic, a manager can invest in a standard game plan to build trust, improve communication, and reduce risk. In summary, an experienced coach can call for a half-dozen plays:

1. Assert ethical values and behavioral expectations at the beginning of a project or relationship.
2. Articulate government or public ethical standards and their applicability to project operations and colleagues.
3. Notify and inform partners/collaborators covered by government or public service standards.
4. Support self-governance by private-sector and nonprofit participants.
5. Prepare all parties for full disclosure and accountability.
6. Broadcast the principle of inexcusable ignorance; familiarity with public service's ethical standards is the responsibility of all parties.

It is not so much a matter of a level playing field as of playing in the same ballpark. Similar challenges and their related risks prompted President Kennedy to propose the first codification of federal conflict-of-interest legislation (some dating to Civil War scandals). In a message to Congress on April 27, 1961, he argued as follows: "This need to tap America's human resources for public purposes has blurred the distinctions between public and private life. It has led to a constant flow of people in and out of business, academic life and government. It has required us to contract with private institutions and call upon part-time consultants for important public work. It has resulted in a rapid rate of turnover among career government employees. . . . And, as a result, it has gravely multiplied the risk of conflicts of interest while seriously complicating the problem of maintaining ethical standards."

Case: Manager's Mark

The title of this case cues thinking of the subordinate as the manager's victim and also of the manager's leaving a mark on a subordinate through modeling.

Mark, a sharp young analyst in the governor's central budget shop, excelled as a junior member of the legislative liaison team. He then used all his vacation to recover from his first legislative session, with its usual bruising pressures and late nights. As his direct supervisor, you are pleased with his fine job.

Mark comes to you with a problem. He would like to leave a half-hour early for a few days to beat the crosstown rush hour delays that cut into the visiting hours at the hospital where his father is recuperating from surgery. He also requests a morning off to take his father home and get him settled in.

Of course, you are concerned about maintaining regular office discipline and about the impact on morale of what could look like privileged treatment. Mark's position qualifies for compensatory time but only with prior, signed authorization. You are certainly not going to direct that he start using—or, more accurately, abusing—his accumulated sick leave. Yet unpaid personal leave hardly seems fair after the job he has done.

What do you say? What do you do? Is this your problem?

What ethical issues are raised? Does compassion outweigh other values here?

What effect on Mark's future performance could your decision have? Is this concern your responsibility? (The tools in Chapter Six may help here.)

What Are Your Options? Check the responses with which you agree.

_____ 1.   Fraudulently back date authorization for compensatory time because good managers take risks for good employees—meaning that telling the truth and obeying the law rank well behind loyalty and productivity in *your* office.

_____ 2.   Tell Mark he has earned the time; you will sign the time cards because of *his* very special attitude or effort—a trivial falsification (for the public good?) but arbitrarily applied, meaning that rules and regulations do not apply to Mark.

For your information: A recent General Accounting Office investigation into sick leave usage by retiring employees in the General Services Administration found required authorizing and approval documentation missing (General Accounting Office, 1989, p. 54).

_____ 3.   Tell Mark to leave early and you will sign the time cards, just as you would try to accommodate any productive, cooperative employee— meaning that you generalize the treatment and take responsibility for breaking the work rules.

For your information: A colleague recounts how after many extra hours and late nights at the old U.S. Civil Service Commission, he was directed by his boss *not* to charge an upcoming vacation to vacation time.

_____ 4.   Tell Mark you cannot do anything without personnel's okay, but you do understand rigid enforcement of all the petty regulations drives good people out of government and breeds clock-watching in those who stay—meaning that passing the buck and demoralizing platitudes fail to solve the problem or motivate the employee.

_____ 5.   Hint to Mark about the available sick leave—meaning that lying or cheating is acceptable in a good cause, especially if it is Mark's lie, not yours.

_____ 6.   Explain to Mark that no personal business is allowed on government time and you cannot appear to play favorites, so there is nothing you can do, and then turn back to the papers on your desk—simultaneously failing to solve the problem and showing Mark the utility of hiding behind the rules.

_____ 7.   Tell Mark always to reserve some vacation time and that his lack of foresight causes a problem you cannot be expected to solve—ignoring the problem, blaming Mark, and avoiding responsibility.

8. _____

(Your resolution)

Would your response be different if Mark's performance were marginal?
- Does different performance warrant different treatment?
An old administrative precept calls for authority commensurate with responsibility. Would giving managers more latitude in situations such as this promote an ethical environment?
- Would latitude deprive a manager of a protective refuge?
- Is the risk of arbitrary treatment worth it from the employee's perspective? The public's? Yours?

Chapter 10

Building
an Ethical Agency

Routine agency operations set the organization's ethical tone, and this chapter advocates agency operations structured to support and promote ethical action. Laying out objections lets managers lay them aside—the venture is possible, desirable, and banks on prudential management. The chapter itemizes feasible agency interventions through which managers build ethical concerns directly into daily routine and expected conduct. An ethics impact statement integrates ethics soundly and methodically into agency decisions, and agency audit and risk-assessment tools contribute to the building of an ethical agency. A case study portrays in an agency setting several of this book's main themes.

An agency is an abstraction, legal authority, and set of relationships. It does not really have moral obligations. These are reserved for individuals. Asserting an agency's moral responsibility actually symbolizes ethical responsibilities imposed on its members by the agency's officers, management, statutory authority, and functional mission.

A new item on the public service agenda is building ethical organizations. This is a symbol, too, a shorthand way of speaking about forging administrative relations, systems, processes, procedures, and standards that fortify the ethical individual, bolster ethical reasoning, nourish ethical dialogue, and inject ethical concerns into routine operations—admittedly, a tall order.

Most likely, we will go the route of fusion, described in the introduction, by taking both the compliance and integrity roads to this goal. The reason is that neither alone has worked satisfactorily. A report of the congressional General Accounting Office (1981, p. 1) advises, "Agencies need to develop programs that aggressively implement standards of employee conduct and actively promote ethical behavior."

If we agree on the goal and route, there still remains the question of the best vehicle: How can we move the item off the agenda and into office operations?

Abstract answers include linking personal and public ethics through organizational practices and procedures, promoting an organizational framework to buttress ethical integrity and responsibility, supporting ethical practitioners, and sustaining ethical reasoning and behavior within public agencies. These are really skeletal goals that beg to be fleshed out with concrete proposals for action. This chapter offers proposals in three categories: agency operations, a model ethics audit and risk-assessment strategies, and an ethics impact statement.

Other agencies, jurisdictions, and business practices are a rich source of tested ideas. The resulting ethics agenda draws on a mix of actual practices, the author's imagination, and suggestions that surfaced in discussions and meetings. For example, at ASPA's 1989 ethics conference, the session devoted to institutionally operationalizing ethics aired almost two dozen proposals, including "an explicit factor in recruiting, hiring, and promoting people" and accountability for ethical conduct through performance appraisals. The Education and Training Working Group at the conference urged publicizing positive models, the object of the Exemplar's Project initiated under Terry Cooper's guidance. Leadership's critical role emerged strongly at the Conference Board's 1990 business ethics conference.

Agency Operations

A very first step is usually to formulate a written policy, often as an adopted code, and some of the items listed here are part of managing the code (examined in Chapter Eight). Experiences with codes and with public and corporate ethics programs flag stable, ongoing attention, which works better than fits and starts. That entails *an ethics program with leadership at the center*. Senior managers' reputations and behavior plus their commitment to the agency's ethics program are vital to its success. Although rarely as cheap as the old adage would have us believe, talk *is* important. Officers' and managers' participation in programs and signing off on communications, from office memos and house newsletters to budgets and news releases, do play a role.

But talking commitment is not enough. Public employees are sensitive to the flow of real resources, an expressive nonverbal cue in any organization. Staff time and real dollars that go for training, incentives, performance, and ethical aspects of agency policies and practices will be used by agency staff members to meter the authenticity of the talk and the priority of public service ethics in the agency. By way of clarification, what do *you* think is the more meaningful communication, fine words at a staff meeting or disregarded negligence and padded budget estimates? Why would colleagues and employees think otherwise?

Ethics can be built into daily routine and expected conduct. Ethical reasoning can be made (1) creditworthy, (2) recognized, and (3) routinely expected. How? (Let us omit individualized tools for decision making such as the ethics responsibility statement in Exhibit 6.4.) A baker's dozen of feasible techniques can contribute to making ethics a standard dimension of management, decision making, and agency operations. These intervention techniques are laid out in Exhibit 10.1. The list converts into a training tool when we ask ourselves to identify items most effective in our own office, items least effective in our own office, items we intend to bring back to the office, and items we would like our supervisor to introduce.

These proposals load another set of duties on the human resource function, but as a state personnel manager quipped about new ethics-based tasks, "Why not? We handle everything that people care about, even parking. Especially parking."

This agenda lands on every manager's desk, and earnest attention is a tough, constant demand. That managers teach subordinates by doing is hardly a trailblazing idea, but it needs to be extended directly to *ethical* aspects of behavior in the agency. More than modeling is needed, however. Any one and any number in the agency can play in this game. At every level and in every type of unit, there is something to be done to improve the ethical climate. The whole team can and should participate. It is the manager's job to see that they do. Ethics is not a spectator sport.

Surely, integrity-based, positive ethics can be integrated into an agency's operations. The widespread institutionalization of the merit principle over the past century shows that we *can* transform the way we do everyday business. It may be a slow, frustrating process, and there is much to learn. Woodrow Wilson

---

Exhibit 10.1. Intervention Techniques for Integrating Ethics into Agency Operations.

Do both compliance and integrity training and counseling.

Give briefings on common ethical problems on the job for new hires.

Give termination briefings on potential post-employment problems.

Designate senior manager(s) for integrity issues, separate from compliance/investigative unit.

Require annual sign-off on prospective commitment and compliance.

Attend to ethical values and character in recruitment.

Integrate ethical performance into promotional exams and annual reviews; link ethical behavior to incentives.

Publicize positive, noteworthy role models.

Raise ethical concerns at meetings and through regular communication channels.

Train middle managers to recognize and commend subordinates' statements about ethical concerns.

Review management practices and administrative routines at every level and in every type of unit in the organization.

Get the whole team—all employees, all levels, all units—to participate; ethics is not a spectator sport.

Give earnest attention to ethical treatment of subordinates, clients, and others.

([1887] 1987, p. 16) warned over a century ago, "In government, as in virtue, the hardest of hard things is to make progress."

Five Objections. Wilson also noted in a less frequently cited quote, "We go on criticizing when we ought to be creating" ([1887] 1987, p. 16). All new ideas ignite derivative problems, and an ethics agenda is no exception. West Virginia, "trying to recover both morally and financially from the loss of over $200 million through the mismanagement of state investment funds" (Hall, 1989, p. 20), pronounced itself the thirty-sixth state to create an independent ethics commission. The speaker of the West Virginia House of Delegates and cosponsor of the state's 1989 ethics act reviewed objections to the legislation. His arguments (Chambers, 1989, p. v) are relevant to objections to administrative ventures. "'You can't legislate morality' was a common refrain for those who questioned the need for comprehensive ethics legislation. The bureaucracy of ethics regulations . . . seemed to outweigh any benefits. To some, an ethics law was merely window dressing, unlikely to change how real public officials act except to complicate being one. Inertia, rather than opposition, presented the greatest difficulty."

There are five major objections to agency action: (1) the substitution of ritual for responsibility, (2) ethical behavior as exception, not rule, (3) red tape, (4) behavior modification, and (5) the double-edged threat of vigilante ethics. Because we can lay them aside only by meeting them, let us take each one in turn.

The first objection views ritualistic compliance as a poor but likely proxy for ethics. It is valid as far as it goes, but it does not go far enough. Institutional mechanisms do endanger the broader goal by threatening to substitute formalistic compliance for ethical responsibility. But must they? Can we accommodate new concerns in administrative routines without trivializing fundamental principles? The answer is, "Of course." That is what responsive, innovative public management is all about.

The second objection is keyed to defining ethical behavior as the exception, not the rule, by rewarding managers for ethical behavior. Some managers, noses wrinkled in distaste, resist linking ethical behavior to professional rewards or financial incentives. Unless we are willing to ignore ethics altogether, this objection undercuts the former by leaving no alternative except routinizing ethics as an ordinary habit in daily operations. Public administration is at a point of choice.

The third objection hoists the red flag of red tape, a symbol of excessive bureaucratic routine derived from the banding once tied around legal papers and official documents in England. Regulations and procedures should be instrumental in the achievement of objectives, not valued for their own sake, and few public practitioners are particularly fond of rules and paperwork. Even the Occupational Safety and Health Administration (the OSHA of labor regulations) subscribes to this attitude. In remarks delivered at ASPA's 1989 ethics conference, the deputy assistant secretary of the U.S. Department of Labor said, "OSHA's mission is to assure America's workers safe and healthful working conditions. Therefore, our priorities are not paperwork or statistics or litigation. Our priority is safeguarding the workplace" (McMillan, 1989, p. 1).

This attitude does not preclude necessary or desired rules and procedures. Participants from state and local jurisdictions at the same conference used a voluntary survey to petition for more direction and guidelines, which translates into rules and procedure. This voiced need was one of the few statistically significant differences between these participants and their federal counterparts (Keehley, 1990).

Federal employees already *enjoy* detailed standards and full-blown ethics programs with a heavy compliance slant. The OGE surveyed ninety-nine federal agencies' activities in 1989 and discovered that more than one-half (52 percent) of all agency responses linked ethics programs' goals to implementation (U.S. Office of Government Ethics, 1990a, p. 23). Understanding standards (29.4 percent of responses), oversight of financial disclosure (15.5 percent), post-employment advising (4.4 percent), and developing improved standards (2.8 percent) fall in this category, compared to employee awareness (28.4 percent) and "other" (19.4 percent). Further, the single most commonly used training materials are agency regulations (1990a, p. 26).

A questionnaire published in *City & State* (1989, p. 105) verified the perceived need for procedures at the state and local levels. The questionnaire drew responses from 456 readers (40 percent were in city government, 18 percent in county or state government, and 19 percent in special districts or school districts); 62 percent indicated that the jurisdiction has an ethics law. Fully 85 percent responded yes to the question "Should state and local governments implement ethics legislation?" while 46 percent said no to "Do you think your government's ethics law is being enforced?"

Federal, state, and local managers undoubtedly and pragmatically would resist intricate, paper-laden, and immoderate proposals. Three rules of thumb let us respond to the need without adding unduly to the administrative burden. First, ethics do's, like ethics don'ts, should be as few as necessary and as simple as possible to do the job. Second, instead of force-feeding prototypical packages or universal remedies, ethics programs are best tailored to the administrative realities in different jurisdictions and agencies. The third rule of thumb identifies the internal, direct clients of agency interventions as the ethical managers and employees who want to do the right thing (see Chapter Eight). These guidelines explain why the proposed ethics impact statement follows the contours of the simpler, shorter environmental assessment instead of the more rigorous environmental impact statement (sometimes as long as 150 to 300 pages).

The fourth objection is to modifying behavior. It can be raised against all work routines and rules, including laws and standards of conduct. Yes, they modify behavior; that is what they are for. Yes, some people will spend a great deal of time figuring a way around them, and some will *have to* in order to do their job. A case in point is how performance is adapted to its measure; recall the old story about sanitation workers watering down garbage because their productivity was measured by tonnage.

Then again, other people will ignore the spirit in favor of rigid application, as a case from Philadelphia reveals. This is the city portrayed as "corrupt and contented" at the turn of the century by muckraker Lincoln Steffens ([1904] 1982). Philadelphia's extensive ethics code dates to 1963. A decision issued by its commission prohibited municipal employees from being foster parents (who were defined as contracted agents with the city) because full-time employment meant that they could not receive additional government payments (Potamianos, 1990).

Cases throughout this book suggest that these problems are endemic. An annual sign-off can address them explicitly by targeting *next year's* performance and *future* commitment; it allows everyone a good-faith promise instead of assuring a few pointless lies.

The upshot of the most carefully crafted ethics program may not be entirely what the public manager would want. Human imagination being what it is, some perverse behavior is predictable. Yet if we reject proposals until perfection is guaranteed, in effect we reject all change.

The fifth and final objection to agency action sees these proposals as a modern version of that sword hanging over Damocles. The threat is double-edged. One edge cuts into productivity: more shackles on the manager menace public service. The other is at our neck: the potential for harassment and coercion in an abstract sphere about which people disagree. For this and other reasons, procedural protections are crucial to an agency's ethics program (see Chapter Eight).

Proposals that bear on personnel generally, but especially on recruitment and promotion, provoke legitimate concern about fourth amendment rights and unreasonable search. The backlash against polygraphs, reference and credit checks, urinalyses, and blood tests invites nightmarish visions about the probable response to public agencies' use of so-called integrity tests (honesty screening). Usually paper-and-pencil instruments, such tests are very much in vogue in the corporate world (Deutsch, 1990, p. 29); an estimated 5,000 to 6,000 businesses use them for screening and selecting job applicants, usually for nonmanagerial, low-skill jobs (U.S. Congress, 1990, p. 11). The congressional Office of Technology Assessment (OTA) defines these tests as "written tests designed to identify individuals applying for work in such jobs who have relatively high propensities to steal money or property on the job, or who are likely to engage in behavior of a more generally 'counterproductive' nature" (U.S. Congress, 1990, p. 1). In the latter instance, the OTA mentions *time theft* such as sick leave abuse (see Chapter Nine) as an example. The OTA finds no clear evidence for or against the tests predicting dishonest behavior. "Errors in test results, potential discriminatory impact, and potential violations of privacy raise important public policy issues pertaining to the use of integrity tests" (U.S. Congress, 1990, p. 10).

The Employee Polygraph Protection Act of 1988 prohibits most private employers from using lie detectors for screening applicants or testing employees, but the law does not affect federal, state, and local governments. In 1989, the Supreme Court upheld drug testing for government employees who operate hazardous equipment or carry weapons; later that year, the Court ruled that mandatory drug testing without prior labor union approval is permitted for rail and airlines employees.

Some current "good ideas" are negative, obsessed with compliance, and even demoralizing. Do these threats bid managers to hold out for no risk and do nothing? Or can managers go ahead and rely on an ancient virtue to minimize risk?

Prudence. Managers can and should move ahead, prudentially. The success of an agency's ethics agenda turns on its managers' prudence, in the age-old meaning of wisdom and caring for the community and general good. It demands the rejection of its modern corruption into personal expediency or self-interest.

In the *Nicomachean Ethics* (Book VI), Aristotle associates *practical wisdom* with the statesman who is concerned with right action; others, solely concerned with right thinking, may indulge in purely abstract wisdom. Edmund Burke and others have argued that "although principles are necessary, they are not enough. They must be applied to concrete reality by a type of practical reasoning which Burke called prudence" (Canavan, 1963, p. 606). Prudence tempers the impeccable with the practical in order to pursue the ideal, not simply substitute the doable. Recall that pragmatism is built into the initial decision-making model in Chapter Two.

Public managers are, by and large, creative, judicious, and capable of conceiving of positive, nonthreatening ways of incorporating ethics into agency procedures. In annual reviews, for example, the criterion could be self-defined by having the employee respond to the question "What do *you* do to contribute to the ethical operations or practices in this agency?" A more directed device is shown in Exhibit 10.2. A contractual format is suitable for an annual sign-off on prospective code commitment and compliance, as shown in Exhibit 10.3 from New York City. Both illustrate the practical importance of trust and oath giving (Chapters One and Two), along with personal commitment.

Considering the volume of paper crossing a manager's desk, flagging important communication becomes an art. Interestingly, while written standards are distributed by most (eighty-nine) of the federal agencies surveyed on their 1989 ethics programs, more than one-half (fifty-six) never require certification that the material was read, and only two-fifths (forty-one) of the ninety-nine agencies surveyed require certification by new employees (U.S. Office of Government Ethics, 1990a, p. 24).

A city manager offers a word of advice for prudent managers with first-rate ethics programs. Expect mistakes. "It then becomes important to deal with them quickly and openly. An analysis and discussion with staff on why the

Exhibit 10.2. A Simple But Complete Performance Appraisal.

This appraisal is from Gary B. Brumback, "Institutionalizing Ethics in Government," *Public Personnel Management*, 1991, *20*. Reprinted by permission.

	Yes	*No*	*Explain* (in addendum)
Did you meet all objectives?	____	____	X
*Was your manner of performance positive:	____	____	X
On the managerial factor?	____	____	X
On the professional/technical factor?	____	____	X
On the general conduct and ethics factor?	____	____	X
Is there clear evidence you significantly exceeded one or more objectives?	____	____	X
(If yes, describe below, attach or reference)	____	____	X
Reviewer's concurrence?	____	____	X
Employee and reviewer's signatures and dates:			

*See [Manual or] Performance Handbook.

Exhibit 10.3. Certification of Receipt.

This certification is from the City of New York and is provided courtesy of Stephen Rolandi.

> I have received a copy of New York City's Code of Ethics and I agree to familiarize myself with its provisions, and to abide by its terms.
>
> SIGNATURE _____
>
> PRINT NAME _____
>
> DATE   _____

ethical impropriety occurred and how to prevent such an occurrence in the future is essential" (Bonczek, 1990, p. 7).

Rules of Thumb. Rules of thumb for the prudential manager are culled from this and earlier chapters and listed here as general guidelines for ready reference. They speak to managers' decisions about both ethical issues and ethics in the agency (see Exhibit 10.4). Serving public managers best when combined with the fundamentals shown on page 109 in Exhibit 6.2, these rules of thumb give purpose and direction to ethical action in the agency and to agency intervention techniques.

Ethics Impact Statement and Process

The proposed ethics impact statement (EthIS) provides for a decision-making process that integrates several analytic methods and tools laid out in this book. Figure 10.1 charts the steps in this process. Formally adopted (and adapted), it

Exhibit 10.4. Rules of Thumb.

The "rule of thumb" derives from English common law that permitted the head of house-hold to beat the spouse using a stick with a diameter no larger than the thumb. (Gender references in original formulation are removed to meet contemporary standards.)

Danger! Justifying an action in the name of a greater good or higher authority, instead of taking action for the sake of that purpose (Chapter One).

Disobedience is preferred to illegality—refuse an illegal directive (Chapter Two).

Public position may not be used for dissent as a citizen (Chapter Two).

Ethical public service rejects naïveté and cynicism and opts for hard-headed optimism (Chapter Two).

Respect for future generations is a test for the public interest (Chapter Three).

Empathy is another test of commitment to the public interest (Chapter Three).

A public manager's first task is fixing the problem and only secondarily fixing the blame (Chapter Four).

Ethical neutrality strips the humanity from managers and service recipients; dehumanizing the victims denies the ethical element (Chapter Four).

In public service, the search is for compatibility and balance, reconciliation and accommodation (Chapter Five).

Impartial open-mindedness is the first-order test of genuine empathy in public service (Chapter Five).

The impartial public manager is ethically driven, not ethically empty (Chapter Five).

Danger! Militant claims to moral superiority (Chapter Five).

Where to draw the line? The more *un*ethical one judges a behavior, the less likely one will practice it or tolerate others' doing it (Chapter Seven).

Ethics is not a toggle switch. Ethical managers exercise reasonable selectivity among responsibilities (Chapter Six) and choose their battles in a principled way (Chapter Seven).

Danger! The slippery slope and losing the capacity to make moral judgments or act on them (Chapter Seven).

Ethical managers and employees are the internal, direct clients of agency intervention (Chapter Eight).

In a diversifying work force, some behaviors need rethinking; others need full-scale remodeling (Chapter Nine).

In a collaborative setting, put ethical issues and standards on the table, right up front (Chapter Nine).

Ethics do's, like ethics don'ts, should be as few as necessary and as simple as possible to do the job (Chapter Ten).

Tailor operations to specific administrative realities (Chapter Ten).

A responsible manager seeks to minimize opportunities and temptation and encourage integrity, both personal and institutional (Chapter Ten).

procedurally secures a role for ethical analysis in agency deliberations, particularly over policies and regulations. Another application is critiquing potent standard operating procedures in the agency. An individual manager can apply the process informally to working through the wrenching dilemma that seems an inevitable part of public service. The design is deliberately slanted toward process rather than outcome because *the objective is to integrate systematically ethical analysis into decision making.* The goal is to amplify managers' thinking, not usurp it.

An EthIS or kindred framework can help add ethical analysis to the decision maker's formidable inventory, customarily amassed through years of cultivating new skills and mastering new techniques. Take inventory for a moment. Counting in dollars? Use cost-benefit analysis. Accounting for nonquantifiable factors? Turn to cost-effectiveness analysis. Pull out a standardized format for fiscal notes when proposed legislation calls for cost estimates. Develop performance and productivity measures. Apply evaluation techniques and statistical analysis. Attack the project with program evaluation and review techniques (PERT). Today public managers must puzzle over scenarios worked up on a spreadsheet or scrutinize once-novel variables in environmental impact statements, risk assessments, and comparable worth analyses. The point is, in order to assist decision making and improve decisions, each analytic skill adds new techniques, technical tools, and some new vocabulary. Responsible for specialized knowledge that keeps accumulating, public managers in effect sign up for lifelong learning.

Ethical analysis is no different. It makes comparable intellectual demands. Like the other items in the inventory, it is sound only when used soundly. An EthIS must be properly applied, at the right time, in carefully selected situations. Perhaps there is one major difference: it cannot be farmed out to paid consultants or outside authorities. (Expert advice and external assistance are appropriate in the fact-finding and analytic stages.) The process is dynamic, consultative, participatory, and cooperative (versus adversarial). But it is *not* perfunctory. Ethics involves individual responsibility for moral judgments and choices. The last step in the process, signing the EthIS, is not a hollow symbol; it is a critical component of the seven-step process. Ethics responsibilities cannot be delegated, bought, or temporarily rented.

For efficiency's sake and to minimize the administrative burden and paperwork, the EthIS is patterned after the environmental impact assessment. It is a shorter, simpler, streamlined version of a formal environmental impact statement. The acronym EthIS distinguishes the process from its environmental kin. The Council on Environmental Quality (1987) in the Executive Office of the President issued regulations for implementing the National Environmental Policy Act, the underlying charter for environmental protection nationally. Many recommendations that follow are adaptations of these regulations (40 CFR 1500–1508).

Step One: Feasibility

Timing. Because the objective is ethical action, not after-the-fact justification, the EthIS process begins in planning, when a proposal's initial feasibility is appraised and before a decision is made.

Exclusion. Answers to Rion's questions in Chapter Six, "Why is this bothering me?" and "Is it my problem?" asked at the agency level may mean that no ethics impact statement is prepared. Proposals with no significant ethical facets either

Figure 10.1. Ethics Impact Statement Process.

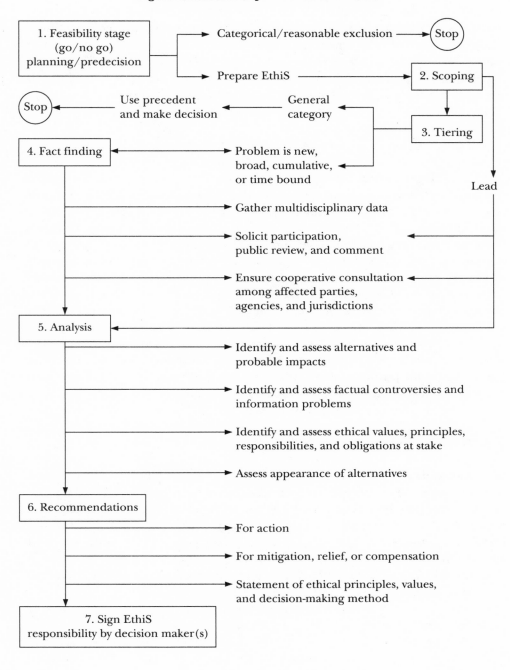

individually or cumulatively can be excluded categorically. Note, however, that an ethical dimension permeates all significant decisions. Because ethics for public managers is linked to behavior, proposed agency actions that will not practically be affected by EthIS (for example, a legal mandate) or emergency responses in which delay constitutes a decision (crisis management) may be reasonably excluded. Yet, an EthIS on otherwise reasonably excluded actions may yield ideas for corrective action and/or statutory change (activating the inventive resolution from Chapter Six).

Step Two: Scoping

A decision to prepare an EthIS initiates scoping, "an early and open process for determining the scope of issues to be addressed and for identifying the significant issues related to a proposed action" (40 CFR 1501.7). *Scope* refers to "the range of actions, alternatives, and impacts to be considered" (1508.25). A pilot diagnosis exercises selectivity again and sets boundaries. That can be accomplished by asking Rion's question "What is the ethical concern?" and responding in terms of Cooper's formulation of obligation as responsibility *for* and accountability as responsibility *to*. The diagnosis is used to identify and eliminate insignificant elements. Relevant criteria in scoping include severity of impacts, controversy and uncertainties, and gravity of values and principles at stake.

At this point, a *lead* senior manager is designated, appropriate staff members are assigned, and a reporting date is set. A team may include a low-level line manager for purposes of responsibility and effectiveness. "The person performing the task is in an ideal position to assess the outcomes of the action in terms of human impact" (Denhardt, 1988, p. 147).

Step Three: Tiering

The lead manager satisfies a core value in public service, efficiency, by forestalling repetition. Where appropriate, the manager folds the proposal into an umbrella category keyed to general ethical (versus legal or pragmatic) criteria and makes the decision by using precedent and logic. This potential shortcut also checks for consistency. The EthIS process proceeds only with new, broad, or cumulative factors or when a review is suitable. Note that past decisions may be time bound. As a check on obsolescence, the manager can consider revisiting dated decisions.

Step Four: Fact-Finding

Many decision-making models begin with getting the facts, getting them all, and getting them straight. Realistically, there are informational limits that are best set by preliminary stakeholder analysis (see Chapter Seven). On the other hand, inexcusable ignorance scuttles the whole EthIS process. Exhibit 4.2 (page 70) poses general but critical questions about information. It is imperative to identify legal obligations and mandates. Chapter Four raises three questions about the legal context so critical to public service.

Because a wide sweep in fact-finding helps minimize bias, error, and omission in the analytic stage, the process calls for multidisciplinary data. An inclusive sweep covers four categories of information about *facts* and *values:* objective, subjective, quantitative, and qualitative. Expert opinion and advice are solicited at this step and the next. Preliminary stakeholder analysis is crucial to designing meaningful participation and consultation.

At some point, too much information complicates matters instead of clarifying them. "[A]rriving at ethical decisions requires a greater tolerance for ambiguity than does arriving at decisions based on empirical evidence alone" (Denhardt, 1988, p. 120). When to stop collecting facts and to proceed to the next step is a decision critical to the process.

Step Five: Analysis

The EthIS team selects an ethical analytic framework at this stage. Criteria underlying selection are discussed in Chapter Six. A truly momentous issue or having no team consensus calls for the application of several frameworks or one framework that combines different ethical perspectives (see checklist in Exhibit 6.1, page 105). Possible analytic techniques include one or more of the following: identifying values or principles at risk (Exhibits 1.2 and 1.3, pages 23 and 28); assessing and ranking responsibilities by rigor, perhaps using tools 1 through 3 discussed in Chapter Six; and/or using the stakeholder diagnostic presented in Exhibit 7.1 (page 122). Note that federal regulations for environmental impact statements require disclosure of all major opinions, points of controversy, and incomplete or unavailable information.

In this stage, substance is assessed and so is appearance. The latter's separate entry in Figure 10.1 symbolizes its eminence in public service, not its analytic isolation from the assessment of alternatives and probable impacts.

Step Six: Recommendations

Once obligations, impacts, principles, and values have been sorted out and selected in step five, the EthIS now recommends an action or decision. The go/no-go decision model in Chapter Two honors legal and pragmatic boundaries in ethical decision making. In a true dilemma, the fundamental obligation to serve the public interest implies reconciliation where possible (see Chapters Three and Five). As a result, the team successively corrects and modifies proposals. In that context, a rigorous obligation to avoid doing harm implies that the team's goal is to minimize harm and reduce any adverse impact on values, principles, and/ or stakeholders (see Chapter Six). The end result is that the decision maker (or makers) identifies the public interest by proposing an action, discloses the decision-making method, and recommends action triggered by the proposal that he or she considers obligatory.

As for the document, its general style and overall format can parallel the environmental impact regulations: concise rather than wordy, clear prose, plain language, and comprehensible to the general public.

Step Seven: Responsibility

The importance of taking responsibility for a decision has already been discussed in Chapters Four and Six. The format for the ethics responsibility statement to be signed by the EthIS team members and the agency head can be adapted from the model statement shown in Exhibit 6.4 (page 116) or a similar declaration. A simple statement might read, "I certify that the attached policy, regulation, or procedure is recommended after due consideration of its ethical dimensions."

There remain, of course, the implementation and evaluation processes once the decision is made.

Pros and Cons of Ethics Impact Statements

The EthIS and similar instruments promise advantages not too different from evaluation assessments (Wholey, 1983, p. 103). The list is tempting: assist in setting priorities and realistic objectives, identify early on the problems and needed corrections in policy or regulation, pinpoint unsettled issues and unanticipated effects for legislative proposals or executive decision, and inform decision makers and the public.

As an *action-forcing device,* an ethics impact statement can contribute to resolving disputes quickly and fairly, one of the stated goals of environmental impact statements (40 CFR 1501.1[c]). The EthIS process, like its parent model, has the paradoxical potential for accomplishing just the opposite. As a *disclosure instrument,* it could freeze action by increasing political opposition over newly clarified controversies and stakes. Even with subdued enthusiasm, one can still admit that an ethics impact statement reserves a role and formalizes a process for ethical analysis. At minimum, it is an advocacy device and learning tool for ethical reasoning and ethical decision making in the agency.

More modest, usually noninstitutional, frameworks for probing public policy's ethical aspects have been and are now being developed for those "unperceived angles and forgotten dimensions" (Fischer, 1983, p. 32). Managers may prefer to insert an examination of the normative elements of operating procedures, policy, and other decisions into evaluation techniques already in place.

Agency Ethics Audit

The agenda outlined in this chapter is double-pronged. A jurisdiction's or agency's ethics program realistically cannot be divorced from compliance issues. Legally enforceable standards and controls play an important part in establishing a fair, productive, and supportive workplace. Complying with agency procedures and obeying rules *are* important. But an agency's ethics program need not and should not focus exclusively on the adequacy of and compliance with internal controls and legal prohibitions. It can also target ethical reasoning and its role in the organization by expanding workaday priorities to managers' receptivity to ethical considerations and the scope for ethical deliberation in the agency. The aim is to move on both fronts.

Before we agree on what needs to be done, it makes sense to evaluate current practice, problems, and potential. A practical, accessible tool is necessary for assessing the agency as an ethical environment. The resource at the end of the book offers a model ethics audit designed to profile the agency's strengths and deficiencies and produce an action agenda in a format appropriate for periodic review. It functions somewhat like an audit manual in less regulated jurisdictions and more informal agencies. The word *model* is aimed at encouraging adaptation to each agency's peculiarities. (Given Washington's elaborate standards of conduct, formal ethics offices and systems, and control mechanisms and audit procedures, the model audit necessarily serves in federal offices as a diagnostic tool or vulnerability checklist.)

An audit absorbs managers' time and energy, along with staff resources. Even allowing that any operation can be improved, no manager can do it all, and all at once. Some realistic selectivity is needed. A quick overview can give a reading on urgency and criticality. This can be done using the mapping diagnostic in Figure 1.2 (p. 30). A serious mismatch between preference and practice could move the full-fledged audit to high priority on a manager's agenda.

A cautionary note is in order here. At a hearing on HUD, a senator asked, "What's the thermometer that you inject into an agency to get an immediate readout of the health of that agency?" Then-chairman of the President's Council on Integrity and Efficiency, William M. Diefenderfer, III, answered, "Well, unfortunately, I don't think the level of the technology is at the level of the thermometer. It's more the hand to the brow that maybe your mother did to establish whether or not you have a fever. So it's not a perfect instrument" (U.S. Senate, 1990).

Assessing Job Risk

Job vulnerability assessment is a related method limited to identifying potential snags or staff that need special assistance. A form of risk assessment, it concentrates on compliance, detection, and enforcement. For fraud or other abuses, "[a]n initial step is learning to recognize indicators of the presence of fraud or of the potential for it" (U.S. Department of Defense, 1984, preface).

The GAO analyzed fraud cases from 1976 to 1979 and found that federal employees were responsible for 29 percent of the attributable cases (General Accounting Office, 1981, p. 1). Using a Delphi technique to pool expert judgments and statistical techniques to analyze responses, the GAO identified fifty-two factors affecting relative job exposure. The GAO's method is not meant to predict the behavior of individual incumbents but to play the odds on certain jobs. It rests on a proportional relationship between problems and opportunities, all else held constant (General Accounting Office, 1981, p. 10). For example, the position of food inspector ranked high on relative vulnerability among the jobs selected for evaluation. A poor "integrity record" (reported misconduct) or reputation did not appear to influence rankings in a test evaluation; the second-highest exposure was awarded another position with "an excellent integrity record" (General Accounting Office, 1981, p. 11).

Isolation and discretion are defining characteristics for the food inspector's job. If the manager's objective is to minimize temptation and opportunity among line employees assigned off-site discretionary leverage, then the implication of the GAO's study is that preventive action (subject to position count and budget constraints) calls for teaming employees and frequent rotation among partners and sites.

A deputy attorney general in the U.S. Department of Justice reports that the number of federal convictions for corruption among public servants nationally increased 400 percent between 1977 and 1986; in 1986 alone, federal indictments resulted in over 1,000 convictions of corrupt public officials at all government levels (Burns, 1987, p. 46). National patterns of arrest and prosecution indicate that there are some standard high-risk job functions, but because the data come from enforcement, only known or reported areas are flagged.

Assuming that ingenuity outpaces detection, analysis necessarily lags behind novel abuses. Computer crime once fit this category but is now the focus of special security and many publications, including *Computers: Crimes, Clues and Controls*, prepared by the President's Council on Integrity and Efficiency (1986) as a management guide. Nonetheless, much more needs to be done. In *The Cuckoo's Egg* (1990), Cliff Stoll, stalker of viruses and worms, rebukes government, academic, law enforcement, and other personnel for carelessly and thereby dangerously downplaying or mismanaging computer security.

If one suspects that white-collar crime is especially ingenious and therefore undetected to some degree, then the fact that recurring abuses are so pedestrian comes as no surprise. Some traditions are honored even in the face of vigorous enforcement efforts. "Almost every area of public service has its distinctive forms of corruption, with variations cropping up at different levels of government across the country" (Burns, 1987, p. 46). Typical patterns and related examples include police selling protection; case fixing; contract bid rigging and kickbacks; regulatory crimes involving building and utility inspectors, licensing, and land use; judicial conflicts of interest; election crimes, including ballot and campaign finance fraud; narcotics-related abuses, such as firearms violations; and graft of all kinds.

The Prize. Some local governments prove that America is still the land of opportunity. No stranger to corruption, cities provoked the reform movement of the Progressive Era at the turn of the century and its literary genre, muckraking. Old-time, big-city machine politics is associated with corruption for all the right reasons. George W. Plunkitt of New York's former Tammany machine bestowed upon us the standard specimen of conflict of interest: "Everybody is talkin' these days about Tammany men growin' rich on graft, but nobody thinks of drawin' the distinction between honest graft and dishonest graft. There's all the distinction in the world between the two. . . . There's an honest graft, and I'm an example of how it works. I might sum up the whole thing by sayin': 'I seen my opportunities and I took 'em' " (quoted in Riordan, 1974, p. 7).

Edward Koch's third term as New York City's mayor began in January 1986 and provides a wealth of more recent examples. *City for Sale* (Newfield and Barrett, 1989) lays them out with an impassioned outrage very much in the muckrakers' tradition.

Present-day Chicago is famous for many things, machine politics and corruption among them. A study of official misconduct in Chicago and Cook County, part of the Chicago Ethics Project, identified almost 400 incidents between 1970 and 1987 and found that nearly two-thirds of the cases implicated municipal officials and employees (ChicagoMetro Ethics Coalition, 1989, p. 3; Gardiner and Malec, 1987). Law enforcement, involving police, sheriffs, and courtroom personnel, accounted for 30 percent of the municipal cases. Regulation, covering inspection, licensing, permits, and citations, constituted the second-largest category at 27 percent of municipal cases; *expediting* was a major subcategory. Other municipal cases involved city departments of the treasurer, streets, water, consumer affairs, and finance/revenue. Of all 400 cases in the city and county over the period, 53 involved government contracting. As for positions, the lineup for cited offenders was one-half, line employees; one-quarter, elected officials; and one-quarter, department heads, supervisors, managers, and appointed board members (ChicagoMetro Ethics Coalition, 1989, p. 3). (The researchers suggested a strategy of public mobilization for combatting corruption [Gardiner and Malec, 1989].)

In his celebrated autobiography, Lincoln Steffens wrote of corruption in Los Angeles's early days. Seemingly foreseeing the contemporary scene described in Tom Wolfe's *The Bonfire of the Vanities* (1987), Steffens argued that "society really offers a prize for evil-doing: money, position, power." He concluded that the fault lies not so much with Adam, Eve, or even the serpent. "Now I come and I am trying to show you that it was, it is the apple" ([1931] 1974, p. 289).

Big-city government is big business, and that offers a chance for big but ill-begotten prizes. (Just think of the opportunities in economic development alone.) From the business front, Laura Nash prescribes "facing up to fallibility." "When you couple the undeniable pervasiveness of human fallibility with the age-old temptations of money and power, the need for a deliberate exploration of the moral challenges of management becomes clear" (1990, p. 3).

The Lesson. Responsible managers try to reduce temptation through routine procedures and controls. Concerned with creating a supportive environment for compliance but also for ethical behavior, *a manager seeks to minimize opportunities and temptations and to encourage integrity, both personal and institutional.* This managerial responsibility of prevention applies to government no less than to nonprofit or other components of public service. In response to the HUD scandal, high-risk, vulnerable areas identified with incipient problems were marked for preventive action across dozens of federal agencies.

The many steps along the introduction's fusion road to a supportive ethical environment partly follow a paper trail. As Paul Appleby (1951, p. 169) rightfully pointed out, "The bureaucratic substructure and its red tape often provide the bulwark of agency conscience."

Case: The Many Victims of Abuse and Neglect

This case is loosely adapted from data in Finholm's "Social Work Tests Body and Soul," 1989, pp. A1, A12–13.

A social worker resigns from the state's child welfare agency in frustration, he says, over the state's reneging on its promise of resources to help his careworn clients. When he took the job, he did not know that bilingual case workers like himself end up with a higher caseload than other social workers. With little professional training and a self-taught specialty in child abuse and neglect (his bachelor's degree is in primary education), he finds himself juggling a caseload well above the standards set by the Child Welfare League of America.

Experts point out that such overloading contributes to high turnover. Other contributing factors are dangerous sites designated for teams, although often no co-worker is available; walking down infested hallways hearing death threats shouted by an abusive parent; an agency manual specifying clothing a social worker can run in; spending a big part of each work week on paperwork and court reports; and having to tell a child the court's decision while the custodial parent lies stoned on the couch.

To a manager responsible for subordinates' performance and professional well-being as well as meeting the agency's mission, the turnover means untrained, raw recruits backing up others on their way to burnout. But what good does it do if a burned-out cynic stays on the job?

How would you handle the resigning case worker? Would you try to retain him?
– Who would benefit? At what costs and to whom?
Would you instruct the next recruit to keep his or her caseload tolerable by forgetting to mention any bilingual skills? To lie if asked? Why?
Would you come forward and volunteer information to a public interest group filing a lawsuit against the agency for failing to protect abused and neglected children? Why?
Who are the victims here, and what interests are at stake?

- Are they equally important? How do you decide?

Are there *any* situations in which responsibilities to internal stakeholders outweigh those to external stakeholders?

- Are the answers identical for the case worker, supervisor, and agency?
- How could a manager discriminate among responsibilities to all stakeholders?

Note: In response to a class-action lawsuit accusing the state of violating abused and neglected children's constitutional rights, a U.S. District Court in December 1990 ordered comprehensive changes in Connecticut's child welfare agency. They range from training requirements to caseload reductions and improved procedures. Because eight similar suits have been filed around the country, the decree is especially significant (Barden, 1990, p. B1). Patricia Wilson-Coker, the agency member on the mediation panel that developed the settlement noted, "Everyone says that it's about the children. . . . It's about the social workers, too. Inside the system, you know you give 150 percent, and you know it's not enough" (Tuohy and Finholm, 1990, p. A8).

The pattern of job satisfaction among public employees parallels the general public's, with survey data showing about one-half of all public employees "very satisfied" with their jobs. They are somewhat more likely to describe their lives as "exciting" (Lewis, 1990, p. 225).

In your opinion, is job satisfaction related to ethical behavior?
- How? Whose?
- Are fair labor practices related to building an ethical agency?

Can an agency operate ethically even without the resources to accomplish its mission fully? What is the reasoning behind your response?

What would *you* do to build a more ethical agency?
- What does a more ethical agency entail in this case?
- What would you do first? Then what? Why?

In your view, can an agency provide a work environment that supports ethical behavior?
- Should it?
- What does this entail in your agency?

Afterword

The Job Ahead

A few indelible words summarize the many values, diverse responsibilities, and anticipated trajectory of ethical public service. The preamble to the U.S. Constitution states, "We the people of the United States, in order to form a more perfect Union, establish justice, insure domestic tranquility, provide for the common defense, promote the general welfare, and secure the blessings of liberty to ourselves and our posterity, do ordain and establish this Constitution for the United States of America."

Who guards the guardians? Juvenal's renowned question from the second century, *Quis custodiet ipsos custodes?* is a permanent fixture in American public service. A version of it appears on the masthead of COGEL's newsletter, *Guardian,* and opened the Tower Commission's (1987) narrative on its investigation into the Iran-Contra affair. The question begets innumerable answers: oversight and watchdog agencies, internal controls, grand juries and congressional investigations, the courts, criminal statutes, and enforced standards of conduct. Rules and regulations on their own are inadequate guarantees of ethical behavior.

Fine public service and good government rely first and foremost on good people with the character, cause, and courage to do the right thing. By oath, office, and profession, public managers voluntarily commit themselves to thoughtful, ethical action. Ethics in public service is a perpetual responsibility to implement and comply with the law, to serve the public interest, to avoid doing harm, to hold the future in stewardship, and to accommodate clashing definitions of what is right and important in public life.

The job ahead is no more and no less. From here we can see the twenty-first century.

Agency Ethics Audit

Does your agency (or jurisdiction, association, or operation) sustain and promote ethical decision making and ethical behavior?

Apply each question or standard to your agency.
Check column 1 if answer is yes, high, usually.
Check column 2 if answer is maybe, medium, sometimes.
Check column 3 if answer is no, low, never.
Check column 4 if response varies from agency's established goal.
Check column 5 if response varies from preferred, reasonable goal.

EXPLICIT POLICY

	1	2	3	4	5

1. Do written policies and procedures exist?
2. If yes, is the primary theme proscriptive, coercive, punitive, threatening—encouraging obedience (versus prescriptive, positive, promoting responsibility)?
3. If yes, is it distributed and explained in detail (handbook, briefing, training)
   (a) to all employees?
   (b) to new recruits, new hires?
   (c) to vendors, clients, consultants, others?
4. If yes, are general standards (example, appearance of impropriety) explained clearly and practically?
5. If yes, are systematic, confidential, responsive mechanisms (hot line, financial disclosure) in place for identifying violations?
6. If yes, do accused and complainant have due process protections?
7. If yes, is legal compliance (example, corruption) the sole concern?
8. Is written policy referred to in decision making?
9. If no, are shared, general guidelines easily available from other sources (state, professional code)?
10. If no, is top management satisfied with behavior in agency (versus uninterested)?

Apply each question or standard to your agency and check the appropriate column:
1 = yes, high, usually; 2 = maybe, medium, sometimes; 3 = no, low, never; 4 = varies from
set goal; 5 = varies from preferred, reasonable goal.

EXPLICIT POLICY, continued

	1	2	3	4	5

11. If no, is ethics handled by informal culture (role model, un-
    written "rules of the game")?
12. Your standard

_____

_____

OPERATIONS and PROCEDURES

	1	2	3	4	5

13. Does efficiency override other values? (Does agency mission
    override ethical concerns?)
    Would the following agree:
    (a) service recipients?
    (b) line employees?
    (c) middle managers?
    (d) _____ ?
14. Can employees perform job and fulfill duties without
    breaking
    (a) laws?
    (b) agency's rules/procedures?
15. Are ethical standards referred to in decision making or
    explanations?
16. Are competing obligations among line or operational em-
    ployees ignored (example, caseload versus intervention
    effectiveness)?
17. Do middle and top managers acknowledge and commend
    subordinates' raising ethical issues in discussions, meetings,
    analyses? (Is ethics dialogue encouraged?)
18. Do internal memos, in-house newsletters, press releases,
    other communications refer to fairness, honesty, public in-
    terest, other public service values?
19. Is there a systematic procedure for flagging normative/ethi-
    cal issues
    (a) in decision making?
    (b) in agency operations/routines?
20. Do documented development and review procedures specifi-
    cally and explicitly treat ethical dimensions of
    (a) proposed policy?
    (b) proposed regulations?
21. Is assistance available for resolving ethical questions (versus
    pursue violations)?
    (a) committee or ombudsman?
    (b) designated senior manager?
22. If yes, is before-the-fact advice available on ethical (not com-
    pliance) issues?
23. The last time something important went wrong, did a man-
    ager take responsibility and corrective action (versus job
    protection and damage control)?
24. If a survey were taken in the agency, would
    (a) most employees rate the immediate supervisor as trust-
        worthy, truthful, fair?

Apply each question or standard to your agency and check the appropriate column:
1 = yes, high, usually; 2 = maybe, medium, sometimes; 3 = no, low, never; 4 = varies from set goal; 5 = varies from preferred, reasonable goal.

	1	2	3	4	5
OPERATIONS and PROCEDURES, continued					

(b) most first-line managers say service users or clients (rather than management, procedures, or employees) count in agency operations or decisions?

25. Does recruitment consider ethical concerns or character (versus only technical qualifications)?

26. Does promotion consider ethical dimensions of performance (versus only productivity or longevity)?

28. Are statements of values and ethical principles included in
    (a) plans/forecasts?
    (b) budgets?
    (c) performance standards?
    (d) policy statements?
    (e) _____ ?

29. Is all relevant information (examples, error margin, assumptions, underlying estimates) disclosed in
    (a) plans/forecasts?
    (b) budgets?
    (c) performance standards?
    (d) policy statements?
    (e) _____ ?

30. Do budget worksheets show evidence of intended padding (exaggeration/distortion)?

31. Are efforts made to ensure that the following are reasonable (within employee's competence), accurate, and valid:
    (a) productivity measures?
    (b) performance standards?
    (e) _____ ?

32. Are policies (and training) up-to-date in terms of
    (a) new technologies (examples, computerized information and privacy, data integrity)?
    (b) new service or procedural mandates?
    (c) new clients/service recipients?
    (d) new collaborators?
    (e) other agency issues _____ ?

33. Do the terms *responsibility* and *public interest* come up in discussion/documents?

34. Are ethical aspects of the following relationships outside the agency confronted in discussion or documents:
    (a) contracting out?
    (b) public-private partnerships?
    (c) intergovernmental collaboration?
    (d) _____ ?

35. Your standard

_____

_____

Apply each question or standard to your agency and check the appropriate column:
1 = yes, high, usually; 2 = maybe, medium, sometimes; 3 = no, low, never; 4 = varies from
set goal; 5 = varies from preferred, reasonable goal.

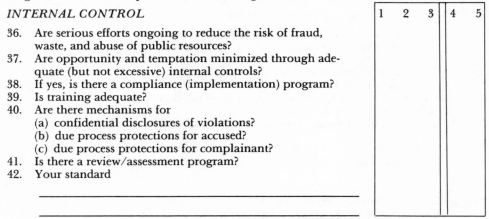

INTERNAL CONTROL

	1	2	3	4	5

36. Are serious efforts ongoing to reduce the risk of fraud, waste, and abuse of public resources?
37. Are opportunity and temptation minimized through adequate (but not excessive) internal controls?
38. If yes, is there a compliance (implementation) program?
39. Is training adequate?
40. Are there mechanisms for
    (a) confidential disclosures of violations?
    (b) due process protections for accused?
    (c) due process protections for complainant?
41. Is there a review/assessment program?
42. Your standard

_____

_____

Auditor: _____   Audit Date: _____

Problems Identified (column 4 or 5 checked)   Causes

1.   1.

2.   2.

3.   3.

4.   4.

5.   5.

Recommendations   Implemented (date)

1.   ☐ _____

2.   ☐ _____

3.   ☐ _____

4.   ☐ _____

5.   ☐ _____

References

Allison, G. T. "Public and Private Management: Are They Fundamentally Alike in All Unimportant Respects?" In J. M. Shafritz and A. C. Hyde (eds.), *Classics of Public Administration.* (2nd ed.) Chicago: Dorsey Press, 1987, pp. 510–529.

American Arbitration Association. *Resolving Your Disputes.* AA155-20M-6/89. New York: American Arbitration Association, 1989.

American Bar Association. *Professional Discipline for Lawyers and Judges.* Chicago: National Center for Professional Responsibility for the Joint Committee on Professional Discipline, American Bar Association, 1979.

American Bar Association. *Model Code of Professional Responsibility and Code of Judicial Conduct.* Chicago: National Center for Professional Responsibility and the American Bar Association, Aug. 1980.

American Bar Association. *Model Rules of Professional Conduct and Code of Judicial Conduct.* Chicago: American Bar Association, Aug. 1983.

American Institute of Certified Public Accountants. *Code of Professional Conduct as Adopted January 12, 1988 and Bylaws and Implementing Resolutions of Council as Amended January 12, 1988.* New York: American Institute of Certified Public Accountants, 1988a.

American Institute of Certified Public Accountants. *Code of Conduct Bylaws as of June 1, 1988.* New York: American Institute of Certified Public Accountants, 1988b.

American Society for Public Administration. *Ethics Resource Notebook.* Developed for ethics conference sponsored by the American Society for Public Administration, Washington, D.C., Nov. 12–15, 1989.

Ansberry, C. "Advice from Headhunters: You're Not CEO Material." *Wall Street Journal,* July 14, 1987, p. 35.

Appleby, P. H. "Ethics in the National Government." Testimony given at hearings before a subcommittee to study Senate Concurrent Resolution 21 (establishment of a commission on ethics in government) of the Committee on Labor and Public Welfare, U.S. Senate. Washington, D.C.: U.S. Senate, 1951, pp. 165-171. (Committee print.)

Appleby, P. H. "Government Is Different." In J. M. Shafritz and A. C. Hyde (eds.), *Classics of Public Administration*. (2nd ed.) Chicago: Dorsey Press, 1987, pp. 158-164. (Originally published in *Big Democracy*. New York: Knopf, 1945.)

Arendt, H. *Eichmann in Jerusalem: A Report on the Banality of Evil*. (rev. ed.) New York: Penguin, 1964.

Associated Press/Media General. National adult telephone survey, Sept. 6-14, 1988.

Bailey, S. K. "Ethics and the Public Service." *Public Administration Review*, 1964, *24*, 234-243.

Barbanel, J. "Happy Land Arrest Order Ignored in 1989." *New York Times*, Apr. 3, 1990, p. B1.

Barden, J. C. "Panel to Direct Child Welfare in Connecticut." *New York Times*, Dec. 21, 1990, pp. B1, B4.

Barnard, C. *The Functions of the Executive*. Cambridge, Mass.: Harvard University Press, 1938.

Barringer, F. "Changing Times Turn Tables on a 'Saint' of the Stalin Era." *New York Times*, Mar. 21, 1988, pp. A1, A7.

Beauchamp, T. L., and Pinkard, T. P. *Ethics and Public Policy: An Introduction to Ethics*. (2nd ed.) Englewood Cliffs, N.J.: Prentice-Hall, 1983.

Behrman, J. N. *Essays on Ethics in Business and the Professions*. Englewood Cliffs, N.J.: Prentice Hall, 1988.

Berger, J. "In School Bureaucracy, Despair at the System." *New York Times*, Feb. 5, 1990, pp. A1, B2.

Bergsman, S. "Employee Conduct Outside the Workplace." *HRMagazine on Human Resource Management*, 1991, *36*, 62-64.

Betti, J. A. Remarks to the Best Practices Forum, Defense Industry Initiative on Business Ethics and Conduct. Washington, D.C. June 7, 1990. (Duplicated.)

Bok, S. *Lying: Moral Choice in Public and Private Life*. New York: Vintage Books, 1978.

Boling, T. E., and Dempsey, J. "Ethical Dilemmas in Government: Designing an Organizational Response." *Public Personnel Management Journal*, 1981, *10*, 11-19.

Bonczek, S. J. "Clean Up with Ethics Code, Dedicated Leadership." *City & State*, Aug. 27, 1990, 7.

Boren, J. H. Testimony given to the Subcommittee on Investigations and Oversight of the Committee on Public Works, U.S. House of Representatives, June 22, 1971.

Bowman, J. S. "Whistle-Blowing in the Public Service: An Overview of the Issues." *Review of Public Personnel Administration,* 1980, *1,* 15–28.

Bowman, J. S. "The Management of Ethics: Codes of Conduct in Organizations." *Public Personnel Management Journal,* 1981, *10,* 59–66.

Bowman, J. S. Responses to survey conducted in spring 1989 of members of the American Society for Public Administration. In *Ethics Resource Notebook,* pp. 7, 107–108. Developed for ethics conference sponsored by the American Society for Public Administration, Washington, D.C., Nov. 12–15, 1989.

Bowman, J. S. "Ethics in Government: A National Survey of Public Administrators." *Public Administration Review,* 1990, *50,* 345–353.

Bowman, J. S., and Elliston, F. A. *Ethics, Government and Public Policy: A Reference Guide.* Westport, Conn.: Greenwood Press, 1988.

Bowsher, C. A. "Resolving the Savings and Loan Crisis: Billions More and Additional Reforms Needed." GAO/T-AFMD-90-15. Testimony given before the Senate Committee on Banking, Housing and Urban Affairs, Apr. 6, 1990. Washington, D.C.: General Accounting Office, 1990.

Brackman, A. *The Other Nuremberg: The Untold Story of the Tokyo War Crimes Trials.* New York: Morrow, 1987.

Broad, W. J. "Pervasive Decline of Staff Stunts NASA, Critics Say." *New York Times,* Sept. 9, 1990, pp. 1, 32.

Brown, M. T. *Working Ethics: Strategies for Decision Making and Organizational Responsibility.* San Francisco: Jossey-Bass, 1990.

Brownlow Committee. "Report of the President's Committee on Administrative Management." In J. M. Shafritz and A. C. Hyde (eds.), *Classics of Public Administration.* (2nd ed.) Chicago: Dorsey Press, 1987, pp. 90–95. (Originally published 1937.)

Brumback, G. B. "Institutionalizing Ethics in Government." *Public Personnel Management,* 1991, *20.*

Bukkyo Dendo Kyokai. *The Teaching of Buddha.* (509th rev.ed.) Tokyo: Toppan Printing Co., 1987.

Burnham, D. *A Law Unto Itself: Power Politics and the IRS.* New York: Random House, 1990.

Burns, A. I. "Combatting Public Corruption." *Investigators' Journal,* 1987, *3,* 46–47.

Campbell, V. C. " 'Total Quality': A Framework for Ethics." In *Business Ethics Report,* pp. 20–21. Highlights of Bentley College's eighth national conference on business ethics, Oct. 26–27, 1989.

Canavan, S. J. "Edmund Burke." In L. Strauss and J. Cropsey, (eds.), *History of Political Philosophy.* Chicago: Rand McNally, 1963, pp. 601–620.

Caperton, G. "Foreword." In R. T. Hall, *The West Virginia Governmental Ethics Act: Text and Commentary.* Charleston, W.Va.: Mountain State Press, 1989.

Carren, P. M., and Seal, R. T. "The Challenges of CRAG." *Government Contract,* 1989, *6,* 3–10.

Carter, J. *Why Not the Best?* New York: Bantam Books, 1976.

Catron, B. L., and Denhardt, K. G. *Ethics Education in Public Administration and Affairs: Research Report and Recommendations.* Washington, D.C.: National Association of Schools of Public Affairs and Administration, Oct. 1988.

Chambers, R. "Introduction." In R. T. Hall, *The West Virginia Governmental Ethics Act: Text and Commentary.* Charleston, W.Va.: Mountain State Press, 1989.

Chambliss, W. J. *On the Take.* (2nd ed.) Bloomington: Indiana University Press, 1988.

Chandler, R. C. "A Guide to Ethics for Public Servants." In J. L. Perry (ed.), *Handbook of Public Administration.* San Francisco: Jossey-Bass, 1989a, pp. 602–618.

Chandler, R. C. "Moral Grandeur." Remarks to ethics conference sponsored by the American Society for Public Administration, Washington, D.C., Nov. 12–15, 1989b.

Cheney, D. "Defense Management: Report to the President." Washington, D.C.: U.S. Department of Defense, July 1989. (Duplicated.)

ChicagoMetro Ethics Coalition. "Ethics in Government: The Chicago Experience." Chicago: AMOCO, 1989.

City & State. "Survey of City, County, and State Government Employees." Readership questionnaire, June 19–July 2, 1989. In *Ethics Resource Notebook,* pp. 104–106. Developed for ethics conference sponsored by the American Society for Public Administration, Washington, D.C., Nov. 12-15, 1989.

City of Chicago. *Annual Report of the Board of Ethics.* Chicago: Board of Ethics, 1988.

Cockburn, A. "Beat the Devil." *Nation,* Mar. 26, 1988, pp. 402–403.

Colby, A., Kohlberg, L., Gibbs, J., and Lieberman, M. *A Longitudinal Study of Moral Development.* Monograph of the Society for Research in Child Development, serial no. 200, vol. 48, nos. 1, 2, 1983.

Commission on Accreditation for Law Enforcement Agencies, Inc. *Standards for Law Enforcement Agencies: The Standards Manual of the Law Enforcement Agency Accreditation Program.* Fairfax, Va.: Commission on Accreditation for Law Enforcement Agencies, Inc., Jan. 1989.

Common Cause. *A Model Ethics Law for State Government.* Washington, D.C.: Common Cause, Jan. 1989a.

Common Cause. *Conflict of Interest Legislation in the States.* Washington, D.C.: Common Cause, Sept. 1989b.

Commonwealth of Massachusetts. *Annual Report of the State Ethics Commission.* Boston: State Ethics Commission, 1988.

Commonwealth of Massachusetts. *Annual Report of the State Ethics Commission.* Boston: State Ethics Commission, 1989.

Congressional Budget Office. *Federal Liabilities Under Hazardous Waste Laws.* Washington, D.C.: Congressional Budget Office, May 1990.

Congressional Quarterly. *Watergate: Chronology of a Crisis.* Vols. 1, 2. Washington, D.C.: Congressional Quarterly, 1974.

Cooper, T. "Hierarchy, Virtue, and the Practice of Public Administration." *Public Administration Review,* 1987, *47,* 320–328.

Cooper, T. *The Responsible Administrator: An Approach to Ethics for the Administrative Role.* (3rd ed.) San Francisco: Jossey-Bass, 1990.

Council of State Governments. *Blue Book, Campaign Finance, Ethics & Lobby Law.* Lexington, Ky.: Council on Governmental Ethics Laws, 1986–1987.

Council of State Governments. *Blue Book, Campaign Finance, Ethics & Lobby Law.* Lexington, Ky.: Council on Governmental Ethics Laws, 1988–1989.

Council of State Governments. *Blue Book, Campaign Finance, Ethics & Lobby Law.* Lexington, Ky.: Council on Governmental Ethics Laws, 1990.

Council on Environmental Quality. Executive Office of the President. *Regulations for Implementing the Procedural Provisions of the National Environmental Policy Act.* 40 CFR ps 1500–1508 (as of July 1, 1986). Document 0-184-736. Washington, D.C.: U.S. Government Printing Office, 1987.

Cowan Commission. *Option Reports Prepared for the Commission to Draft a Code of Ethics for Los Angeles City Government.* Los Angeles: Cowan Commission, Oct. 1989a.

Cowan Commission. *Ethics and Excellence in Government.* Final Report and Recommendations of the Commission to Draft an Ethics Code for Los Angeles City Government. Los Angeles: Cowan Commission, Nov. 1989b.

Cox, A. Testimony given at hearings before the Subcommittee on Oversight of Government Management of the Committee on Governmental Affairs, U.S. Senate, Apr. 12–13, 1988. Washington, D.C.: U.S. Government Printing Office, 1988, pp. 4–148.

Defense Industry Initiative on Business Ethics and Conduct. *1989 Annual Report to the Public and the Defense Industry.* Washington, D.C.: Defense Industry Initiative on Business Ethics and Conduct, Feb. 1990.

Denhardt, K. G. *The Ethics of Public Service, Resolving Moral Dilemmas in Public Organizations.* Contributions in Political Science, no. 195. Westport, Conn.: Greenwood Press, 1988.

Denhardt, K. G. "The Management of Ideals: A Political Perspective on Ethics." *Public Administration Review,* 1989, *49,* 187–193.

Deutsch, C. H. "Pen-and-Pencil Integrity Tests." *New York Times,* Feb. 11, 1990, sec. 3, pt. 2, p. 29.

Dobel, J. P. "Integrity in the Public Service." *Public Administration Review,* 1990, *50,* 354–366.

Dostoyevsky, F. "Notes from the Underground." In *The Best Short Stories of Fyodor Dostoyevsky* (D. Magarshack, trans.). New York: Random House, n.d.

Downs, A. *Inside Bureaucracy.* Boston: Little, Brown, 1967.

Dreiford Group. *Managing Ethical Issues: Executive Level.* Bethesda, Md.: Dreiford Group, 1988.

Drucker, P. F. "What Is 'Business Ethics'?" *Public Interest,* 1981, *63,* 18–36.

Drucker, P. F. "How to Manage the Boss." *Wall Street Journal*, Aug. 1, 1986, p. 16.

Drucker, P. F. "The Non-Profit's Quiet Revolution." *Wall Street Journal*, Sept. 8, 1988, p. 30.

Drucker, P. F. *The New Realities*. New York: Harper Collins, 1989.

Egan, T. "Oregon Lists Illnesses by Priority to See Who Gets Medicaid Care." *New York Times*, May 3, 1990a.

Egan, T. "In West, a Showdown Over Rules on Grazing." *New York Times*, Aug. 19, 1990b, pp. A1, A20.

Enos, G. "Early Retirement Gains Popularity, but States Pay Price." *City & State*, Aug. 27, 1990, p. 2.

"Fact File: Attitudes and Characteristics of This Year's Freshmen." Survey by American Council on Education and Higher Education Research Institute at the University of California, Los Angeles. *Chronicle of Higher Education*, Jan. 24, 1990, pp. A33–A34.

Fair Political Practices Commission. *Political Reform Act of 1974 as Amended to January 1, 1990*. Sacramento: State of California, Fair Political Practices Commission, 1990.

Fedders, J. M. "Text of Resignation Letter." *New York Times*, Feb. 27, 1985, p. D5.

Feigenbaum, E. D., Larsen, J. L., and Reynolds, B. J. (eds.). "A Model Law for Campaign Finance, Ethics, and Lobbying Regulation." Lexington, Ky.: Council on Governmental Ethics Laws, 1990. July 1990 Proposed Draft for Adoption.

Finholm, V. "Social Work Tests Body and Soul." *Hartford Courant*, Dec. 10, 1989, pp. A1, A12–13.

Fischer, F. "Ethical Discourse in Public Administration." *Administration & Society*, 1983, *15*, 5–42.

Frederickson, H. G. "Toward a New Public Administration." In J. M. Shafritz and A. C. Hyde (eds.), *Classics of Public Administration*. (2nd ed.) Chicago: Dorsey Press, 1987, pp. 424–439.

Frederickson, H. G. "Public Administration and Social Equity." *Public Administration Review*, 1990, *50*, 228–237.

French, P. A. *Ethics in Government*. Series in Occupational Ethics. Englewood Cliffs, N.J.: Prentice-Hall, 1983.

Fuchs, L. "Maya Angelou." *Facing History and Ourselves News*, Winter 1989–1990, pp. 12–13.

Fulghum, R. *All I Really Need to Know I Learned in Kindergarten*. New York: Ivy Books, 1988.

Gallup Organization. "Who Do We Trust?" *Gallup Report*, (279), Dec. 1988.

Gallup Organization. National telephone surveys, Aug. 1977, July 1981, May 1983, July 1985, and Feb. 1990.

Garcia, K. J. "Prognosis Gloomy for Trauma Network." *Los Angeles Times*, Apr. 10, 1990, pp. B1, B8.

Gardiner, J. A., and Malec, K. L. "Measurement Issues in the Study of Official Corruption: A Chicago Example." *Corruption and Reform*, 1987, *2*, 267–278.

Gardiner, J. A., and Malec, K. L. "Mobilizing Public Opinion Against Corruption: A Report to the Chicago Ethics Project." *Corruption and Reform*, 1989, *4*, 107–121.

General Accounting Office. *Framework for Assessing Job Vulnerability to Ethical Problems*. FPCD-82-2. Washington, D.C.: General Accounting Office, Nov. 4, 1981.

General Accounting Office. *Ethics Enforcement: Process by Which Conflict of Interest Allegations Are Investigated and Resolved*. GAO/GGD-87-83BR. Washington, D.C.: General Accounting Office, June 1987.

General Accounting Office. *Ethics Enforcement: Results of Conflict of Interest Investigations*. GAO/GGD-88-34. Washington, D.C.: General Accounting Office, Feb. 1988.

General Accounting Office. *The Public Service: Issues Affecting Its Quality, Effectiveness, Integrity, and Stewardship*. GAO/GGD-89-73. Washington, D.C.: General Accounting Office, June 1989.

General Accounting Office. Office of Public Affairs. *Reports and Testimony: July 1990*. Washington, D.C.: General Accounting Office, 1990, pp. 50–51.

Gilligan, C. *In a Different Voice: Psychological Theory and Women's Development*. Cambridge, Mass.: Harvard University Press, 1982.

Gilman, S. C. "Many Hands, Dirty Hands, and No Hands: Bringing Applied Ethics to Public Management." *Practicing Manager*, 1989, *9*, 20–26.

Goodpaster, K. E. "Ethical Frameworks for Mangement." Harvard Business School Case 9-384-105. Boston: Harvard Business School Case Services, 1983.

Goodpaster, K. E. "Some Avenues for Ethical Analysis in General Management." Harvard Business School Case 9-383-007, (rev. ed.) Boston: Harvard Business School Case Services, 1984.

Goodsell, C. T. *The Case for Bureaucracy: A Public Administration Polemic*. (2nd ed.) Chatham, N.J.: Chatham House, 1985.

Gorlin, R. A. (ed.). *Codes of Professional Responsibility*. (2nd ed.) Washington, D.C.: Bureau of National Affairs, 1990.

Graham, G. A. *Morality in American Politics*. New York: Random House, 1952.

Graham, G. A. "Ethical Guidelines for Public Administrators: Observations on Rules of the Game." *Public Administration Review*, 1974, *34*, 90–92.

Gulick, L. "Notes on the Theory of Organization." In L. Gulick and L. Urwick (eds.), *Papers on the Science of Administration*. New York: Institute of Public Administration, 1937, pp. 1–45.

Guy, M. E. *Ethical Decision Making in Everyday Work Situations*. Westport, Conn.: Quorum Books, 1990.

Haas, L. J. "Budget Focus." *National Journal*, Aug. 5, 1989, p. 2014.

Hall, R. T. *The West Virginia Governmental Ethics Act: Text and Commentary*. Charleston, W.Va.: Mountain State Press, 1989.

Hardin, G. "The Tragedy of the Commons." In G. Hardin, *Exploring New*

Ethics for Survival. New York: Viking, 1972, 250-264. (Originally published in *Science,* 1968, *162,* 1243-1248.)

Harmon, M. "The Responsible Actor as 'Tortured Soul': The Case of Horatio Hornblower." In B. L. Catron and H. D. Kass (eds.), *Images and Identities in Public Administration.* Newbury Park, Calif.: Sage, 1990, pp. 151-182.

Hart, D. K. "Social Equity, Justice, and the Equitable Administrator." *Public Administration Review,* 1974, *34,* 3-11.

Heclo, H. "Bureaucratic Dispositions." In D. L. Yarwood (ed.), *Public Administration, Politics and the People.* New York: Longman, 1987, pp. 44-50.

Hill, I. "Common Sense and Everyday Ethics." *Accountability,* Newsletter of the LAC Regional Financial Management Improvement Program, U.S. Agency for International Development, 1990, *5,* p. 2.

Hirschmann, N. J. "Freedom, Recognition, and Obligation: A Feminist Approach to Political Theory." *American Political Science Review,* 1989, *83,* 1227-1244.

Hummel, R. P. *The Bureaucratic Experience.* (3rd ed.) New York: St. Martin's Press: 1987.

International Journal of Public Administration. 1989, *12* (entire issue).

Jennings, B. "Too Much of a Good Thing?" *State Government,* 1989a, *62,* 173-175.

Jennings, B. "Ethics in Government: There Still Is Hope." Reprinted in *Ethics Resource Notebook* developed for ethics conference sponsored by the American Society for Public Administration, Washington, D.C., Nov. 12-15, 1989, 23-29. Originally published in *World and I,* May 1989b.

Johnson, M. "A Filmmaker's Odyssey." *Facing History and Ourselves News,* Winter 1989-1990, pp. 18-21.

Jos, P. H., Tompkins, M. E., and Hays, W. S. "In Praise of Difficult People: A Portrait of the Committed Whistleblower." *Public Administration Review,* 1989, *49,* 552-561.

Josephson Institute. *Preserving the Public Trust: Principles of Public Service Ethics, Standards of Conduct & Guidelines for Government Decision Making.* Marina del Rey, Calif.: Josephson Institute for the Advancement of Ethics, Government Ethics Center, 1990.

Josephson, M. *Power, Politics, and Ethics: Ethical Obligations and Opportunities of Government Service.* (3rd ed.) Marina Del Rey, Calif.: Josephson Institute for the Advancement of Ethics, 1989.

Jotman, M. *George Washington's Expense Account.* New York: HarperCollins, 1988.

Judd, R. R. "Ethics Codes and Commissions: Legislation and Litigation in 1989." Paper prepared for the annual meeting of the Council on Governmental Ethics Law, New Orleans, Dec. 6, 1989.

Kane, Parsons and Associates for *Parents Magazine.* National adult telephone survey, Jan. 15-31, 1989.

Keehley, P. Untitled draft report on results of survey conducted at ethics conference sponsored by the American Society for Public Administration, Washington, D.C., Nov. 12–15, 1989. Department of Political Science, University of Utah, Spring 1990.

Keller, B. "Chernobyl Plant Being Mismanaged, Pravda Charges." *New York Times,* Apr. 25, 1988, pp. A1, A6.

Keller, E. K. (ed.). *Ethical Insight, Ethical Action: Perspectives for the Local Government Manager.* Washington, D.C.: International City Management Association, 1988.

Kernaghan, K., and Langford, J. W. *The Responsible Public Servant.* Halifax, Canada: Institute for Research on Public Policy and Institute of Public Administration of Canada, 1990.

King, M. L., Jr. "Letter from Birmingham City Jail." Apr. 16, 1963. Philadelphia: American Friends Service Committee, May 1963.

Kohlberg, L. "Stages of Moral Development as a Basis for Moral Education." In B. Munsey (ed.), *Moral Development, Moral Education, and Kohlberg.* Birmingham, Ala.: Religious Education Press, 1980, pp. 15–98.

Kohlberg, L. *The Philosophy of Moral Development, Moral Stages and the Idea of Justice.* Vol. 1. New York: HarperCollins, 1981.

Koran [*The Holy Qur'an*]. Text, trans., and commentary by Abdullah Yusuf Ali. Beirut, Lebanon: Dar Al Arabia, 1968.

Kouses, J. M. "Why Businessmen Fail in Government." *New York Times,* Mar. 8, 1987, Sec. 3, p. 3.

Kurtz, H. "Why We Blew the HUD Story." *Washington Post,* Nov. 12, 1989, p. D5.

Lewis, C. W. *Scruples & Scandals: A Handbook on Public Service Ethics for State and Local Government Officials and Employees in Connecticut.* Storrs: Institutes of Public Service and Urban Research, University of Connecticut, 1986.

Lewis, C. W. "Iran-Contra Hearings Highlight Conflicting Ethical Standards." *Hartford Courant,* July 19, 1987, pp. D1, D4.

Lewis, G. B. "In Search of the Machiavellian Milquetoasts: Comparing Attitudes of Bureaucrats and Ordinary People." *Public Administration Review,* 1990, *50,* 220–227.

Lilla, M. "Ethos, 'Ethics,' and Public Service." *Public Interest,* 1981, *63,* 3–17.

Lindblom, C. E. "The Science of 'Muddling Through.'" *Public Administration Review,* 1959, *19,* 79–88.

Lipset, S. M., and Schneider, M. *The Confidence Gap, Business, Labor, and Government in the Public Mind.* (rev. ed.) Baltimore, Md.: Johns Hopkins University Press, 1987.

Lipsky, M. *Street-Level Bureaucracy: Dilemmas of the Individual in Public Services.* New York: Basic Books, 1980.

Louis Harris and Associates. National surveys, Feb. 1977, Nov. 1977, Aug. 1978, Nov. 1984, and Nov. 1985.

McCullough, H. M. "Ethics in the City of Angels." *COGEL Guardian,* Apr. 30, 1990, pp. 1, 6.

McMillan, A. C. Remarks delivered at ethics conference sponsored by the American Society for Public Administration, Washington, D.C., Nov. 12-15, 1989.

Marini, F. (ed.). *Toward a New Public Administration: The Minnowbrook Perspective.* Scranton, Pa.: Chandler Press, 1971.

Maskell, J. H. "Ethics Laws and Regulation in the Federal Sector: Executive and Legislative Branches." Paper presented at ethics conference sponsored by the American Society for Public Administration, Washington, D.C., Nov. 12-15, 1989.

Mauro, F. J., and Benjamin, G. (eds.). *Restructuring the New York City Government: The Reemergence of Municipal Reform.* Proceedings of the Academy of Political Science. Montpelier, Vt.: Capital City Press, 1989.

Mensen, T. P. "Ethics and State Budgeting." *Public Budgeting & Finance,* 1990, *10,* 95-108.

Mertins, H., Jr., and Hennigan, P. J. *Applying Professional Standards and Ethics in the '80s.* (2nd ed.) Washington, D.C.: American Society for Public Administration, 1982.

Miale, F. R., and Selzer, M. *The Nuremberg Mind: The Psychology of the Nazi Leaders.* New York: Quadrangle, 1975.

Milgram, S. "The Dilemma of Obedience." In D. L. Yarwood (ed.), *Public Administration, Politics and the People.* New York: Longman, 1987, pp. 170-175.

Mosher, F. C. (ed.). *Basic Documents of American Public Administration, 1776-1950:* New York: Holmes & Meier, 1976.

Moyers, B. *The Secret Government: The Constitution in Crisis.* Cabin John, Md.: Seven Locks Press, 1988.

Murawski, J. "Congress Out to Cut Pay Gap, But Odds Are Against It." *Congressional Quarterly Weekly Report,* Aug. 25, 1990, *48* 2710-2712.

Nash, L. L. "Ethics Without the Sermon." *Harvard Business Review,* 1981, *59,* 79-90.

Nash, L. L. *Good Intentions Aside, A Manager's Guide to Resolving Ethical Problems.* Boston, Mass.: Harvard Business School Press, 1990.

Nash, N. C. "Troubles Grow for S.E.C. Aide." *New York Times,* Feb. 26, 1985a, pp. D1, D7.

Nash, N. C. "S.E.C. Enforcement Chief Quits, Citing Publicity on Divorce Trial." *New York Times,* Feb. 27, 1985b, pp. A1, D5.

National Institute of Municipal Law Officers. *NIMLO Model Ordinance on Code of Ethics.* Draft prepared by staff attorney J. C. Pinson, Washington, D.C.: National Institute of Municipal Law Officers, Mar. 1990.

National Municipal League. *Model State Conflict of Interest and Financial Disclosure Law.* New York: National Municipal League, 1979.

Neely, A. S., IV. *Ethics-in-Government Laws: Are They Too "Ethical"?* Studies in Legal Policy. Washington, D.C.: American Enterprise Institute for Public Policy Research, 1984.

Nelson, R. F. "Training on Ethics." Paper presented at 1990 business ethics conference sponsored by the Conference Board, New York City, May 1990.

New York State Commission on Government Integrity. *Municipal Ethical Standards: The Need for a New Approach.* New York: New York State Commission on Government Integrity, Dec. 1988.

New York State Department of Civil Service. *New York State Work Force Plan, 1990.* Albany: New York State Department of Civil Service, 1990.

New York Times. National adult telephone surveys, Dec. 14–18, 1985, and Apr. 29–May 1, 1986.

Newfield, J., and Barrett, W. *City for Sale: Ed Koch and the Betrayal of New York.* New York: HarperCollins, 1989.

Nuremberg Charter. In *Trial of the Major War Criminals Before the International Military Tribunal.* Vol. 1: *Official Documents.* Nuremberg, Germany: Secretariat of the Tribunal, 1947.

"Oliver North, Businessman? Many Bosses Say That He's Their Kind of Employee." *Wall Street Journal,* July 14, 1987, p. 35.

Parkinson, C. N. *Parkinson's Law and Other Studies in Administration.* Boston: Houghton Mifflin, 1957.

Patterson, B. H., Jr. *The Ring of Power: The White House Staff and Its Expanding Role in Government.* New York: Basic Books, 1988.

Paul, J. "The New York City Fiscal Crisis." In A. Gutmann and D. Thompson (eds.), *Ethics and Politics: Cases and Comments.* (2nd ed.) Chicago: Nelson-Hall, 1990, pp. 60–73.

Peter, L. J., and Hull, R. H. *The Peter Principle.* New York: Morrow, 1969.

Peters, T. "Contrasting Public and Private Leadership: An Interview with Tom Peters." *State Government,* 1987a, *60,* 241–244.

Peters, T. *Thriving on Chaos.* New York: HarperCollins, 1987b.

Peters, T., and Waterman, R. *In Search of Excellence.* New York: HarperCollins, 1981.

Pfeiffer, D., Levitan, D., and Lavin, M. "Annotated Bibliography on Codes of Professional Conduct." *International Journal of Public Administration,* 1991, *14,* 99–124.

Pollock-Byrne, J. M. *Ethics in Crime and Justice: Dilemmas and Decisions.* Pacific Grove, Calif.: Brooks/Cole, 1989.

Posner, B. Z., and Schmidt, W. H. "Government Morale and Management: A Survey of Federal Executives." *Public Personnel Management,* 1988, *17,* 21–27.

Potamianos, P. "Codes of Ethics in Municipal Government: A Survey of Major Cities." Unpublished paper submitted to author's seminar on administrative ethics at the University of Connecticut, Spring 1990.

President's Blue Ribbon Commission on Defense Management. *Conduct and Accountability: A Report to the President.* June 1986. (Duplicated.)

President's Commission on Federal Ethics Law Reform. *To Serve with Honor: Report and Recommendations to the President.* Washington, D.C.: U.S. Government Printing Office, 1989.

President's Council on Integrity and Efficiency. *Computers: Crimes, Clues and*

Controls: A Management Guide. Washington, D.C.: U.S. Government Printing Office, Mar. 1986.

President's Council on Integrity and Efficiency. *Frontline,* Apr. 1990 (entire issue).

Purdum, T. S. "When Life Itself Is a Conflict of Interest." *New York Times,* Apr. 22, 1990, p. E8.

Raspberry, W. "Give the Candidates Amnesty." *Washington Post,* Oct. 9, 1987, p. A27.

Rawls, J. *A Theory of Justice.* Cambridge, Mass.: Harvard University Press, 1971.

Rest, J. "Developmental Psychology and Value Education." In B. Munsey (ed.), *Moral Development, Moral Education, and Kohlberg.* Birmingham, Ala.: Religious Education Press, 1980, pp. 101–129.

Rice, D., and Dreilinger, C. "Rights and Wrongs of Ethics Training." *Training and Development Journal,* 1990, *44,* 103–108.

Richter, W. L. "Have Ethics Regulations Gone Too Far?" *PA Times,* July 21, 1989.

Richter, W. L., Burke, F., and Doig, J. W. (eds.). *Combatting Corruption, Encouraging Ethics: A Sourcebook for Public Service Ethics.* Washington, D.C.: American Society for Public Administration, 1990.

Rion, M. *The Responsible Manager: Practical Strategies for Ethical Decision Making.* New York: HarperCollins, 1990.

Riordan, W. L. "Honest Graft." In J. A. Gardiner and D. J. Olson (eds.), *Theft of the City: Readings on Corruption in Urban America.* Bloomington: Indiana University Press, 1974, pp. 7–9.

Roberts, E. J. "When Bending the Rules Is Good Business." *Leader's Digest.* Internal Revenue Service, Document 7168 (Rev. 3-90), cat. no. 664226Y, 1990.

Roberts, W. *Leadership Secrets of Attila the Hun.* New York: Warner Books, 1987.

Rohr, J. A. *Ethics for Bureaucrats: An Essay on Law and Values.* (2nd ed.) New York: Marcel Dekker, 1989.

Rohr, J. A. "Ethics in Public Administration: A State-of-the-Discipline Report." In N. B. Lynn and A. Wildavsky, *Public Administration: The State of the Discipline.* Chatham, N.J.: Chatham House, 1990, 97–123.

Roper Organization. National adult personal survey, Aug. 1981.

Roper Organization for *U.S. News and World Report.* National adult survey, June 29–30, 1989.

Rosen, B. *Holding Government Bureaucracies Accountable.* New York: Praeger, 1989.

Ruch, W. A., and Newstrom, J. W. "How Unethical Are We?" *Supervisory Management,* 1975, *20,* 16–21.

Safire, W. "The Pointing Finger." *New York Times,* Mar. 16, 1989, p. A31.

Sakharov, A. "Foreword." In G. Medvedev, *The Truth About Chernobyl.* (E. Rossiter, trans.) New York: Basic Books, 1991.

Sanchez, R. "Enrollment Figures Purposely Withheld, D.C. Audit Alleges." *Washington Post,* June 12, 1990, pp. B1, B8.

Scanlan, C. "What's the Price of Life? Depends Whom You Ask." *Hartford Courant,* July 15, 1990, pp. A1, A7.

Schelling, T. C. "Economic Reasoning and the Ethics of Policy." *Public Interest,* 1981, *63,* 37-61.

Schmitt, E. "2 Out of 3 Women in Military Study Report Sexual Harassment Incidents." *New York Times,* Sept. 12, 1990, p. A22.

Seidman, H., and Gilmour, R. *Politics, Position, and Power: From the Positive to the Regulatory State.* (4th ed.) New York: Oxford University Press, 1986.

Shabecoff, P. "Head of E.P.A. Bars Nazi Data in Study on Gas." *New York Times,* Mar. 23, 1988, pp. A1, A17.

Shklar, J. N. *Ordinary Vices.* Cambridge, Mass.: Belknap Press of Harvard University Press, 1984.

Shkurti, W. J. "A User's Guide to State Revenue Forecasting." *Public Budgeting & Finance,* 1990, *10,* 79-94.

Simon, H. *Administrative Behavior.* New York: Macmillan, 1947.

Solomon, J. "As Cultural Diversity of Workers Grows, Experts Urge Appreciation of Differences." *Wall Street Journal,* Sept. 12, 1990, pp. B1, B13.

Sprinthall, R., and Sprinthall, R. C. "Value and Moral Development." *Easier Said Than Done,* 1988, *1,* 16-22.

Steffens, L. "Philadelphia: Corrupt and Contented." In W. J. Murin (ed.), *Classics of Urban Politics and Administration.* Oak Park, Ill.: Moore, 1982, pp. 134-161. (Originally published in *The Shame of the Cities.* New York: Hill & Wang, 1904.)

Steffens, L. "Los Angeles and the Apple." In J. A. Gardiner and D. J. Olson (eds.), *Theft of the City: Readings on Corruption in Urban America.* Bloomington: Indiana University Press, 1974, pp. 285-289. (Originally published in *The Autobiography of Lincoln Steffens.* San Diego, Calif.: Harcourt Brace Jovanovich, 1931.)

Stein, H. (ed.). "The Glovis-Ballinger Dispute." In *Public Administration and Policy Development: A Case Book.* The Inter-University Case Program. San Diego, Calif.: Harcourt Brace Jovanovich, 1952, pp. 77-87.

Stewart, D. W. "Managing Competing Claims: An Ethical Framework for Human Resource Decision Making." *Public Administration Review,* 1984, *44,* 14-22.

Stillman, R. J., II (ed.). *Public Administration: Concepts and Cases.* (3rd ed.) Boston: Houghton Mifflin, 1984.

Stoll, C. *The Cuckoo's Egg: Tracking a Spy Through the Maze of Computer Espionage.* New York: Pocket Books, 1990

Strauss, L. and Cropsey, J. (eds.) *History of Political Philosophy.* (3rd ed.) Chicago: University of Chicago Press, 1987.

Summers, H. G. "Introduction." In L. J. Matthews and D. E. Brown (eds.), *The Parameters of Military Ethics.* Washington, D.C.: Pergamon-Brassey's International Defense Publishers, 1989.

Taking the Stand: The Testimony of Lieutenant Colonel Oliver L. North. New York: Pocket Books, 1987.

Taylor, M. D. "A Do-It-Yourself Professional Code for the Military." *Parameters: Journal of the U.S. War College,* 1980, *10,* 10–15.

Taylor, S., Jr. "Life in the Spotlight: Agony of Getting Burned." *New York Times,* Feb. 27, 1985, p. A16.

Terkel, S. "Reflections on a Course in Ethics." *Harper's,* Oct. 1973, pp. 11–18.

Thompson, D. F. "Moral Responsibility of Public Officials: The Problem of Many Hands." *American Political Science Review,* 1980, *74,* 905–916.

Thompson, D. F. "The Private Lives of Public Officials." In J. L. Fleishman, L. Liebman, and M. H. Moore (eds.), *Public Duties: The Moral Obligations of Government Officials.* Cambridge, Mass.: Harvard University Press, 1981, pp. 221–247.

Thompson, D. F. "The Possibility of Administrative Ethics." *Public Administration Review,* 1985, *45,* 555–561.

Timmins, W. M. *A Casebook of Public Ethics & Issues.* Pacific Grove, Calif.: Brooks/Cole, 1990.

Tinkham, L. Letter from William B. Donaldson, Mar. 22, 1990. Quoted in unpublished paper submitted to author's seminar on administrative ethics at the University of Connecticut, Spring 1990.

Tong, R. *Ethics in Policy Analysis.* Series in Occupational Ethics. Englewood Cliffs, N.J.: Prentice-Hall, 1986.

Tower Commission. *Tower Commission Report.* The full text of the President's Special Review Board. New York: Bantam Books and Times Books, 1987.

Tranter, R. A. F. "Ethical Problems Today." *Public Management,* 1987, *69,* 2–5.

Tuohy, L. and Finholm, V. "Reforms Ordered for DCYS." *Hartford Courant,* Dec. 22, 1990, pp. A1, A8.

U.S. Bureau of the Census. *Public Employment in 1988.* Series GE-88-1. Washington, D.C.: U.S. Government Printing Office, 1989.

U.S. Congress. Office of Technology Assessment. *The Use of Integrity Tests for Pre-Employment Screening.* OTA-SET-442. Washington, D.C.: U.S. Government Printing Office, Sept. 1990.

U.S. Department of Defense. Office of the Inspector General. *Indicators of Fraud in Department of Defense Procurement.* Washington, D.C.: U.S. Department of Defense, June 1, 1984.

U.S. Department of Defense. *Defense Ethics: A Standards of Conduct Guide for DOD Employees.* IGDG 5500.8, AFU. Washington, D.C.: U.S. Department of Defense, Jan. 1989.

U.S. Department of Health and Human Services. *An Ethics Handbook for Employees of the Department of Health and Human Services.* Washington, D.C.: Office of the Inspector General, U.S. Department of Health and Human Services, June 1989.

U.S. House of Representatives. Committee on Standards of Official Conduct.

Ethics Manual for Members, Officers, and Employees of the U.S. House of Representatives. Washington, D.C.: U.S. Government Printing Office, 1987.

U.S. House of Representatives. "HUD Reform." Hearings before the Subcommittee on Housing and Community Development of the Committee on Banking, Finance and Urban Affairs, Oct. 12, 1989. Serial no. 101-60. Washington, D.C.: U.S. Government Printing Office: 1990a.

U.S. House of Representatives. "Abuses, Favoritism, and Mismanagement in HUD Programs" (Pt. 1). Hearings before the Employment and Housing Subcommittee of the Committee on Government Operations, May 8–June 16, 1989. Washington, D.C.: U.S. Government Printing Office, 1990b.

U.S. Office of Government Ethics. *How to Keep Out of Trouble.* 1987-0-186-363. Washington, D.C.: U.S. Government Printing Office, Mar. 1986.

U.S. Office of Government Ethics. *First Biennial Report to Congress.* Washington, D.C.: U.S. Office of Government Ethics, Mar. 1990a.

U.S. Office of Government Ethics. *The Informal Advisory Letters and Memoranda and Formal Opinions of the United States Office of Government Ethics, 1979–1988.* Washington, D.C.: U.S. Government Printing Office, 1990b.

U.S. Office of Government Ethics. *Resource Materials: Training Course for Deputy Ethics Officials, Seattle.* Washington, D.C.: U.S. Office of Government Ethics, 1990c.

U.S. Senate. "Establishment of a Commission on Ethics in Government." Hearings before a subcommittee to study Senate Concurrent Resolution 21 of the Committee on Labor and Public Welfare. Washington D.C.: U.S. Senate, 1951. (Committee print.)

U.S. Senate. Select Committee on Ethics. *Revising the Senate Code of Official Conduct Pursuant to Senate Resolution 109.* 96th Congress, 2nd sess., Nov. 1980.

U.S. Senate. Select Committee on Ethics. *Rules of Procedure.* Adopted Feb. 23, 1978, and revised as of Jan. 1986. Washington, D.C.: U.S. Government Printing Office, 1986.

U.S. Senate. "Abuses in the Section 8 Moderate Rehabilitation Program." Hearings before the Committee on Banking, Housing, and Urban Affairs, May 17–Oct. 31, 1989. Washington, D.C.: U.S. Government Printing Office, 1990.

United States Military Academy. Associates, Department of Behavioral Sciences and Leadership. *Leadership in Organizations.* (3rd ed.) West Point, N.Y.: United States Military Academy, 1985.

University of Connecticut. Institute for Social Inquiry, for the *Hartford Courant.* Statewide adult telephone surveys, June 7–17, 1987, and Oct. 18, 1989.

Valletta, W. Memorandum on new law on conflicts of interests. Department of City Planning, City of New York, Office of the Counsel, January 5, 1990.

Volcker Commission. *Leadership for America: Rebuilding the Public Service.* Report of the National Commission on the Public Service. Washington, D.C.: National Commission on the Public Service, 1989. (Commission copy.)

Wakham, E. C. "Should ASPA Expel Unethical Members?" *PA Times,* Feb. 1, 1990.

Waldo, D. *The Enterprise of Public Administration.* Novato, Calif.: Chandler & Sharp, 1981.

*Wall Street Journal/*NBC News. National adult survey, July 12, 1987.

Wall Street Journal. Survey of 1,000 corporate executives, Apr. 6, 1988, p. 27.

Walsh, J. "New GFOA Code of Professional Ethics Provides Guidance, Direction." *Government Finance Review,* 1989, *5,* 3.

Walzer, M. "Political Action: The Problem of Dirty Hands." *Philosophy and Public Affairs,* 1973, *2,* 160–180.

Weimer, L. Memorandum on ethics codes, Alaska State Legislature. May 2, 1990.

Wholey, J. S. *Evaluation and Effective Public Management.* Foundations of Public Management Series. Boston: Little, Brown, 1983.

Wildavsky, A. "What Is Permissible So That This People May Survive? Joseph the Administrator." The 1989 John Gaus Lecture. *PS: Political Science & Politics,* 1989, *22,* 779–788.

Wilson, J. "Philosophical Difficulties and 'Moral Development.'" In B. Munsey (ed.), *Moral Development, Moral Education, and Kohlberg.* Birmingham, Ala.: Religious Education Press, 1980, pp. 214–231.

Wilson, J. Q. *Bureaucracy: What Government Agencies Do and Why They Do It.* New York: Basic Books, 1990.

Wilson, T. W. "The Study of Administration." In J. M. Shafritz and A. C. Hyde (eds.), *Classics of Public Administration* (2nd ed.) Chicago: Dorsey Press, 1987, pp. 10–25. (Originally published in *Political Science Quarterly,* 1887, *2,* pp. 197–222.)

Wilson, W. "I Had Prayed to God That This Thing Was Fiction." *American Heritage,* 1990. *41,* 44–53.

Wolfe, T. *The Bonfire of the Vanities.* New York: Bantam Books, 1987.

"Women Take On City Governance." *PA Times,* Sept. 1, 1989, p. 12.

Yankelovich Clancy Shulman. National telephone survey, July 9, 1987.

Yankelovich, Skelly and White. National adult telephone survey, March 2, 1989.

Zimmerman, J. S. "Ethics in Local Government." *Management Information Service Report 8.* Washington, D.C.: International City Management Association, Aug. 1976.

Index